Angels & Tomboys

Angels & Tomboys

GIRLHOOD IN 19TH-CENTURY AMERICAN ART

HOLLY PYNE CONNOR

With contributions by

SARAH BURNS

BARBARA DAYER GALLATI

LAUREN LESSING

NEWARK MUSEUM

Pomegranate
SAN FRANCISCO

Published on the occasion of the exhibition *Angels and Tomboys: Girlhood in Nineteenth-Century American Art,* organized by the Newark Museum.

Exhibition Itinerary

Newark Museum
Newark, NJ
September 12, 2012–January 6, 2013

Memphis Brooks Museum of Art
Memphis, TN
February 16–May 26, 2013

Crystal Bridges Museum of American Art
Bentonville, AR
June 28–September 30, 2013

Major support for the exhibition and catalogue is provided by:

Johnson&Johnson   ART WORKS. arts.gov   New Jersey visitnj.org   ROBERT LEHMAN FOUNDATION, INC.
NEWARK MUSEUM VOLUNTEER ORGANIZATION
FRIENDS OF AMERICAN ART AT THE NEWARK MUSEUM

This exhibition is supported by an indemnity from the Federal Council on the Arts and Humanities.
Supported in part by a grant from New Jersey Department of State, Division of Travel and Tourism.

The Newark Museum, a not-for-profit museum of art, science, and education, receives operating support from the City of Newark, the State of New Jersey, the New Jersey State Council on the Arts/Department of State—a Partner Agency of the National Endowment for the Arts, the New Jersey Cultural Trust, the Prudential Foundation, the Geraldine R. Dodge Foundation, the Wallace Foundation, and other corporations, foundations, and individuals. Funds for acquisitions and activities other than operations are provided by members and other contributors.

Newark Museum | 49 Washington Street | Newark, New Jersey, 07102-3176 | newarkmuseum.org

Published by Pomegranate Communications, Inc., in collaboration with the Newark Museum.

Pomegranate Communications, Inc.
Box 808022, Petaluma, CA 94975
800 227 1428 | www.pomegranate.com

Pomegranate Europe Ltd.
Unit 1, Heathcote Business Centre, Hurlbutt Road
Warwick, Warwickshire CV34 6TD, UK
[+44] 0 1926 430111 | sales@pomeurope.co.uk

© 2012 Newark Museum
Artworks © individual artists or their estates

All rights reserved. No part of this publication may be reproduced or transmitted in any form or by any means, electronic or mechanical, including photocopying, recording, or by any information storage or retrieval system, without permission in writing from the copyright holders.

Unless otherwise indicated, images © and courtesy of the institutions or owners listed in the captions. The Newark Museum has made every effort to trace and contact the copyright holders of both the images and the artworks reproduced in the catalogue; any errors or omissions will be corrected in subsequent editions.

Front cover: Abbott Handerson Thayer, *Angel* (page 74), 1887.
Back cover: John George Brown, *Swinging on the Gate* (page 141), c. 1878–1879.

Library of Congress Cataloging-in-Publication Data

Connor, Holly Pyne, 1952–
 Angels and tomboys : girlhood in nineteenth-century American art / Holly Pyne Connor ; with contributions by Sarah Burns, Barbara Dayer Gallati, Lauren Lessing.
   p. cm.
 Catalog of an exhibition held Sept. 12, 2012–Jan. 7, 2013 at the Newark Museum; Feb. 16–May 26, 2013 at the Memphis Brooks Museum of Art; and June 28–Sept. 30, 2013 at the Crystal Bridges Museum of American Art.
 Includes bibliographical references and index.
 ISBN 978-0-7649-6329-2 (hardcover)
 1. Children in art—Exhibitions. 2. Girls in art—Exhibitions. 3. Art, American—19th century—Exhibitions. I. Newark Museum. II. Memphis Brooks Museum of Art. III. Crystal Bridges Museum of American Art. IV. Title.
 N7640.C66 2012
 704.9'4250973074—dc23
                2012010966

Pomegranate Catalog No. A208
Designed by Patrice Morris

Printed in China

21 20 19 18 17 16 15 14 13 12   10 9 8 7 6 5 4 3 2 1

CONTENTS

6   Foreword
    Mary Sue Sweeney Price

7   Acknowledgments

9   Lenders to the Exhibition

10 The Flowering of Girlhood Narratives, 1850–1870
    Holly Pyne Connor

28 Angel Children: Defining Nineteenth-Century Girlhood
    Holly Pyne Connor

56 Family Matters: Artists and Their Model Girls
    Barbara Dayer Gallati

84 Making Mischief: Tomboys Acting Up and Out of Bounds
    Sarah Burns

106 Roses in Bloom: American Images of Adolescent Girlhood
    Lauren Lessing

133 Plates

168 Exhibition Checklist

175 Contributors

176 Index

183 Trustees and Museum Council

FOREWORD

The Newark Museum continues its historic commitment to the study, display, and publication of American art with *Angels and Tomboys: Girlhood in Nineteenth-Century American Art*. This is the first exhibition devoted exclusively to an examination of nineteenth-century girlhood through exceptional works from the Museum's renowned American holdings, as well as generous loans from other museums and private collections. The accompanying catalogue provides new, thought-provoking scholarship of extensive scope, encompassing the full range of nineteenth-century artists' interpretations of young girls—from androgynous, innocent children to mischievous, free spirits.

The Newark Museum's ongoing dedication to making art accessible to audiences of all backgrounds and ages is reflected in the multilayered interpretations in both the exhibition itself and in the catalogue essays. These commentaries provide a rich cultural context for the individual artworks.

With pleasure, I commend Holly Pyne Connor, Curator of Nineteenth-Century American Art, who conceived of and organized this landmark project. I extend my sincere thanks to her and to the members of the Museum's talented staff who brought this endeavor to fruition. Throughout this undertaking, we have enjoyed partnering with the Memphis Brooks Museum of Art and Crystal Bridges Museum of American Art, the second and third venues of the exhibition.

Angels and Tomboys is supported by generous grants from the National Endowment for the Arts, the Federal Council on the Arts and Humanities, Johnson and Johnson, the Robert Lehman Foundation, the Friends of American Art at the Newark Museum, and the New Jersey Division of Travel and Tourism. The Trustees and staff of the Newark Museum are most grateful for annual operating support received from the City of Newark and the New Jersey State Council on the Arts/Department of State.

We are deeply indebted to the many generous lenders who have committed important works to *Angels and Tomboys*. Without their participation, this exhibition would not have been possible.

Mary Sue Sweeney Price
Director and CEO
Newark Museum

ACKNOWLEDGMENTS

Angels and Tomboys: Girlhood in Nineteenth-Century American Art grew out of a series of encounters with individual masterpieces in the remarkable collection of the Newark Museum. As I researched paintings like Henry Inman's *Children of Bishop George W. Doane,* 1835, and Lilly Martin Spencer's *War Spirit at Home (Celebrating the Victory at Vicksburg),* 1866, I realized that they sparked specific, probing inquiries about artists and the girls they painted even as they invited speculations about broader social, cultural, and artistic issues. When Henry James in 1878 described Daisy Miller, the quintessential American girl, as presenting herself as "an inscrutable combination of audacity and innocence," he highlighted characteristics associated with both the tomboy and the angel, feminine stereotypes that existed throughout the nineteenth century and that are still relevant today. Ranging from sentimental images of girls as pure, passive, and domestic to subversive depictions of adolescents, working children, and adventurous girls, this is the first exhibition and publication to explore such diverse portrayals by painters, sculptors, photographers, and writers. As a broad survey dealing almost exclusively with artists working in the eastern United States, this exhibition paves the way for future, more in-depth investigations.

An undertaking of this scope requires the commitment, hard work, and talent of numerous individuals. I am particularly grateful to our Director, Mary Sue Sweeney Price, who enthusiastically championed the project from its inception, consistently providing support, resources, and encouragement.

The privilege of collaborating with inspiring colleagues has been an enormously enriching experience. At a critical stage, Sarah Burns, Barbara Gallati, Erica Hirshler, Jane Hunter, Lauren Lessing, and David Lubin participated in a stimulating scholarly meeting, which refined the themes of the exhibition. Barbara, Lauren, Sarah, and I have also contributed catalogue essays, which present a wealth of new scholarship.

I am deeply indebted to my dedicated and talented colleagues at the Newark Museum, who have diligently collaborated with me. Exhibit Designer Tracy Long has once again created a beautiful and elegant installation. Associate Registrar Amber Woods Germano coordinated numerous loans with great professionalism and attention to detail. Andrea Hagy, Associate Registrar for Rights and Reproductions, efficiently tracked down obscure images, adroitly handling a huge number of illustrations. Curatorial Assistant Millicent Matthews meticulously and patiently organized countless loan requests. Kristin Curry, Director for Foundation, Corporate, and Governmental Relations, and Anu Malhotra, Grant Writer and Development Associate, wrote endless grant applications. Marketing Communications Manager U. Michael Schumacher worked tirelessly on the exhibition catalogue. Rebecca Buck, Deputy Director for Collection Services, and Antonia Moser, Associate Registrar, were instrumental in our successful application for an indemnity from the Federal Council on the Arts and Humanities. Ted Lind, Director of Education, Linda Gates Nettleton, Assistant Director of Education for Family, Youth and Adult Programs, and Kim Robledo-Diga, Director for Innovation and Learning, created exciting educational programs. Interns Kimberly Fisher, Ellen Crosier, and Jenevieve De Los Santos provided outstanding assistance. Zette Emmons, Manager of Traveling Exhibitions, attentively oversaw the exhibition's tour. My curatorial colleagues, Ulysses Grant Dietz, Mary Kate O'Hare,

Katherine Anne Paul, and Christa Clark, have been an ongoing source of information, support, and humor. They have made working at the Newark Museum an enriching, educational, and thoroughly enjoyable experience.

One of the great pleasures of organizing *Angels and Tomboys* has been viewing works in other museums and private collections and discussing them with fellow curators and scholars. I am particularly indebted to the following individuals, who graciously gave their time and expertise, and in many instances agreed to lend masterworks from the collections that they supervise: Rebecca E. Lawton, Amon Carter Museum of American Art; Teresa A. Carbone, Brooklyn Museum; Sarah Cash, Corcoran Gallery of Art; Christopher B. Crosman and Kevin M. Murphy, Crystal Bridges Museum of American Art; Debra Force, Debra Force Fine Art; Kenneth J. Myers, Detroit Institute of Arts; Paul S. D'Ambrosio, Fenimore Art Museum; Katherine W. Baumgartner, Godel and Co.; Michael Botwinick, Bartholomew F. Bland, and Laura Vookles, Hudson River Museum; Marina Pacini, Memphis Brooks Museum of Art; Elizabeth Mankin Kornhauser and H. Barbara Weinberg, Metropolitan Museum of Art; Elliot Bostwick Davis and Erica E. Hirshler, Museum of Fine Arts, Boston; Bruce Weber, National Academy Museum; Linda S. Ferber and Kimberly Orcutt, New-York Historical Society; Anna O. Marley, Pennsylvania Academy of the Fine Arts; Karl Kusserow, Princeton University Art Museum; Tanya Sheehan, Rutgers; Elizabeth Broun and Eleanor Jones Harvey, Smithsonian American Art Museum; Peter John Brownlee, Terra Foundation for American Art; and William Keyse Rudolph, Worcester Art Museum.

It has been a great privilege to collaborate with the staff at the Memphis Brooks Museum of Art: Cameron Kitchin, Director, and Marina Pacini, Chief Curator; and at Crystal Bridges Museum of American Art: Don Bacigalupi, Executive Director, Christopher B. Crosman, Chief Curator, and Kevin M. Murphy, Curator of American Art.

Working with the team at Pomegranate Communications to produce this beautiful catalogue has been a rewarding experience. I am particularly grateful to Katie Burke, Publisher, Stephanie King, Associate Publisher and Director of Media Relations, Samuel Gilbert, Editor, and Patrice Morris, Designer.

Museums and private collectors from across the country agreed to lend key works in support of this project, and I am extremely indebted to them for their pivotal role in the success of the exhibition.

Holly Pyne Connor
Curator of Nineteenth-Century American Art
Newark Museum

LENDERS TO THE EXHIBITION

Amon Carter Museum of American Art, Fort Worth, TX
Brandywine River Museum, Chadds Ford, PA
Brauer Museum of Art, Valparaiso University, Valparaiso, IN
Brooklyn Museum, Brooklyn, NY
Carnegie Museum of Art, Pittsburgh, PA
Chesterwood, Stockbridge, MA
Chrysler Museum of Art, Norfolk, VA
Colby College Museum of Art, The Lunder Collection, Waterville, ME
Corcoran Gallery of Art, Washington, D.C.
Detroit Institute of Arts, Detroit, MI
Fenimore Art Museum, Cooperstown, NY
George Walter Vincent Smith Art Museum, Springfield, MA
Hirshhorn Museum and Sculpture Garden, Smithsonian Institution, Washington, D.C.
Hudson River Museum, Yonkers, NY
Hyde Collection, Glens Falls, NY
Library of Congress, Washington, D.C.
Memphis Brooks Museum of Art, Memphis, TN
Metropolitan Museum of Art, New York, NY
Museum of Fine Arts, Boston, MA
Museum of the City of New York, NY
National Gallery of Art, Washington, D.C.
Newark Museum, Newark, NJ
New-York Historical Society, New York, NY
Oakland Museum of California, Oakland, CA
Old Print Shop, New York, NY
Pennsylvania Academy of the Fine Arts, Philadelphia, PA
Philadelphia Museum of Art, Philadelphia, PA
Princeton University Art Museum, Princeton, NJ
Private collections
Sheldon Museum of Art, University of Nebraska–Lincoln, NE
Smithsonian American Art Museum, Washington, D.C.
Sterling and Francine Clark Art Institute, Williamstown, MA
Tanya Sheehan Collection, Providence, RI
Taubman Museum of Art, Roanoke, VA
Terra Foundation for American Art, Chicago, IL
Wadsworth Atheneum Museum of Art, Hartford, CT
Whitney Museum of American Art, New York, NY
Winterthur Museum, Winterthur, DE
Worcester Art Museum, Worcester, MA

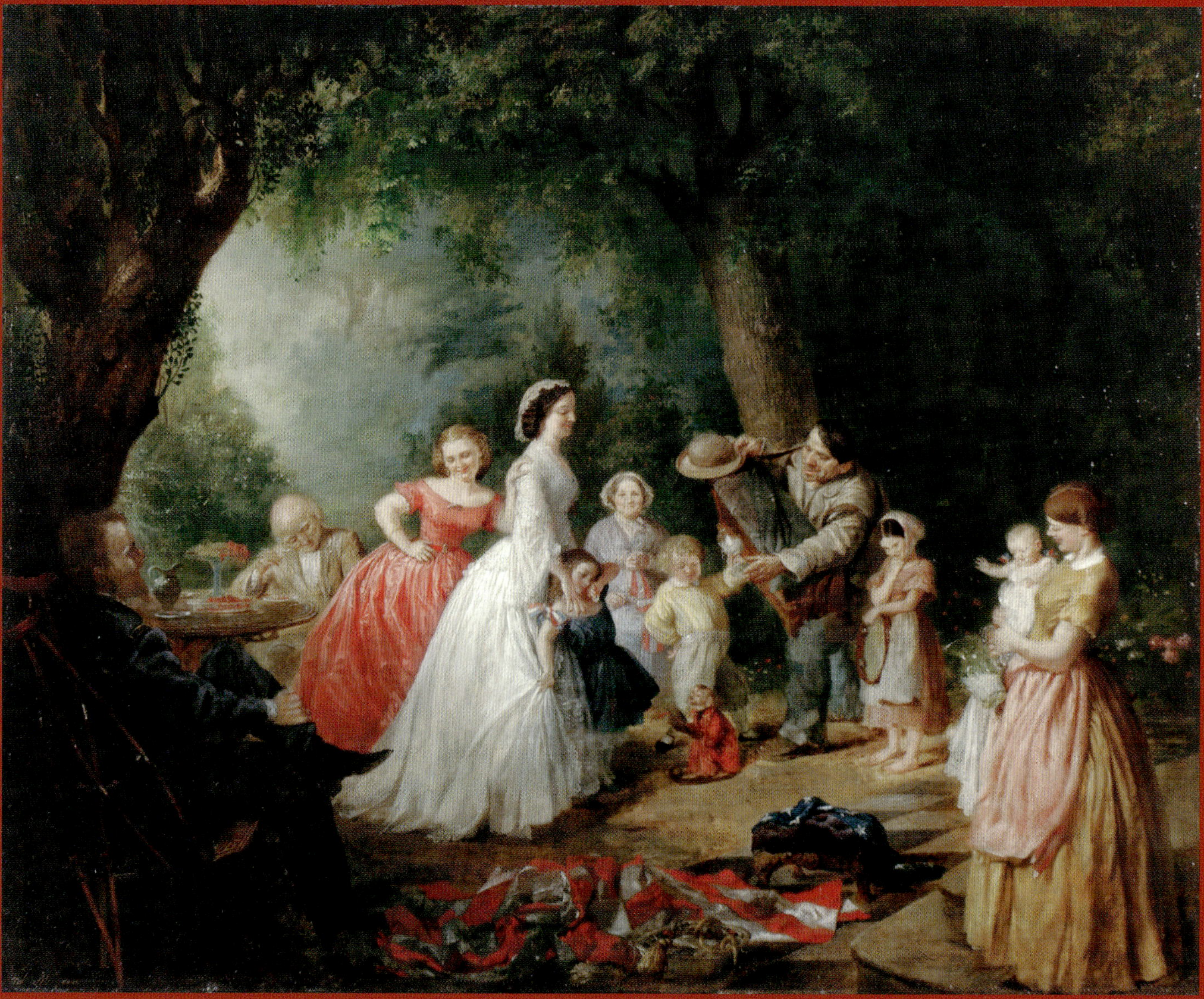

The Flowering of Girlhood Narratives, 1850–1870

HOLLY PYNE CONNOR

Scholars have long noted that American artists' fascination with children began during the Civil War, but the initial interest in girlhood subjects, presented in narrative and genre scenes of everyday life, actually developed a decade earlier, in the 1850s. Commencing with a group of lithographs after paintings by Lilly Martin Spencer, a growing engagement with girlhood was also sparked by an awareness and appreciation of European pictures of children that could be seen in New York City exhibitions and during sojourns abroad. Americans who experienced the horrors of the war years and the disillusionment of the postwar period found solace in reassuring images that captured the perceived security and comfort of home and its female inhabitants, as well as in the portrayal of childhood as an idyllic state enacted in sunny country settings. The 1860s also witnessed the creation of serious pictures by Eastman Johnson, John George Brown, and Spencer in which girls appeared in narratives that commented on topical concerns including family, race, and national destiny. This confluence of events elevated girlhood themes to the canon of American art by the last quarter of the century, as girls took center stage in paintings, watercolors, and prints by American masters.

Before the 1850s, the depiction of girls was primarily confined to commissioned portraits, which used such gendered objects as flowers, dolls, and pets to define the sitters as pure, docile, and domestic.[1] Genre and narrative paintings, however, expanded traditional views of girlhood by creating sentimental and sometimes thought-provoking narratives, with girls presented as active protagonists in relation to other children and adults. As the figures in genre paintings usually represented social types, they provide additional, meaningful avenues to a deeper understanding of attitudes toward girlhood.

During the first half of the nineteenth century, few narrative paintings treated girlhood as their main subject. Only Spencer repeatedly focused on girls and domestic life, subjects that became her specialty.[2] Male genre painters, who were forging an American cultural identity, dealt with masculine themes, including Western expansion, hunting, and politics. George Caleb Bingham, Richard Caton Woodville, Arthur Fitzwilliam Tait, and numerous others almost never painted little girls, inviting speculation that this theme was deemed unworthy of serious consideration by male artists and their patrons. A review of one of the great New York collections of American art, that which Luman Reed amassed from 1832 until his death in 1836, reveals only one painting of a girl, George Whiting Flagg's *The Match Girl,* 1834 (New-York Historical Society), executed in London.[3]

During the same period, boys were popular subjects in the works of William Sidney Mount and David Gilmour Blythe. Mount captured the rowdy activities of country boys, while Blythe focused on urban children, casting them as depraved creatures engaged in disruptive, antisocial behavior. As the art historian Elizabeth Johns noted, "Male artists, consistent with their preoccupation with sovereignty, masculine autonomy, and social control, attended to boys."[4] While girls occasionally appear in the art of

Fig. 1. (opposite) Lilly Martin Spencer, *The Home of the Red, White and Blue,* c. 1867–1868. Oil on canvas, 24 x 30 in. Terra Foundation for American Art, Chicago; Daniel J. Terra Art Acquisition Endowment Fund 2007.1. Image courtesy of Art Resource, NY

Mount and of John Lewis Krimmel, they are minor actors, frequently marginalized in a manner similar to women and African Americans.[5] Before the 1850s, male artists included girls primarily in crowd scenes and family groups, where they comment on intergenerational relationships but rarely take center stage. When boys appear in these antebellum narrative paintings, they enact humorous stories that slyly refer to improper adult behavior. The incorporation of didactic and moral messages in scenes of everyday life has a long history in the European paintings that inspired American artists.[6]

One of the earliest genre paintings prominently featuring a young girl is Asher Brown Durand's *The Peddler*, 1836 (fig. 2). In a rustic home, two girls are portrayed as the main consumers of a peddler's goods. The adolescent daughter holds a colorful piece of fabric, while her younger sister, wearing an unusually large necklace, clutches another piece of jewelry while begging her father for money to purchase these gaudy baubles. Durand's painting was prescient, as the theme of women and girls as consumers was a persistently powerful subject in nineteenth-century art and literature and one that continues today. The same topic is addressed in two paintings, both entitled *The New Bonnet*, one by Francis William Edmonds, 1858 (fig. 3), and the other from 1876 by Eastman Johnson (Metropolitan Museum of Art, New York). In each, the artist dramatically contrasts the values of older and younger generations by depicting vain, fashionably dressed women unconcerned about the financial burden their expensive purchases impose on others. In Edmonds's work, a refined young woman with a pale complexion holds aloft her new possession. Standing in the doorway, silhouetted against a cityscape, is a small working girl whose tanned hands and face indicate outdoor labor. Having delivered the new bonnet, she clutches the empty hat box, a symbol of the barrenness and futility of the young woman's vanity.[7] On a deeper level, Edmonds implies that this self-absorbed woman is bankrupting not only the older generation—her evidently distressed father is holding the bill—but also the next generation, referenced by the delivery girl with the valueless container. At the end of the century, Alice Barber Stephens also juxtaposed a working girl with an affluent woman in *The Woman in Business*, 1897 (fig. 4). While the settings are dramatically different—a rustic home in Durand's painting, an urban residence in Edmonds's work, and the cavernous interior of John Wanamaker's Philadelphia department store in Stephens's grisaille—the themes of female materialism and frivolity connect the three images. In Stephens's poignant scene, a juvenile shop assistant with a sad, serious, and tired expression attends to splendidly dressed shoppers, a compelling comparison of poor and rich. The plight of working children is addressed in Seymour Joseph Guy's *The Crossing Sweeper* (fig. 43, page 64), where similar themes of privilege and exploitation are explored.

The serious social concerns presented in the paintings discussed above are in marked contrast to

Fig. 2. Asher Brown Durand, *The Peddler*, 1836. Oil on canvas, 24 x 34¼ in. New-York Historical Society 1858.26

THE FLOWERING OF GIRLHOOD NARRATIVES, 1850–1870

the humorous depictions produced by Lilly Martin Spencer in the mid-1850s, which are the earliest narrative images focusing solely on American girlhood. Spencer's accomplishments were the result of a confluence of factors, which included the rise of a middle-class market hungry for recognizable and sentimental images, the demand for affordable prints as home decorations, and finally the astute business acumen of Spencer's agent, William Schaus.[8] Schaus had successfully published lithographs after the works of Mount, an established genre painter whose paintings of boys were greatly appreciated as early as the 1830s. The agent is known to have had a close working relationship with the artist, even suggesting subjects for him to paint. As Spencer's primary patron during the 1850s, Schaus probably steered her toward girlhood subjects, recognizing their potential popularity. One of his marketing strategies was to pair lithographs of boys and girls. Pairs of paintings, prints, and sculptures were routinely sold during the nineteenth century, so Schaus combined a proven seller, boyhood, and a relatively new, untried subject, girlhood.[9] Between 1853 and 1858, the agent published and widely distributed five sets of large lithographs based on Spencer's paired images of boys and girls.

Spencer's lithographs were greatly appreciated, even if the estimated one million produced is an exaggeration.[10] As Elizabeth Johns insightfully noted, "That Spencer's images of children were her most popular works and were chosen for lithographs more than any other topic, would seem to reveal the hunger of her viewers for recognition of this suppressed area of emotional experience."[11] Reflecting traditional Victorian attitudes, these lithographs are among Spencer's most conservative and sentimental interpretations of children and would have been marketed to a relatively unsophisticated audience, primarily middle-class women who appreciated their uncomplicated humor.[12] At midcentury, wealthy art collectors were male, as women in most states were legally barred from owning property.

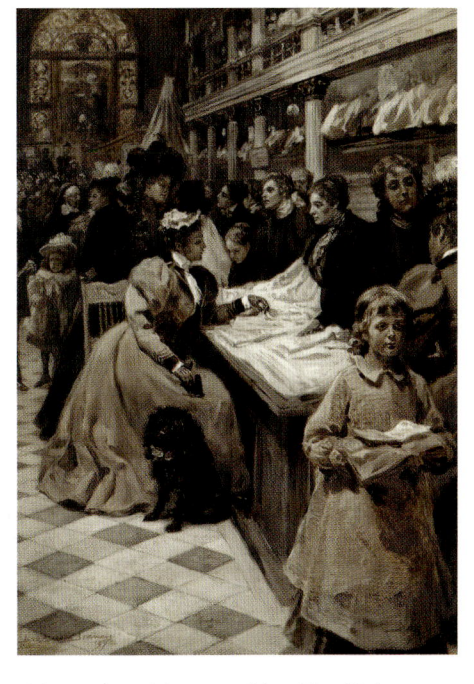

Fig. 3. (left) Francis William Edmonds, *The New Bonnet,* 1858. Oil on canvas, 25 x 30⅛ in. Metropolitan Museum of Art, New York; Purchase, Erving Wolf Foundation and Gift of Hanson K. Corning, by exchange, 1975 1975.27.1. Photograph courtesy of Art Resource, NY
Fig. 4. (right) Alice Barber Stephens, *The Woman in Business,* 1897. Cover for *Ladies' Home Journal,* September 1897. Oil on canvas, 25 x 18 in. Brandywine River Museum; Museum purchase, 1982, made possible through Ray and Beverly Sacks

Women, however, seemed to be taking a more active role in the viewing and perhaps even the buying of art: in such engravings as Francis D'Avignon, after T. H. Matteson, *Distribution of the American Art-Union Prizes at the Tabernacle, Broadway, New York, December 24, 1846* (Metropolitan Museum of Art, New York), for example, numerous women appear in the audience. From the 1840s to the 1860s, countless color prints appeared in illustrated magazines and other publications aimed at woman readers: popular art was thought to reflect feminine taste.[13] By 1883, a writer for the *Art Interchange* blamed Victorian housewives for the excessively cluttered walls of their homes, commenting, "There appears to be a prejudice on the part of women against leaving any considerable portion of the wall space uncovered."[14]

Spencer's series of lithographs of young girls, which sometimes measured as large as thirty-five by twenty-four inches, were intended for framing and domestic display. A similar format links all five in the series: the figure of a single child close to the picture plane. While the children's clothing varies, the backgrounds are blank or ill defined, and only a few objects, such as a pet, toy, or bubble, are included.[15] Reflecting stereotypes, Spencer's little girls are less naughty, less active, and less boisterous than her boys. The final pair, *The Young Teacher* (fig. 5) and *The First Polka* (fig. 6), both published by Schaus in 1858, offer a typical case of behavioral contrasts: a demure girl gently instructs the large dog at her side, while the boy dances energetically with a cat. Spencer's boy is at the center of a scene of youthful mayhem: his drum is punctured, his

Fig. 5. (left) Jean Baptiste Adolphe Lafosse, after Lilly Martin Spencer, *The Young Teacher*, 1858. Lithograph, 35¼ x 24¾. Location unknown.   **Fig. 6.** (right) Jean Baptiste Adolphe Lafosse, after Lilly Martin Spencer, *The First Polka*, 1858. Chromolithograph, 28 x 21 in. Courtesy of the Ohio Historical Society

THE FLOWERING OF GIRLHOOD NARRATIVES, 1850–1870

dancing partner is clearly distressed, and the room is in disarray. On the other hand, a sense of order, much prized by Victorian audiences, pervades the scene over which the young girl presides.

A major theme of Spencer's girlhood prints is the fragility and fleeting nature of childhood, a persistent motif in nineteenth-century visual culture. Printed in 1856, *Oh!* (fig. 7), for instance, depicts a young girl holding a bubble, a common emblem of the transience of youth, while with her other hand she pours out the contents of a small pitcher, another reference to the passage of time. As the little girl bends forward, her dress slips down, revealing her shoulder and part of her chest. Elizabeth Johns has convincingly discussed the sensual quality of the exposed bodies of Spencer's young girls, while David Lubin has made similar, but more extensive and disturbing, observations regarding the erotic aspects of the seminaked, prepubescent girls in the paintings of Guy. While twenty-first-century viewers frequently find these images disconcerting, scholar Wendy J. Katz offers a more benign interpretation, writing that the loose, revealing clothing in Spencer's images "suggests their unconstrained nature, offering maximum freedom and 'natural' growth in comparison to adult constriction."[16]

Although few of these paired lithographs survive, their importance as the first sustained and widely distributed group of girlhood images should not be underestimated. Eager to purchase sentimental and accessible images as home decorations, the expanding middle class was responsible for the success of Spencer's girlhood prints. Schaus and other print firms—Currier and Ives was founded in 1857—tapped into this new, burgeoning market, creating and distributing vast numbers of colored lithographs and other prints. Since women presided over the domestic sphere, they were encouraged to beautify their homes, making them refuges from worldly concerns. A woman artist like Spencer was viewed as particularly well suited to producing images for that new market.[17]

Spencer's girlhood lithographs parallel the literary developments of the period, as women writers were engaged with girlhood themes as well. Years before Louisa May Alcott published *Little Women*, 1868–1869, Susan Warner and Maria Susanna Cummins focused on the plight of girls in their best-selling novels. Ellen Montgomery, the heroine of Warner's *The Wide, Wide World*, 1850, and the young orphan Gerty in Cummins's *The Lamplighter*,

Fig. 7. Jean Baptiste Adolphe Lafosse, after Lilly Martin Spencer, *Oh!*, 1856. Lithograph, 24½ x 19½ in. Printer: William Schaus, NY; Imp. Fois Delarue, Paris. Courtesy of Louisa May Alcott's Orchard House

1854, are memorable characters, whose trials and tribulations had great appeal for female readers. As Nina Baym observed, "It is widely agreed that since the middle of the nineteenth century, no book can hope for popular success if it does not attract large numbers of women readers, because women were and are the majority of readers in America."[18]

In the mid-1850s, another indicator of the marketability and timeliness of girlhood subjects was that talented male artists, including Eastman Johnson and William Morris Hunt, embraced girlhood themes for the first time. Both men's initial exposure to paintings of girls was in Europe, where the theme was a staple. When they returned to America in 1855, each produced pictures in which girls were the primary focus, recognizing that this popular European subject was ripe for exploration, and no doubt hoping that their wealthy and sophisticated East Coast patrons would agree.

Hunt's sustained engagement with girlhood scenes began in 1853, when he was living in the French village of Barbizon, studying and working with Jean-François Millet, the renowned painter of peasant life. Under Millet's influence, Hunt's subject matter and style changed noticeably, as he began to paint humble, contemplative domestic scenes, often depicting girls engaged in simple activities like spinning and reading. Back in America, Hunt briefly continued painting young girls: in 1856, he produced *Girl with Cat* (fig. 25, page 45) and also finished *The Violet Girl* (Museum of Art, Rhode Island School of Design, Providence), which he had begun in France about 1851.[19] These paintings have a seriousness and a depth of feeling that connect them to Millet's art rather than to Spencer's sentimental and lighthearted lithographs. Hunt's commitment to girlhood was fleeting, as by 1859 he had turned his attention to portraiture, but Johnson's interest lasted until the end of the 1880s. His first American foray into girlhood narratives was probably *The Pets,* 1856 (fig. 24, page 44), which reflects his appreciation of the seventeenth-century Dutch genre paintings that he studied at The Hague from 1851 to 1855. That painting's rapid sale to William Wilson Corcoran, one of the few collectors purchasing contemporary American art at midcentury, would have signaled to Johnson that the girlhood topic, slighted by earlier genre painters (with the exception of Spencer), had a potential audience among influential, affluent patrons.[20]

By 1857, artists no longer had to travel to Europe to view pictures of girls by French painters, as the Parisian firm of Goupil, Vibert, and Company began mounting a series of New York City exhibitions that included numerous childhood scenes. In this regard, Goupil's shows were in stark contrast to those held at the National Academy of Design, the American Academy, and the American Art-Union, where girlhood images seldom appeared before the 1860s. Goupil's exhibition catalogues mention several paintings of girls by Pierre-Édouard Frère, Jean Louis Hanon, and Théophile Emmanuel Duverger. In the 1857 catalogue, Frère's works were given the distinction of being grouped under a special heading, "Scenes in Humble Life," a description that applied to other artists' works listed in the brochure.[21] By exhibiting paintings of adorable girls, Goupil further legitimized and popularized this genre.

An 1857 article in the *New York Times* applauded the Goupil exhibition, praising the French painters as part of the leading school in contemporary art and describing Frère as "a poet in feeling and in fidelity. There is no object essential to his theme, which is too trivial in his eyes to be treated with patient truth . . . The affection of childhood, its whims, its vagaries, its pretty, preposterous dreams—the pains and pleasure of youth—some innocent drama or simple incident of domestic life; these he treats with a sympathetic

THE FLOWERING OF GIRLHOOD NARRATIVES, 1850–1870

earnestness... The interest in home and in childhood is characteristic of a very large class of French artists, as it is a trait of the national character." The writer then encouraged professional and amateur artists to attend the exhibition and to consider "the importance of a careful study of this collection during the short remaining time of its presence among us."[22] Goupil's fifth exhibition, held in 1866 and 1867, included works by English and Flemish artists; girlhood paintings were again well represented.

Repeatedly acclaimed in the American press, Frère's paintings (e.g., fig. 8) exerted a strong influence on a number of American painters, particularly Johnson, who in the 1860s adopted Frère's use of humble settings, confined spaces, and single figures, often young girls. As late as 1875, the influence of the French artist can still be seen in *Ice Skater* (fig. 63, page 88), which portrays an adorable little girl alone in a rustic interior. American critics continually linked Johnson and Frère: in 1866, Clarence Cook wrote, "How little reason we have to envy France her Edouard Frère, when we have a man like Eastman Johnson, as able to do for our rural life what Frère does for France, and with no less quiet beauty and homely truth."[23] Even the independent-minded Winslow Homer singled out Frère as an artist that he wanted to surpass. Explaining Frère's popularity, art historian Gabriel P. Weisberg noted that he "represented the lower classes with a purity and wholesomeness that in the Victorian age alleviated the very real misery and struggle that other Realists dedicated themselves to revealing."[24]

While Frère's subject matter, compositions, and realistic style were influential, Johnson employed girlhood subjects to explore contemporary American issues, even the controversial topics of race and slavery. In the late 1850s and early 1860s, for example, he created a number of paintings of African American girls, including *Hannah amidst the Vines,* 1859 (Georgetown University Art Collection, Washington, D.C.); *The Freedom Ring,* 1860 (Hallmark Fine Art Collection, La Jolla, California); and *Union Soldiers Accepting a Drink,* circa 1865 (fig. 9). The small scale and highly unusual themes of these works indicate that they were probably experimental, conceived for personal reasons rather than for public display. *Hannah amidst the Vines* is the most conventional of the group, capturing the blossoming sensuality of a mulatto adolescent, but *Union Soldiers Accepting a Drink* addresses complex national concerns about the fate of African Americans at the close of the Civil War.

Fig. 8. Pierre Édouard Frère, *Supper with a Friend,* n.d. Oil on panel, 12 x 9¾ in. Private collection

Fig. 9. Eastman Johnson, *Union Soldiers Accepting a Drink,* c. 1865. Oil on canvas, 17½ x 21½ in. Carnegie Museum of Art, Pittsburgh; Heinz Family Fund 1996.45

THE FLOWERING OF GIRLHOOD NARRATIVES, 1850–1870

At the center of the composition stands a small and solitary black girl. She is in the shadows, symbolizing the oppression of slavery and the uncertainty of the present, but above her head is a lush bower of leaves and flowers silhouetted against a vivid blue sky, suggesting a brighter and more promising future. As so often in Johnson's work, generations are contrasted. The young girl is associated with natural freshness and renewal, whereas the two older women flanking her suggest servitude and work: the one on the right pours drinks for two Union soldiers, and the distant figure on the left may be engaged in manual labor. As an emblem of the future, the girl represents a new generation of African Americans, whose destiny, although still undecided, has the potential for a different path from that of her elders.[25]

While *Union Soldiers Accepting a Drink* looks to the future, Johnson's *Corn Husking*, 1860 (fig. 10), evokes the past, as it is a nostalgic celebration of the productivity, simplicity, and wholesomeness of the farming community. In a dark, cavernous barn, filled with newly harvested corn symbolizing the abundance of nature, three generations appear. A virile yeoman carrying a huge basket of corn on his shoulders dominates the composition. Like the heroic French peasants of the Barbizon School, Johnson's farmers allude to the manual work, communal lifestyle, and family bonds associated with nineteenth-century rural life at a time of increasing urbanization and industrialization. Framing the iconic figure of the yeoman are a courting couple and a grandfather with his granddaughter. Beginning in the 1850s, girls were frequently paired

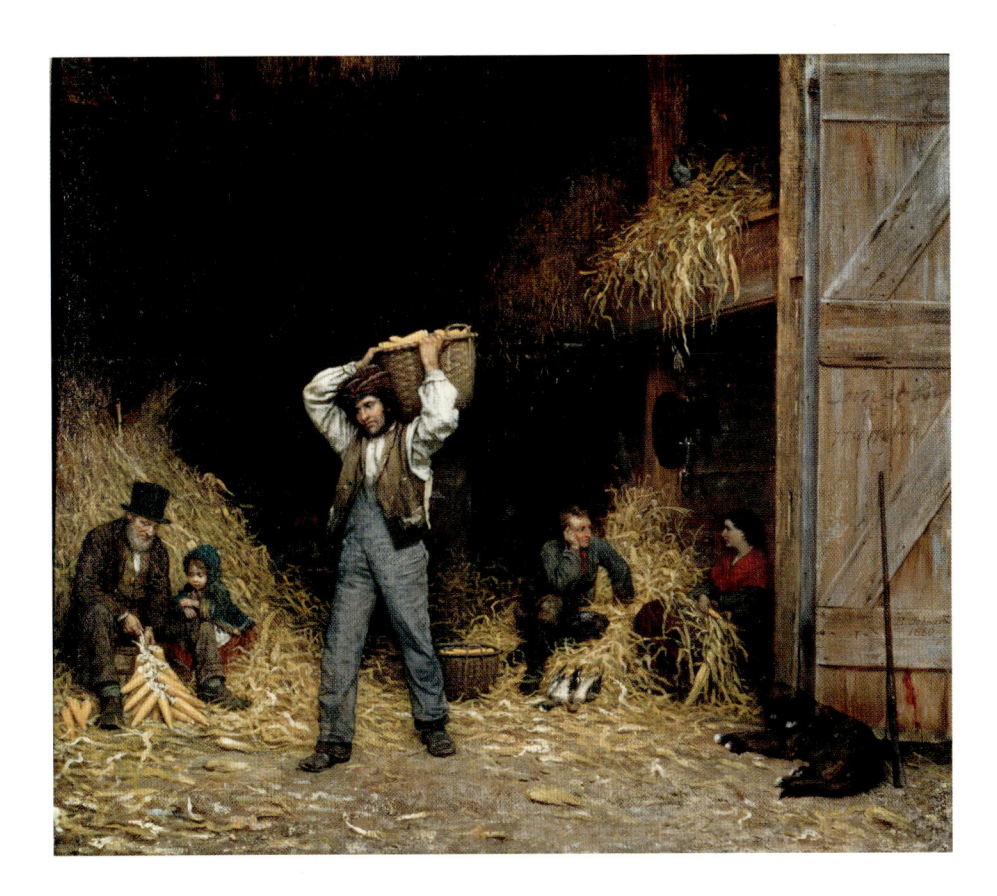

Fig. 10. Eastman Johnson, *Corn Husking,* 1860. Oil on canvas, 26½ x 30¼ in. Everson Museum of Art; Gift of Hon. Andrew D. White 19.116

Fig. 11. John George Brown, *Vanity,* 1899. Oil on canvas, 24 x 18 in. Newark Museum; Gift of Dr. J. Ackerman Coles, 1920 20.1212

THE FLOWERING OF GIRLHOOD NARRATIVES, 1850–1870

with grandfatherly types, an emotional juxtaposition in which the promise of youth is contrasted to the frailty of old age.[26] Embedded in the barn's huge pile of corn husks, as if she too is a fruitful product of the harvest, Johnson's little girl attentively watches her industrious grandfather. Dressed in patriotic red, white, and blue, a color scheme repeated throughout the painting, the adorable granddaughter evokes a healthy, harmonious, and prosperous future for the nation, a painful irony as the country was on the brink of civil war.[27]

The 1860s witnessed a flowering of girlhood subjects, as Johnson, Guy, Brown, Spencer, and Jerome Thompson produced images of carefree, healthy youths frequently in country settings that served as refreshing antidotes to the horrors of war.[28] These artists tended to paint sentimental scenes in a realistic style, which appealed to an emerging middle-class art patronage.[29] During this decade, Brown was instrumental in popularizing girlhood subjects. As art historian Martha Hoppin noted, he was initially drawn to courtship scenes of boys and girls indebted to English narrative painting, but during the second half of the 1860s, he turned to images of solitary girls in woodland settings, rendered in a tight, detailed Pre-Raphaelite style.[30] Often saccharine and escapist, these narrative works occasionally address powerful social concerns. *Watching the Woodpecker,* 1866 (fig. 38, page 60), painted immediately after the Civil War, is particularly noteworthy as one of the few midcentury genre paintings of girlhood that suggests the devastation of the conflict. Dressed in red, white, and blue, with her hands clasped modestly in front of her, this child of nature looks pensively upward with a glance that is reminiscent of Baroque saints in prayer. Leaning against a massive tree whose base has been disfigured by deep cuts of an ax, perhaps a reference to the destruction of the recent war, she seems to embody hope and solace. Brown has placed the figure outside the security of the domestic sphere, but she is enveloped and protected by the natural world and by her purity. Brown again addressed Civil War issues in *The Peacemaker,* 1867 (location unknown), where another girl dressed in red, white, and blue courageously separates two fighting boys. By the mid-1870s, Brown began focusing on urban scenes, primarily of boys working in the streets of New York City, but also produced paintings of little girls selling flowers (e.g., fig. 11). Like their country cousins, these urban working children are healthy, well fed, and not in the least threatening.[31]

During the Civil War and the years immediately following, happy families presided over by confident women and girls secure in the domestic sphere resonated with a nation traumatized by death and violence. The sanctity of the home and the amiability and innocence of young girls had great appeal to artists and their patrons, as part of what Ann Douglas termed the "feminization of American culture."[32] Spencer produced two powerful topical paintings that featured mothers and daughters: *War Spirit at Home (Celebrating the Victory at Vicksburg),* 1866 (fig. 70, page 96), and *The Home of the Red, White and Blue,* circa 1867–1868 (fig. 1). These two allegorical works reflect Spencer's deeply felt attitudes toward family, new feminine roles, and the state of the nation at a time of tremendous social change and upheaval. The bleak vision of family and home presented in *War Spirit at Home* is underscored by disorder and gender disruptions, including an overwhelmed, distracted mother and her energetic tomboy daughter. Spencer's gloomy, claustrophobic, and messy interior contravenes the clean and neat Victorian ideal. Instead, the artist portrays a household, and by implication a society, in the throes of turmoil, even chaos, caused in part by the absent father and the resulting lack of all patriarchal authority.

Fig. 12. Bessie Potter Vonnoh, *Enthroned,* 1902; cast 1906. Bronze, 12 x 8 x 10 in. Colby College Museum of Art; The Lunder Collection

Spencer's subversive and highly pessimistic intent is underscored when viewed in the context of the advice literature of the period, which emphasized the importance of order. "Order . . . is the essential prerequisite of every truly efficient action," T. S. Arthur wrote in *Advice to Young Ladies,* 1860. "Without it, nothing can be done well; with it, there is no duty in life that may not be rightly performed."[33] Arthur then criticized a household similar to the one depicted by Spencer, where a mother neglects her domestic responsibilities to follow the news of the day: "Worse behaved children, or a more disorderly household, we have never seen. The mother was a capital thinker, but that was all."[34] Spencer's grim commentary on the emotional and physical toll that the war took on family life is particularly evident when *War Spirit at Home* is compared to the 1866 Currier and Ives lithograph entitled *Training Day* (fig. 71, page 97), which provided the initial inspiration for her painting. The sentimental print situates a happy household in a light-filled and tidy room where the mother tenderly holds her infant and a smiling maid ignores her work to delight in the children's playful antics.

Painted about two years after *War Spirit at Home, The Home of the Red, White and Blue* is an optimistic work, offering hope for the nation. Three generations cheerfully interact in a sunny, verdant setting, which may suggest an earthly Eden; different ethnic groups share in the harmless fun provided by the Italian musician's monkey. Spencer's painting has serious social implications, offering a new direction for America, one in which mothers and daughters will rebuild and direct the traumatized country. The artist underscores the painting's national themes with her title, the tattered American flag, and the red, white, and blue dresses of the mother and her two daughters, who are the focus of the composition. Dressed in white, the mother occupies the highest part of the picture, emphasizing her matriarchal power. Her younger daughter timidly clutches her dress as if for protection, while the older child is independent and confident, suggested by her active, assertive pose of hand on waist.

By placing the sewing box near the torn flag, Spencer indicates that mother and daughters will repair and restore the ravaged nation. Immediately after the Civil War, many espoused Harriet Beecher Stowe's belief, articulated in the April 1866 issue of the *Atlantic Monthly,* that Americans were "called on to set the example of a new state of society—noble, simple, pure and religious; and women can do more towards this even than men, for women are the real architects of society."[35] In *The Home of the Red, White and Blue,* Spencer cast mothers and daughters as the bedrock of social stability and harmony. In a particularly subversive vignette, the artist placed the father, a wounded Union soldier with the smiling features of Spencer's husband, in the shadows, where he appears marginalized and immobile. Spencer's radical agenda is particularly apparent when her painting is contrasted to *Enthroned,* a work created about thirty-four years later by another talented woman artist, the sculptor Bessie Potter Vonnoh (fig. 12). Vonnoh aspired to a timeless beauty and tenderness, welding the figures of a mother and her three daughters into a harmonious composition, while Spencer engaged contemporary social issues that resonated with her on a profoundly personal level.

A literary parallel to the mothers and daughters of *The Home of the Red, White and Blue* is the Marsh family of Louisa May Alcott's best-selling domestic novel *Little Women,* written during the same period that Spencer created her allegory of a reconstructed America. The painting and the novel captured the postwar mood of a nation hungry for reassuring images of loving, devoted mothers and daughters who are resilient and courageous. The female empowerment displayed in *The Home of the Red, White and Blue* reinforces statements made by historian Alice Fahs, who argued that immediately after the war, writers presented new, active models of domesticity for women and the nation.[36]

Well before female readers made *Little Women* such a great success—by 1870 Alcott was the most well-known and highly paid author in America—they had expressed their enthusiasm for girlhood themes. From 1864 to 1870, Alcott completed three novels focusing on girls. Her first novel, *Moods*, 1864, detailed the romantic predicaments of the adolescent Sylvia, who dies at the end of the tale; it was a literary and financial disappointment.[37] Assessing the novel in the July 1865 issue of the *North American Review*, Henry James was highly critical, writing: "We are utterly weary of stories about precocious little girls. In the first place, they are in themselves disagreeable and unprofitable objects of study; and in the second, they are always the precursors of a not less unprofitable middle-aged lover."[38] In a remarkable change of opinion, which may have been predicated in part on the enormous success of *Little Women*, James decided to make the heroine of his first novel, *Watch and Ward*, 1871, a "precocious little girl."[39]

James's reassessment was part of the greater acceptance and appreciation of girlhood that occurred throughout the 1870s. It was then that Thomas Eakins and Winslow Homer turned their attention to this topic for the first time, while artists already invested in the theme—Johnson, Guy, Brown, and Spencer—continued their engagement. When Eakins returned to Philadelphia in 1870 after four years in Europe, he painted a number of works depicting girls in domestic interiors, including *Home Scene*, circa 1871 (fig. 50, page 72), and *Elizabeth Crowell with a Dog*, circa 1874 (fig. 51, page 73). Like Hunt and Johnson, Eakins was drawn to this subject after living abroad; like Hunt, his interest was brief, intense, and fruitful. Never before had Eakins been away from home for so long, and the themes of home and its female inhabitants resonated. His interpretations of girlhood were highly personal: he not only employed two of his sisters, Margaret and Caroline, as models in the former work, and an intimate friend, Elizabeth Crowell, in the latter, but both paintings are set in the Eakins home. Although he perpetuated prevailing stereotypes by assigning women and girls to the domestic sphere, the artist broke with tradition in his characterizations of Caroline, who is engaged and intellectually curious, and Elizabeth, who appears strong, willful, and controlling. Harbingers of the post–Civil War generation of women, Caroline and Elizabeth are portrayed as types of the New Woman, who had increased personal and professional opportunities.[40]

Homer too would have a fleeting but productive engagement with girlhood subjects in the 1870s. While Eakins placed his figures in dark, claustrophobic, almost brooding interiors, Homer and later William Merritt Chase painted girls in lush outdoor settings. Homer was attracted to this subject during a period when he was experimenting with the watercolor medium and painting outdoors. As the majority of his girlhood depictions are watercolors, it is intriguing to speculate about the extent to which he connected subject and medium. Amateur female painters, including Homer's beloved mother, Henrietta Benson Homer, were expected to use watercolors in their pictures of children, flowers, and fruits, subjects considered appropriate for woman artists. Although the American Society of Painters in Water Colors, founded in 1866, championed the medium, in the 1870s, watercolors were typically employed as studies or sketches for finished oil paintings. Always sensitive to the properties of his materials, Homer chose watercolors for his girlhood scenes because their luminosity, spontaneity, and freshness reinforced his lighthearted, sunny country themes. His tiniest watercolors often portray girls, suggesting that he viewed girlhood as a minor subject, one that did not provide the opportunity to explore the profound themes that he developed in his oil paintings.

In Gloucester during the summer of 1873, Homer had focused on boyhood themes in his watercolors, but five years later, at Houghton Farm in Mountainville, New York, he concentrated on country girls. Inspired by the verdant, rural setting, Homer created a large body of work in which girls tend sheep, pick apples, and luxuriate in the warm, bright light of summer. As art historian Helen Cooper noted, Homer was influenced by French Barbizon painting in his interpretation of these rustic types, particularly the art of Millet, which he saw in France in 1866 and 1867.[41] In many of Homer's girlhood watercolors, the female figures appear with sheep, seated or lying on the ground, with the curves of their hips and buttocks echoing the undulating forms of the lush landscape that surrounds them. Clearly, Homer associated girls with the animals they tended and with earthly and animal fecundity. The Houghton Farm watercolors were a huge financial and critical success when twenty-three were shown at the American Water Color Society's 1879 exhibition. Writing in 1882, George Sheldon attributed part of the success to the engaging subject, stating, "Winslow Homer . . . never fully found himself until he found the American shepherdess."[42]

By the last quarter of the nineteenth century, the acceptance and popularity of girlhood subjects among serious artists was widespread. William Merritt Chase repeatedly used his charming daughters as models, particularly his eldest, Alice Dieudonnée, known as Cosy, who sat for her father on countless occasions. These strikingly tender paintings show the girl embracing her mother (fig. 57, page 79), dramatically dressed in a fancy hat and orange sash (fig. 56, page 78), and posing uncomfortably in her mother's black dress (fig. 55, page 77). As with Eakins's paintings of his sisters, Chase's depictions of his daughters were deeply personal and profoundly moving images. Many combine elements of portraiture and narrative painting, a melding adopted by other painters of girlhood in the last decades of the nineteenth century, including George Fuller and John Singer Sargent. This conflation of portraiture and narrative paintings is evident in two of the greatest nineteenth-century girlhood paintings, both by the immensely talented Sargent: *The Daughters of Edward Darley Boit,* 1882 (Museum of Fine Arts, Boston) and *Carnation, Lily, Lily, Rose,* 1885–1886 (Tate, London). By the time Sargent created these two masterworks, girlhood had become an established subject in American art.

1. For a full discussion of the symbolic objects or attributes in girlhood portraits, see my other essay in the present catalogue: "Angel Children: Defining Nineteenth-Century Girlhood," 28–55.
2. In the 1840s, Spencer produced numerous small sketches of girls, indicating an early interest in this subject. See Robin Bolton-Smith and William H. Truettner, *Lilly Martin Spencer, 1822–1902: The Joys of Sentiment,* exhibition catalogue (Washington, D.C.: Smithsonian Institution Press, 1973), 94–100, 109.
3. Ella M. Foshay, *Mr. Luman Reed's Picture Gallery: A Pioneer Collection of American Art* (New York: Abrams, 1990). A review of the paintings listed in the two volumes of *National Academy of Design Exhibition Record, 1826–1860* (New York: New-York Historical Society, 1943) confirms that genre painters only began to exhibit and probably to paint girlhood subjects in the 1850s, although portraits of girls were exhibited regularly as early as the 1830s.
4. Elizabeth Johns, *American Genre Painting: The Politics of Everyday Life* (New Haven, CT: Yale University Press, 1991), 170.
5. On rare occasions, Mount exhibited girlhood subjects at the National Academy of Design: in 1830, he exhibited *Girl and Pitcher* (location unknown), and a decade later he showed *The Blackberry Girls,* 1840 (Joslyn Art Museum, Omaha, NE). His engagement with this theme was extremely limited.
6. The influence of seventeenth-century Dutch and Flemish genre paintings on the art of Francis William Edmonds is discussed in H. Nichols B. Clark's *Francis W. Edmonds: American Master in the Dutch Tradition,* exhibition catalogue (Washington, D.C., and London: Amon Carter Museum and Smithsonian Institution Press, 1988).
7. While Johnson's painting is obviously indebted to that of Edmonds, Edmonds was probably influenced by John Lewis Krimmel's 1821 aquatint *The Return from Boarding School* (Library Company of Philadelphia), which also shows a bonnet and a bill. I examined the theme of the new bonnet in "City-Country Contrasts in American Genre Paintings, 1830–1860" (Ph.D. dissertation, Rutgers, 1996), 150–164.
8. After serving as the New York agent of the Paris-based firm Goupil, Vibert, and Company from 1848 to 1852, Schaus founded his own company.
9. Mount's paired lithographs of African Americans may have influenced Schaus's decision to sell Spencer's prints as pairs; the first set of paired lithographs after Spencer's works portrayed an African American boy and girl: *Power of Fashion,* 1853, and *Height of Fashion,* 1854.
10. "Art Items," *Philadelphia Daily Evening Bulletin,* March 3, 1870, 2; quoted in Laura Groves Napolitano, "Nurturing Change: Lilly Martin Spencer's Images of Children" (Ph.D. dissertation, University of Maryland, 2008), 131.
11. Johns, *American Genre Painting,* 170.
12. Spencer's patrons are a subject that warrants further investigation. Elizabeth Johns writes that Spencer's work was perceived "as appealing to, and good for, a large, relatively inexperienced, and uneducated audience." See her *American Genre Painting,* 162. Wendy J. Katz convincingly argues that many of Spencer's prints were sold by peddlers in small rural towns. See her "Lilly Martin Spencer and the Art of Refinement," *American Studies* 42, no. 1 (Spring 2001): 24.
13. Peter C. Marzio, *The Democratic Art: Pictures for a Nineteenth-Century America; Chromolithography, 1840–1900* (Boston: David R. Godine, 1979), 125–126.
14. *Art Interchange,* July 19, 1883, 13; cited in Marzio, *Democratic Art,* 128n58.
15. Robin Bolton-Smith and William H. Truettner mention three set of prints: *Power of Fashion,* 1853, and *Height of Fashion,* 1854; *Oh!* and *Hush,* both 1856; and *My Birthday Present,* 1856, and *The Young Soldier,* 1856. See *Lilly Martin Spencer,* 40–41, 145–146, 156–157. I would argue that there are two additional sets, each pairing a young boy and a girl: *The Little Navigator* and *The Little Sunshade,* both 1854; *The First Polka* and *The Young Teacher,* both 1858. While Spencer's lithographs of girls are consistently larger than those of boys, the latter two pairs have similar compositions and dimensions and the same date. It is noteworthy that few of Spencer's prints have survived, indicating that these highly sentimental images were not particularly valued or appreciated during the twentieth century.
16. Johns, *American Genre Painting,* 170–174; David M. Lubin, *Picturing a Nation: Art and Social Change in Nineteenth-Century America* (New Haven, CT: Yale University Press, 1994), 205–271; Katz, "Lilly Martin Spencer and the Art of Refinement," 19.
17. Johns, *American Genre Painting,* 170–175.
18. Nina Baym, *Woman's Fiction: A Guide to Novels by and about Women in America, 1820–1870* (Ithaca, NY: Cornell University Press, 1978), 277.
19. Martha J. Hoppin, "The Sources and Development of William Morris Hunt's Paintings," in Martha J. Hoppin and Henry Adams, *William Morris Hunt: A Memorial Exhibition,* exhibition catalogue (Boston: Museum of Fine Arts, 1979), 12–13.
20. In 1859 and 1860, Johnson showed three girlhood pictures at the National Academy of Design: *The Pets, Roman Girl,* and *The Freedom Ring.* See *National Academy of Design Exhibition Record, 1826–1860,* 1:271.
21. *The First Exhibition of Paintings by Artists of the French School in New-York,* 1857, 7.
22. "The French Exhibition," *New York Times,* November 25, 1857. I am indebted to Kimberly Fisher for finding this review.
23. Clarence Cook, "National Academy of Design," *New-York Daily Tribune,* July 4, 1866, 5; cited in Teresa A. Carbone and Patricia Hills, *Eastman Johnson: Painting America,* exhibition catalogue (New York: Brooklyn Museum of Art, 1999), 146.
24. Gabriel P. Weisberg, *The Realistic Tradition: French Painting and Drawing, 1830–1900,* exhibition catalogue (Cleveland: Cleveland Museum, 1980), 100.

25. I agree with Patricia Hills's interpretation of this painting, which I have expanded to include generational issues. See Hills, "Painting Race: Eastman Johnson's Pictures of Slaves, Ex-Slaves, and Freedmen," in Carbone and Hills, *Eastman Johnson: Painting America,* 138.

26. In 1852, Christian Schussele produced one of the earliest genre paintings to juxtapose an old man with a young girl. That work, entitled *Contrasts* (location unknown), also focused on the disparities between rich and poor. See Hermann Warner Williams Jr., *Mirror to the American Past: A Survey of American Genre Painting, 1750–1900* (Greenwich, CT: New York Graphic Society, 1973), 173. While living in The Hague in 1853, Johnson painted *The Card Players* (Shannon's Fine Art Auctioneers), which includes a young girl and her grandfather. Thomas Waterman Wood's *The American Farmer,* 1874 (New York State Historical Association, Cooperstown), which includes an ancient farmer and a diminutive girl, appears to be indebted to Johnson's *Corn Husking.* In 1875, Johnson again returned to the theme of young girl and old man in *What the Shell Says* (Fine Arts Museums of San Francisco, San Francisco, CA).

27. After the birth of his only child, Ethel, in 1870, Johnson sometimes produced works in which his spirited daughter served as a model, occasionally capturing her as a tomboy (fig. 49).

28. In the 1860s, genre painter Thompson produced a number of works in which a brother and sister are situated in a peaceful, pastoral landscape. See Lee M. Edwards, "The Life and Career of Jerome Thompson," *American Art Journal* 14, no. 4 (Autumn 1982): 19–22. "Guy began to paint genre scenes of children about 1861, taking his cue from Brown, who started to picture children in rustic country settings by 1859." See Bruce Weber, "Seymour Joseph Guy: 'Little Master' of American Genre Painting," *The Magazine Antiques* 31, no. 4 (November 2008): 144.

29. Linda Ayres, "The American Figure: Genre Paintings and Sculpture," in *An American Perspective: Nineteenth-Century Art from the Collection of Jo Ann and Julian Ganz, Jr.* (Washington, D.C.: National Gallery of Art, 1981), 51.

30. Martha Hoppin, *The World of J. G. Brown* (Chesterfield, MA: Chameleon Books, 2010), 22–36, 45–61.

31. Charles Cromwell Ingham's *The Flower Girl,* 1846 (Metropolitan Museum of Art, New York, NY), was one of the earliest paintings of a female flower seller, but Ingham's is considerably older than Brown's children and lacks their innocence. For a brief discussion of the erotic overtones in Ingham's painting, see John Caldwell and Oswaldo Rodriguez Roque, *American Paintings in the Metropolitan Museum of Art* (New York: Metropolitan Museum of Art, 1994), 1:402–403.

32. Ann Douglas, *The Feminization of American Culture* (New York: Noonday Press, 1998).

33. T. S. Arthur, *Advice to Young Ladies on Their Duties and Conduct in Life* (Philadelphia: J. W. Bradley, 1860), 40.

34. Ibid., 42.

35. Harriet Beecher Stowe, "The Chimney-Corner for 1866," *Atlantic Monthly,* April 1866, 494.

36. Alice Fahs, "The Feminized Civil War: Gender, Northern Popular Literature, and the Memory of the War, 1861–1900," *Journal of American History* 85, no. 4 (March 1999): 1476–1480.

37. Sylvia is similar to the New Woman heroines of Henry James and Edith Wharton—Daisy Miller and Lilly Bart—who also die at the end of their stories.

38. Henry James, review of *Moods,* by Louisa M. Alcott, *North American Review,* July 1865, 276; quoted in Louisa May Alcott, *Moods* (New Brunswick, NJ: Rutgers University Press, 1991), 219.

39. *Watch and Ward* is the story of a young girl who becomes the interest of a "middle-aged lover." He adopts her and then grooms her to become the perfect wife—for himself. James's literary fascination with young girls would continue, and several figure prominently in his greatest works: Pansy in *The Portrait of a Lady,* 1880–1881; Maisie in *What Maisie Knew,* 1897; Flora in "The Turn of the Screw," 1898; and, perhaps the most memorable, Daisy in *Daisy Miller,* 1878.

40. Debra Williams Hanson, "Thomas Eakins' Home Scenes of the 1870s" (Ph.D. dissertation, Virginia Commonwealth University, 2005), 26.

41. Helen A. Cooper, *Winslow Homer Watercolors,* exhibition catalogue (Washington, D.C.: National Gallery of Art, 1986), 52–65.

42. G. W. Sheldon, *Hours with Art and Artists* (1882; repr., New York: Garland, 1978), 140; quoted in Cooper, *Winslow Homer Watercolors,* 62.

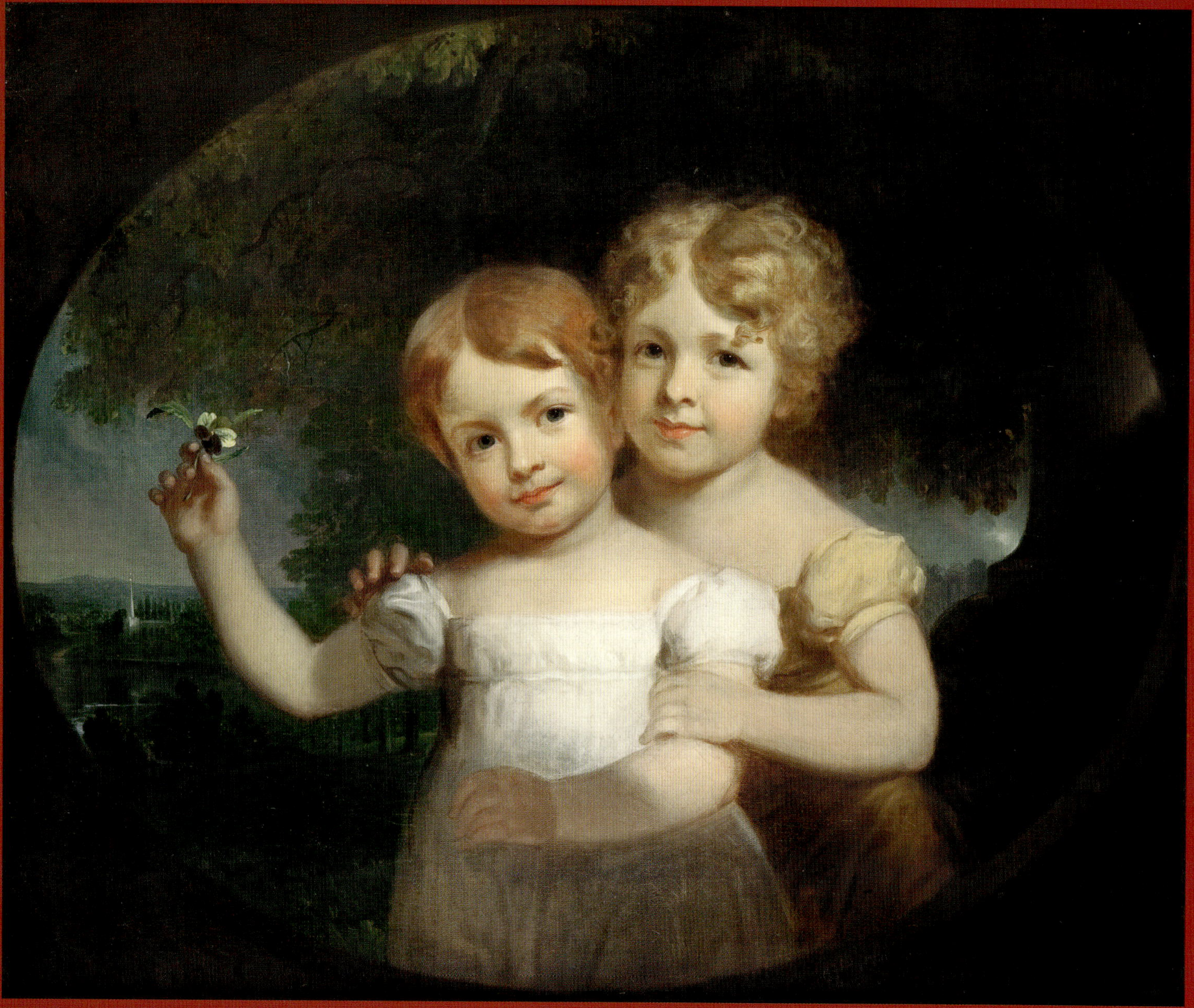

Angel Children

Defining Nineteenth-Century Girlhood

HOLLY PYNE CONNOR

Nineteenth-century American artists employed poses, settings, and the symbolic objects known as attributes to define the personalities of the young girls they portrayed, frequently presenting them as the "angel children" mentioned by Louisa May Alcott in her best-selling 1868–1869 novel, *Little Women*.[1] The most common attributes were flowers, pets, and dolls, all of which reinforced stereotypic views of girls as demure, domestic, dependent, and sweet. These traditional attributes have a long history in European art, where they formed a well-known pictorial vocabulary; their pervasive use in American art, literature, and popular culture shows that painters and their audiences understood their deeper significance. Even before the nineteenth century, American artists were aware of gendered attributes and their meanings through reproductions of European pictures. During the second half of the century, however, artists became increasingly cosmopolitan, traveling to Europe where they studied the great art of the past, mining it for ideas and inspiration, but also transforming it to achieve their own personal artistic objectives.

Throughout the nineteenth century, infants and young children were characterized as angelic and androgynous, since parents wanted to de-emphasize the sexual identity of their children.[2] As this attitude extended to clothing, with both boys and girls wearing dresses, the task of deciphering the sex of young children in portraits and genre paintings can be extremely difficult for twenty-first-century audiences not conversant with Victorian attitudes. Upon close inspection, however, subtle clues, such as attributes, can indicate the sex, personality, and even the future expectations for the young subjects.

Since adults wanted to view young children as asexual, they treated male and female infants and toddlers in the same way. Child-raising manuals recommended identical routines and diets for small boys and girls, and babies of both sexes were allowed to be physically active and to behave in a boisterous manner.[3] "Our sons and daughters start even," the advice writer Marion Harland wrote in 1882. "Green apples disagree as surely with one as the other, and the same kind and amount of hard play have the like sequence of fatigue."[4] Infants and toddlers were attired in loose, comfortable dresses and robes so that they could easily be changed, kept dry, and freely move their limbs. Boys and girls wore dresses until the age of around five or six, when boys were "breeched" (put into trousers). Infant dresses were made of white cotton, as it could be washed and bleached without fading; white was also the preferred color as it symbolized purity, a virtue associated with childhood.[5] Hairstyles were not always the same but could be confusing: boys with long, flowing curls and girls with short, cropped hair appeared regularly in paintings, sculptures, photographs, and prints.

Historians have noted that the practice of attiring babies in dresses, regardless of sex, began in America as early as the seventeenth century. Young children were clothed in long robes or petticoats to prevent them from crawling, which was viewed as bestial rather than human behavior. During the seventeenth and eighteenth centuries, childhood was seen as a period of innate sinfulness and physical limitation,

Fig. 13. (opposite) Henry Inman, *Children of Bishop George W. Doane*, 1835. Oil on canvas, 25 x 31¼ in. Newark Museum; Purchase 1959, Louis Bamberger Bequest Fund 59.83

attitudes derived from the sixteenth-century writings of Protestant Reformation theologian John Calvin. Calvin promoted the idea that children were born in sin and needed strict discipline to overcome their inherently wicked natures. American Puritans regarded childhood as a time of moral and physical deficiency, even depravity, in part because infants were unable to control their emotions and bodily functions. Parents encouraged their children to stand upright and walk as early as possible, since straight posture was associated with respectability and morality.[6] As infant mortality rates remained extremely high until the end of the nineteenth century, parents were also painfully aware that childhood was a dangerous time. By encouraging children to act in a mature fashion and by dressing them as adults at an early age, parents hoped their young children would survive this perilous period.[7] For example, in the double portrait *Elizabeth Clarke Freake (Mrs. John Freake) and Baby Mary* (fig. 14), painted about 1670 by an unknown artist, the infant girl appears as a miniature adult. She is attired in a costume similar to that worn by her mother, and her upright pose is stiff and unnatural. Historian Joseph E. Illick has speculated that the child may have been wearing a corset to keep her body erect: it may well be that the artist and the child's parents wanted to present her as capable of standing, even though she was too young to assume this pose without assistance.[8] Indeed, Mary's posture is highly contrived, and she would not have been able to sustain it through the long sittings required to complete the portrait.

Fig. 14. Unknown artist, *Elizabeth Clarke Freake (Mrs. John Freake) and Baby Mary,* 1671–1674. Oil on canvas, 42½ x 36¾ in. Worcester Art Museum, Worcester, MA; Gift of Mr. and Mrs. Albert W. Rice 1963.134

By the beginning of the nineteenth century, however, young children were being depicted in a radically different manner, indicating dramatic changes in attitudes about nature and nurture. Nestled in the laps of their mothers, babies and even older children were characterized as adorable and loving, rather than as small, independent adults. During the eighteenth century, Enlightenment ideas as articulated in the writings of John Locke and Jean-Jacques Rousseau began to erode earlier views about the depravity of children. Locke wrote that at birth children were like blank slates whose future characters were shaped by their environment and by the education and training provided by parents and teachers. Rousseau, on the other hand, thought that young children were natural, spontaneous beings who had not been corrupted by what he considered the pernicious influences of civilization. Increasingly, childhood was viewed as a unique stage in human development, and children were thought to be innocent rather than depraved or sinful. By the end of the eighteenth century, the Enlightenment ideas of Locke and Rousseau had influenced European writers and artists, who developed and popularized what is now referred to as the Romantic concept of childhood, emphasizing the naturalness and purity of youth.

European ideas profoundly affected nineteenth-century American attitudes toward children, inspiring artists and writers to characterize children as asexual, angelic beings.[9] The two figures in Henry Inman's *Children of Bishop George W. Doane*, 1835 (fig. 13), appear to be more feminine that masculine. Not only do they appear in the high-waisted dresses inspired by the French Empire style popular in the 1820s and 1830s, but one of the figures also holds a flower, the most common attribute of femininity as well as a popular symbol of childhood fragility. In fact, the children were the sons of an Episcopal bishop of New Jersey. William Croswell Doane, age three, is dressed in white and grasps a pansy in his hand, while behind him is his five-year-old brother, George Hobart Doane, who lovingly embraces his sibling. While flowers were a pervasive emblem of childhood and femininity, the pansy has a number of specific meanings, one of which is religious. As pansies are composed of three different colors, they are associated with the Holy Trinity: the Father, Son, and Holy Ghost. The pansy's religious meaning resonates in Inman's double portrait, particularly as the flower is held over the illuminated spire of a distant Gothic Revival church. Inman's reference to the Holy Trinity, a key Christian doctrine, emphasized the boys' religious upbringing and the family's faith.[10] The setting is also highly symbolic, since the children appear behind a stone portal, which acts as a barrier between them and the viewer, alluding to the belief that childhood is a unique stage in human development, separate from the world of adults. By situating the figures in a lush landscape, whose verdant branches frame the boys' heads, Inman referenced the Romantic idea that childhood was a natural, spontaneous, and uncorrupted state. These two boys are children of nature, an idea that originated in the European art and literature of the late eighteenth century.

The sex of the Doane children would be difficult to determine if the sitters were unidentified, but through the research of the art historian Jennifer Yunginger, a greater understanding of the different hairstyles, jewelry, accessories, and attributes of boys and girls has become available.[11] By analyzing a group of early nineteenth-century folk portraits, Yunginger realized that boys' hair is usually parted on the side, while girls' hair is parted in the middle. Another determining factor can be the sitter's jewelry. Although girls wear bracelets, necklaces, and rings, boys are rarely shown with jewelry. Throughout the eighteenth and nineteenth centuries, coral was the most popular material for children's jewelry and was also applied to toy rattles, as it was thought to have protective properties as a charm against illness and evil.

In a series of portraits that the renowned folk artist Ammi Phillips painted in the 1830s, the male and female sitters wear identical red dresses with white trim, but only the girls have coral necklaces. While on one level these pictures underscore Phillips's standard working method of using the same clothing, pose, and accessories for multiple portraits, they also dramatically illustrate the desire of adults to downplay the sexuality of their young children by having identical wardrobes for girls and boys. In Phillips's 1834 portrait *Andrew Jackson Ten Broeck—Age One Year, Six Months* (fig. 15), the male sitter appears in a bright crimson dress with white detailing on the waist and sleeves, red shoes, and long white pantaloons. The female sitters in three other Phillips portraits painted in the 1830s wear dresses that are almost identical to the one worn by Ten Broeck: *Girl in a Red Dress* (fig. 16), which was made in 1835 or so; *Girl in Red Dress with Cat and Dog*, 1830 (American Folk Art Museum, New York); and *Girl in Red Dress with Dog* (private collection), dated between 1830 and 1835. All four sitters have short, androgynous haircuts, which further obscures their sexual identity, while an identical brown dog appears in the lower corner of each composition, perhaps as a symbol of fidelity. Although small details such as shoe color and lace trim vary slightly from portrait to portrait, the works are remarkably alike.[12]

Clues to the gender of the sitters are, however, provided. In addition to the necklaces previously mentioned, the settings are different. The boy is seated next to a hickory tree, while each of the girls appears in a room decorated with a rug and upholstered furniture. During the nineteenth century, there were separate spheres for males and females: women and girls were meant to inhabit the home, while men and boys were expected to engage in worldly activities.[13] Doctors, educators, and ministers promoted the concept that girls and women were biologically, intellectually, and temperamentally different from boys and men. Girls, like grown women, were thought to be emotional and nurturing. Their domain was the home, where family duties and domestic activities occupied their lives. Older girls were frequently encouraged to curtail their physical activity and their academic pursuits, while older boys prepared for active lives in competitive commercial and professional environments.

In portraits, settings and attributes can be employed to refer to personality traits viewed as either masculine or feminine, or can allude to the sitter's role in society. Although the outfits worn by

Fig. 15. Ammi Phillips, *Andrew Jackson Ten Broeck—Age One Year, Six Months* (detail), 1834. Oil on canvas, 39 x 34 in. Private collection

Fig. 16. Ammi Phillips, *Girl in a Red Dress,* c. 1835. Oil on canvas, 32⅜ x 27⅜ in. Terra Foundation for American Art, Chicago; Daniel J. Terra Collection 1992.57. Photograph courtesy of Art Resource, NY

the brother and sister painted by Phillips around 1832 are similar, the subjects are holding different attributes (figs. 17 and 18). Attired in a red dress, the boy holds a hammer, a masculine object, while his sister in pink holds over her womb a strawberry, a predominantly feminine attribute frequently associated with fertility. The brother also appears to stand, but his sister sits, a passive pose. Although pink is now associated with little girls, color was not used to identify children's sex until the early twentieth century.

The figure in *The Goying Child* (fig. 19), painted between 1832 and 1835 by an unknown, self-taught artist, is often thought to be female as the sitter is attired in a distinctive yellow calico dress with matching pantaloons. In fact, the child is a young boy who has not been breeched. A number of masculine attributes surround the figure. The whip he holds is a symbol of male power and authority, while the dog at his feet is also a clue to his sexuality—dogs appear more frequently in male portraits as symbols of loyalty and, sometimes, submission. Towering over the landscape, the boy has an upright, rigid, and commanding pose. On the other hand, the sexual identity of the sitter in *Girl with Flowers* (fig. 20) of about 1840, also by an unknown, self-taught artist, is unambiguous. The title announces that the child is female; the figure holds flowers; and her demeanor is passive. The artist placed her next to a large table, a juxtaposition that emphasizes her small stature and vulnerability, while her stance is relaxed and tranquil as she leans against the table as if for support. The sweetness and fragility of girlhood are the dominant themes of this work, underscored by the bunch of dainty flowers, the sitter's angelic and luminous countenance,

Fig. 17. Ammi Phillips, *Boy in Red,* c. 1832. Oil on canvas, 23½ x 20 in. Princeton University Art Museum; Gift of Edward Duff Balken, Class of 1897 Y1958-75. Photograph by Bruce M. White

and her beautiful salmon-colored dress. Another significant difference between the two portraits mentioned above is their settings. The girl is in an interior, while the boy is outdoors, again suggesting separate male and female spheres.

Although the gender of infants and toddlers is often ambiguous, older girls are easily identifiable by their dress, hairstyles, and demeanor. As girls matured, they were expected to abandon their energetic and uninhibited ways and behave in a demure and dignified fashion, while their skirts were gradually lengthened to cover their legs and feet. With puberty, adolescents were strapped into corsets, their hair was tightly bound, and their mobility was further restricted by heavy, floor-length dresses. "The transition from childhood to girlhood, when a little girl has had an almost unlimited freedom of out-of-door life," Lucy Larcom recounted in her engaging 1889 autobiography, *A New England Girlhood,* "is particularly the toning down of a mild sort of barbarianism, and is often attended by a painfully awkward self-consciousness."[14] Like many other women of her generation, Larcom was painfully aware of the emotional stress accompanying the difficult transition from youth to adolescence, a subject discussed in Lauren Lessing's essay in this volume (see pages 106–132).

For women and girls, flowers were the most common attribute, and they appear in close proximity to female figures in paintings, sculptures, prints, and photographs.[15] Flowers appear on the bodies of women and girls, in their hair, on their breasts, or as part of the fabric design of their clothing. As Meg Marsh comments in *Little Women,* "Mother said real flowers were the prettiest ornament for a young girl."[16] Girls were even encouraged to assume the

Fig. 18. Ammi Phillips, *Girl in Pink,* c. 1832. Oil on canvas, 23½ x 20 in. Princeton University Art Museum; Gift of Edward Duff Balken, Class of 1897 Y1958-74. Photograph by Bruce M. White

Fig. 19. Unknown artist, *The Goying Child,* c. 1832–1835. Oil on wood, 42 x 25¼ in. Newark Museum; Anonymous gift, 1938 38.213

Fig. 20. Unknown artist, *Girl with Flowers,* c. 1840. Oil on canvas, 36⅛ x 29 in. Newark Museum; Purchase 1931, Felix Fuld Bequest Fund 31.145

role of flowers in the games they played, as discussed in Lydia Maria Francis Child's *The Little Girl's Own Book,* 1835.[17] In general, flowers symbolized childhood fragility, feminine beauty, and fecundity, but individual flowers also had specific meanings. For example, lilies symbolized purity because of their connection to the Virgin Mary, and roses had multiple meanings, which included beauty and romance.[18] Flower imagery connected children, girls, and women, indicating that all three shared characteristics. Little girls naturally model themselves after their mothers, but women were often infantilized, encouraged to be dependent, subservient, sweet, and emotional. In nineteenth-century art, literature, and popular culture, the pervasive use of the language of flowers indicates that this vocabulary was well-known and understood, although each flower usually had multiple meanings.[19]

The novels of Maria Susanna Cummins, Susan Warner, Henry James, and Louisa May Alcott, among numerous others, provide another lens to view attitudes about girlhood, as young girls are frequent protagonists in these works. James in particular associated girls with flower imagery, providing floral names for the heroines who populate his novels and short stories, including Daisy in *Daisy Miller,* 1878; Flora in "The Turn of the Screw," 1898; and Pansy in *The Portrait of a Lady,* 1880–1881.[20] James used these names symbolically to enhance the depth and complexity of his narratives and to underscore the personality traits of his female characters. The daisy, for example, is an uncultivated meadow flower, and Daisy Miller, while beautiful and appealing, was also wild and unrestrained. She recklessly flouted the conventions of proper female behavior and was eventually ostracized by the expatriate community in Rome. At the beginning of "The Turn of the Screw," little Flora is described as beautiful and pure, but by the end of the tale she has become "hideously hard; she had turned common and almost ugly."[21] Flora's pivotal transformation heightens one of the central mysteries of the tale, which is never fully resolved: whether the two children are innocent or depraved. Finally, Pansy, the illegitimate daughter of Gilbert Osmond and Madame Merle, is referred to as "a little convent-flower" by her father, evoking the religious associations of this flower discussed above.[22]

Painters, sculptors, and photographers repeatedly relied on floral symbolism to provide their images with additional levels of meaning. Most pervasive is the traditional metaphor equating girls with flowers and buds: lovely and delicate. Cultivating flowers was also a traditional feminine pursuit. In *The Female Student; or, Lectures to Young Ladies on Female Education,* 1836, the writer Mrs. Phelps commented, "The cultivation of flowers, and indeed every thing connected with gardening, has a most happy influence upon the disposition as well as the health. I scarcely know of an instance of a lady being at the same time ill-tempered and fond of cultivating flowers . . . To the cheerful they suggest images of hope and happiness, and to the disturbed mind they seem to have the power of imparting serenity."[23]

Picking Flowers, circa 1845 (fig. 21), is an iconic image of girlhood filled with feminine attributes including a cat, bird, house, and flowers. The painting is attributed to Samuel Miller, a self-taught artist who was aware of the long-standing artistic practice of employing gendered objects. The little girl in her bright red dress with white pantaloons, a costume similar to the ones found in the portraits by Phillips discussed above, has a basket of flowers on her arm. The roses represent beauty, with the white rosebuds adding the suggestion of a person too young for marriage; the buttercups at her feet probably allude to childishness; the white house behind the figure seems to refer to the child's future role as wife and mother in the domestic sphere.[24] The figure appears

Fig. 21. Attributed to Samuel Miller, *Picking Flowers,* 1840–1850. Oil on canvas, 44½ x 27½ in. Fenimore Art Museum, Cooperstown, NY N0225.1961

Fig. 22. Cecilia Beaux, *Fanny Travis Cochran,* 1887. Oil on canvas, 35½ x 28½ in. Pennsylvania Academy of the Fine Arts; Gift of Fanny Travis Cochran 1955.12

outdoors rather than in an interior, but she is in a gardenlike setting, which evokes the *hortus conclusus,* where the Virgin Mary and other virtuous women have been pictured.[25]

While flowers were stock attributes in portraits of young girls by self-taught painters, they also appear regularly in the art of more sophisticated, academic artists like John Singer Sargent, Cecilia Beaux, Frank Benson, Abbott Handerson Thayer, William Merritt Chase, and Winslow Homer, among many others. As conservator Judith Walsh had demonstrated, Homer repeatedly incorporated floral symbolism into his art, particularly in the 1860s and 1870s, when he focused on women and girls.[26] During this period, he connected girlhood with buds, flowers, and springtime. Homer's girls typically appear in lush spring or summer landscapes, where they are portrayed as healthy, robust, and removed from the modern world. Although these figures often owed a debt to European peasant imagery, they also celebrated rural values associated with America's past, conveying a nostalgia for a way of life that was rapidly vanishing but was viewed as simple and wholesome. Homer's *Girl and Laurel,* 1879 (fig. 96, page 124), depicts a rural girl dressed in a white apron and bonnet standing in front of a profusion of flowering laurel bushes.[27] Freshness, fecundity, and innocence are Homer's themes, underscored by the early morning light, the spring setting, the white clothing, and the huge blossoms. In nineteenth-century floral dictionaries, the laurel is consistently associated with glory, a meaning the artist probably had in mind, as the painting captures the radiant glory and beauty of the young girl and the natural world surrounding her. Country lasses were viewed as more natural, pure, and industrious than their counterparts in the city, who were thought to be more materialistic and obsessed with fashion, themes that Alcott explored in her novel *An Old-Fashioned Girl,* 1870, at a time when Homer was likewise celebrating country girls.

At the end of the century, girls continued to be associated with floral imagery. While artists employed flowers to impart specific meanings to their interpretations, they also used artistic license in the selection and placement of the blossoms to ensure that their compositions were compelling works of art that satisfied the tastes of their patrons, their sitters, and themselves. In Beaux's memorable 1887 portrait (fig. 22), Fanny Travis Cochran has a colorful bunch of purple, yellow, and white pansies in her lap. As a cosmopolitan artist who was aware of European pictorial conventions, Beaux knew that placing flowers in this suggestive position was a standard device symbolizing fecundity. At the same time, Beaux was probably attracted to the pansy's colors, as they provide a strong accent, reinforcing the luscious yellow of Fanny's sash, which Beaux created specifically for this portrait by buying the fabric and fashioning the voluminous belt.[28] While the pansy has religious associations in Inman's *Children of Bishop George W. Doane,* discussed above, in Beaux's work the flowers probably refer to thoughts and thoughtfulness, their best-known meaning. This reading is strengthened by Fanny's pensive expression: she looks directly at the viewer with a serious air and penetrating gaze, suggesting an alert and keen intelligence.[29]

Like Beaux, Sargent was completely conversant with European portrait conventions, and he often selected costumes for his sitters and props that he deemed appropriate. Floral imagery appears repeatedly in his paintings of young girls, the most famous of which is the stunning *Carnation, Lily, Lily, Rose,* 1885–1886 (Tate, London), which is an iconic image of childhood beauty and innocence. As in numerous other late nineteenth-century pictures of girls and plants, Sargent's title refers to the blossoms rather

Fig. 23. John Singer Sargent, *Katherine Chase Pratt*, 1890. Oil on canvas, 40 x 30⅛ in. Worcester Art Museum, Worcester, MA; Gift of William I. Clark

than the figures, suggesting that the flowers are more noteworthy than the girls. In his 1890 portrait of Katherine Chase Pratt, Sargent also reduced the significance of the sitter by focusing the viewer's attention on the spectacularly lush hydrangeas, which frame the girl in such a way that figure and ground seem to have equal importance (fig. 23). Rather than creating a deeply psychological interpretation of Katherine, Sargent produced a highly decorative composition in which he intimately connected the adolescent girl to the flowers that surround her: the white, lavender, and pale green of the hydrangeas are the same colors as Katherine's flowing dress.[30] Hydrangeas have numerous meanings including boastfulness and heartlessness, which Sargent probably knew.[31] In this portrait, however, the artist seems primarily attracted to the luxurious colors, the abundant blossoms, and perhaps the hydrangea's exotic origins in Japan. In this ornamental painting, girl and flowers are welded together so that figure and ground create a seamless, gorgeous, and striking composition, which visually manifests the common analogy treating young girls like lush and beautiful flowers, but which tends to dehumanize the figure as well.

Girls were also repeatedly paired with small pets, particularly cats and birds. Like these domesticated animals, girls were expected to be docile and obedient. When pets appear in family portraits, their presence may indicate that the pictured animal was part of the household; young children were assigned the care of pets, which became their companions and playmates. The coupling of cats and female figures has a more specific meaning, however, with a long history in European art. In seventeenth-century Dutch genre paintings, for example, cats are symbols of lust and idleness when they are placed in unmade beds, in rooms where women and men are seen drinking together, and in other sexually suggestive scenes. But cats also reference the joys of domesticity: they appear in cozy interiors, near the hearth or asleep on chairs.[32] Nineteenth-century girls were sometimes encouraged to act like cats when playing such children's games as puss in the corner, while Gerty, the heroine of *The Lamplighter*, Maria Susanna Cummins's best-selling 1854 novel, is given both a tiny kitten and, later, a cat as pets.[33] In general, when cats appear in nineteenth-century portraits of children, they are employed as charming accessories and as gendered attributes defining little girls as adorable, domestic, and dependent. In the paintings of such cosmopolitan artists as Thomas Eakins, Eastman Johnson, and Seymour Joseph Guy, however, cats and other pets can evoke more complex and even disturbing associations.

In 1855, Eastman Johnson and William Morris Hunt returned to America after long sojourns in Europe. The following year, each produced a painting of a young girl with one or more pets; as these were not portraits, they were anomalous in American art at the time. Johnson's *The Pets* (fig. 24) is an unsettling narrative painting in which a girl appears in a dingy interior surrounded by a variety of pets. She sits quietly with her hands in her lap and her feet crossed at the ankles, a pose indicating modesty. Like the languid women in the decorative paintings of Thomas Dewing, John White Alexander, and John Singer Sargent at the turn of the century, she seems incapable of action, lacking the energy to move or engage with her environment.[34] Her inertia confines her to the chair and the room while she and the viewer gaze at her pets: a cat sitting on an open cage, a parrot chained to its perch, and a fish in a small bowl. The cage and chain evoke themes of entrapment and oppression; a mood of melancholy pervades the dimly lit interior with its isolated child and shabby rear wall. With its shadowy space and implied male gaze, which is unacknowledged by the girl and therefore surreptitious, *The Pets* prefigures such later paintings by Guy as *Story of Golden Locks,* painted around 1870 (Collection of Mathew Wolf and Daniel Wolf), *Making a Train,* 1867 (fig. 90, page 117), and *Dressing for the Rehearsal,* circa 1890 (fig. 47, page 68). In the latter two works by Guy, however, the implied male gaze is uncanny and voyeuristic.

Hunt's *Girl with Cat* (fig. 25), on the other hand, focuses on the single figure of a young girl shown with a small brown cat nestled on her chest and shoulder. Child and animal are physically connected, underscoring that both are docile, domestic, and passive. Here the cat is employed as a feminine attribute that enhances the sense of stillness and repose, as the viewer is encouraged to imagine the soft purring of the recumbent animal. The artist's main preoccupation, however, is with creating a poetic and evocative image. The deep shadows, mysterious background, and the child's introspective expression establish a mood of reverie and timelessness while paying homage to the art of Jean-François Millet, with whom Hunt had studied and worked while in France the previous year. By attiring the girl in an exquisite old-fashioned pink dress, Hunt disengages the figure from the present and places her in the distant past.

When Thomas Eakins returned to Philadelphia in 1870 after four years in Europe, he too painted a number of works depicting young girls in domestic interiors, including *Home Scene* (fig. 50, page 72) and *Elizabeth Crowell with a Dog* (fig. 51, page 73). In *Home Scene,* Eakins employs two cats to underscore the different personalities, demeanors, and abilities of his sisters. While Margaret sits quietly at the piano with a small immobile cat on her shoulder, Caroline actively writes on a tablet next to a lively feline with an erect tail. By placing Margaret's cat on her shoulder, Eakins stresses that her musical activity is arrested. Conversely, the alert and mobile cat beside Caroline highlights her mental and physical engagement. Caroline intently writes or draws, but her older sister passively gazes with a thoughtful expression. Eakins further contrasts the two sisters by including a musical score beside Margaret's head and a slate near Caroline, suggesting that the elder needs assistance to play the piano successfully, while the younger independently creates her own design or text through the power of her intellect and imagination.[35]

Like Eakins, Guy produced memorable and at times unconventional interpretations of girlhood, which can have ambiguous narratives with sexual undertones. In general, however, the symbolism of his pictures derived from the English narrative paintings he had seen in London during his formative years.[36] Guy often paired female subjects with cats, but he and other artists also associated them with birds, which symbolized spirituality and virtue. Guy's *Girl with Canary (The New Arrival),* painted in 1860 (fig. 26), depicts a young girl looking wistfully at a bird in a cage. While bird and child are

Fig. 24. Eastman Johnson, *The Pets,* 1856. Oil, transferred from academy board to Masonite panel, 25 x 28¾ in. Corcoran Gallery of Art, Washington, D.C.; Gift of William Wilson Corcoran 69.44

Fig. 25. William Morris Hunt, *Girl with Cat,* 1856. Oil on canvas, 42⅛ x 33⅜ in. Museum of Fine Arts, Boston; Bequest of Edmund Dwight 00.504

both captives of the domestic sphere, Guy is also informing the viewer that the girl's virtue is intact, a theme popularized by seventeenth-century Dutch and Flemish genre painters. Numerous other artists, including John Lewis Krimmel, William Merritt Chase, and John Singer Sargent, among others, linked young girls and caged birds; the symbolism was widely understood and appreciated.[37]

Together with flowers and pets, dolls were among the most common objects in the depictions of young girls. These toys served multiple purposes; significantly, they encouraged those who played with them to become nurturing, devoted, and engaged mothers. Treated as if they were real babies that needed care and attention, dolls were cherished companions. Many were sold without clothing, so they provided their owners the opportunity to practice their sewing.[38] Sewing was an obligatory skill for women and girls: "Girls in every station should be instructed in the use of the needle," wrote Marion Harland in 1882. "A knowledge of the rudiments of needle-work should be as much a matter of course as to know the alphabet."[39] Proficiency in making and repairing clothing was taken for granted, while such fancy, decorative works as samplers were viewed as worthwhile pastimes. "The dressing of dolls is a useful as well as a pleasant employment for little girls," wrote Lydia Child in 1835. "If they are careful about small gowns, caps, and spencers, it will tend to make them ingenious about their own dresses, when they are older."[40] Toys were gender-specific. Boys amused themselves with toy soldiers, guns, trains, and boats, acting the part of vigorous adults—strong, brave, assertive, and outgoing; girls' playthings were small and fragile, intended for quiet recreation indoors that anticipated domestic duties.[41]

In *Feeding Dolly (If You Don't Eat It, I'll Give It to Doggie)*, 1890 (fig. 27), William J. McCloskey playfully captures the nurturing instincts of girls, picturing his daughter Eleanor in the dual roles of mother and caretaker.[42] Situated in a sumptuously decorated, dimly lit room, Eleanor feeds her doll, as her stuffed dog stands in attendance on a low stool. While the child takes her imaginary responsibilities seriously, intently focusing on the toy in her lap, the viewer is encouraged to respond in an amused and patronizing manner.[43] McCloskey's title heightens the humor of the piece, providing a narrative in which the child warns her doll that if the food is rejected, it will be given to the stuffed dog.

Sentimental images such as McCloskey's reflect traditional Victorian attitudes about girls' nurturing natures as well as the role that toys played in their social conditioning, but they also show that dolls were playmates, engaging children's imagination and providing entertainment (fig. 28). While McCloskey portrayed his daughter as actively

Fig. 26. Seymour Joseph Guy, *Girl with Canary (The New Arrival),* 1860. Oil on canvas, 12¼ x 9¼ in. Private collection

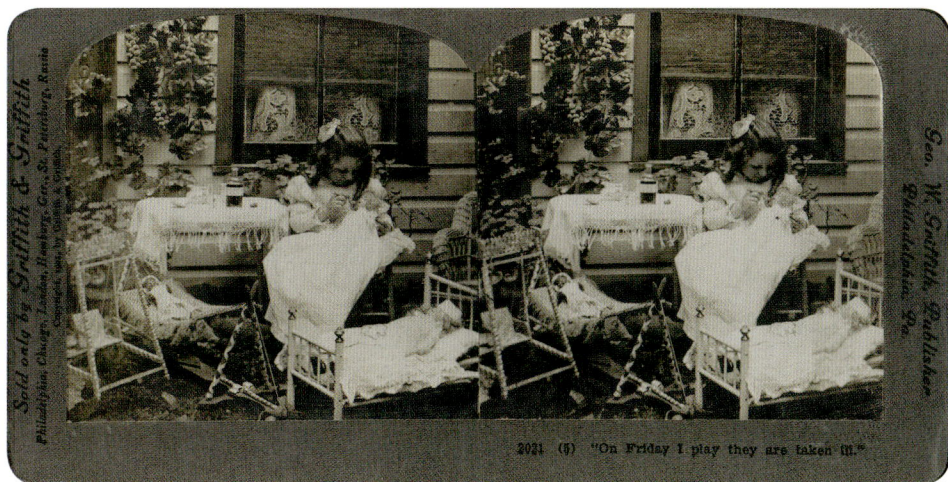

Fig. 27. (above) William J. McCloskey, *Feeding Dolly (If You Don't Eat It, I'll Give It to Doggie)*, 1890. Oil on canvas, 20 x 24 in. Hudson River Museum; Gift of Mrs. Lillie H. Seaman 25.97

Fig. 28. (left) Griffith and Griffith (Philadelphia, PA), *"On Friday I play that they are taken ill,"* 1901. Photograph, 3½ x 7 in. Collection of Tanya Sheehan

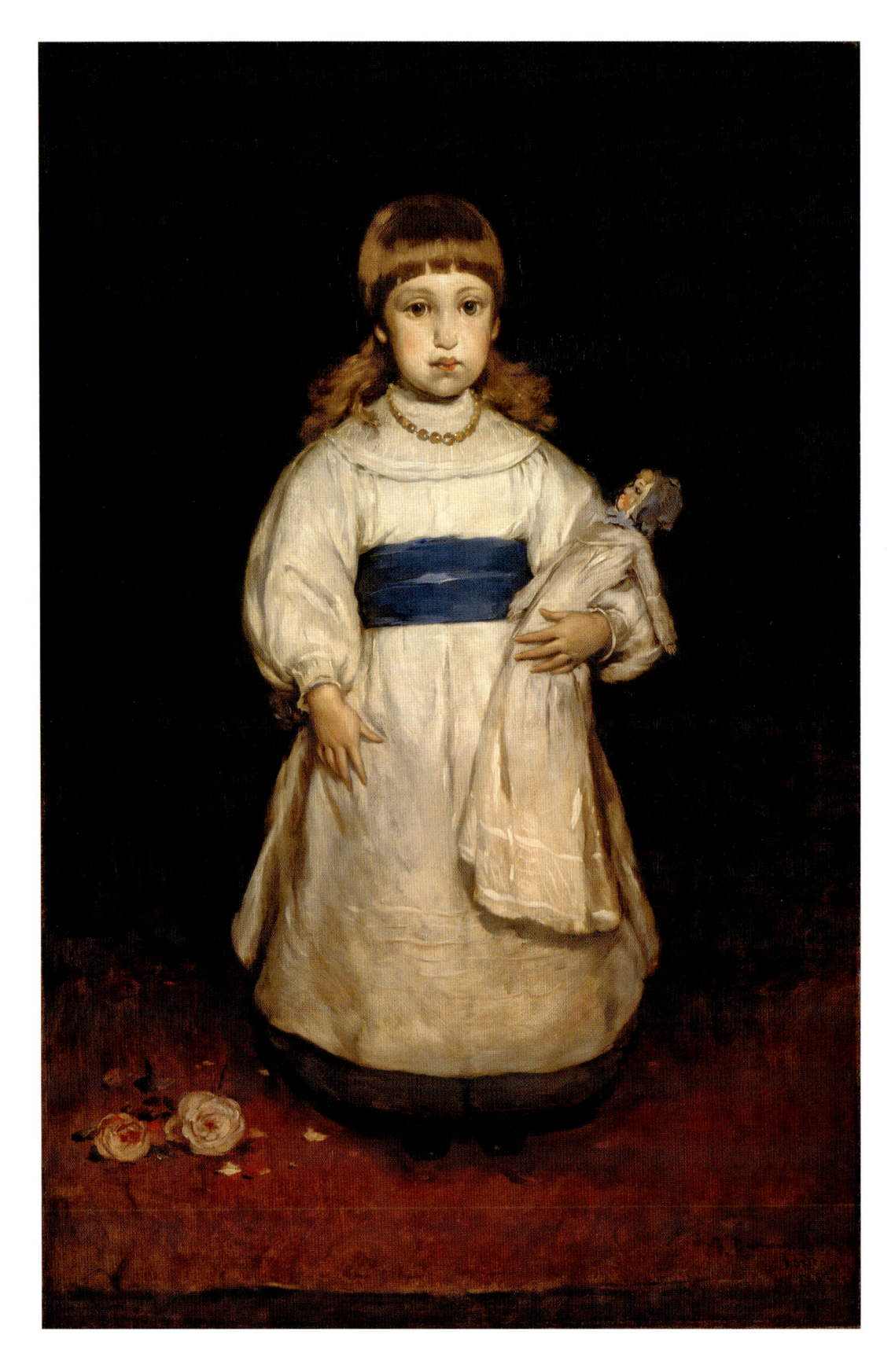

Fig. 29. Frank Duveneck, *Mary Cabot Wheelwright,* 1882. Oil on linen, 50³⁄₁₆ x 33¹⁄₁₆ in. Brooklyn Museum; Dick S. Ramsay Fund 40.87

involved in her make-believe role, Frank Duveneck characterized Mary Cabot Wheelwright as a passive doll in his 1882 portrait (fig. 29). Gently holding a large doll, Mary has a stiff, frozen pose devoid of animation; her expression is blank and lifeless. The artist connected the child with her toy through his choice of costumes and colors: both figures wear white dresses and Mary's blue sash is the same hue as the doll's bonnet. Beside Mary on the floor are two roses, symbols of beauty and perfection, which provide vivid color accents that enliven an otherwise dark foreground. By including two of the most pervasive attributes of girlhood, flowers and a doll, Duveneck underscored the child's loveliness and fragility but also reinforced feminine stereotypes, which defined girls as powerless, passive, and dependent.[44]

While Duveneck characterized Mary Wheelwright as incapable of action, Sargent focused on the energy and vitality of girlhood in his powerful full-length portrait of Ruth Sears Bacon painted in 1887 (fig. 30). Placed in the center of a vortex of energized brushstrokes, Ruth commands the viewer's attention with her penetrating and mesmerizing gaze, suggesting an inquisitive, intelligent mind. This is a memorable depiction: the face is unforgettable, while the painting's immense scale and unconventional composition create a riveting image. Although Sargent, like Duveneck, included a doll in the portrait, his animated child becomes a foil to the lifeless toy. The sketchy, unfinished quality of the background behind the figure suggests the unformed nature of childhood, a pictorial device also used by William Merritt Chase in the portrait of his daughter Cosy in *Did You Speak to Me?* painted around 1897 (fig. 35, page 56).

Rather than capturing unique individuals as Duveneck, Sargent, and Chase had done in the portraits discussed above, William Henry Lippincott presents three recognizable types in his 1895 *Childish Thoughts* (fig. 31). In the artist's fanciful re-creation of a colonial drawing room, a little girl plays happily with her doll, her attractive and fashionably dressed mother plays the piano—a well-known reference to gentility and refinement— and her grandmother quietly knits by the hearth. As the only figure involved in a productive activity, the grandmother attests to the strong work ethic of the previous generation, while her placement immediately in front of the large fireplace connects her to the perceived physical and emotional warmth and sustenance of home, a theme analyzed at length by Sarah Burns.[45] Representing the future,

Fig. 30. John Singer Sargent, *Ruth Sears Bacon,* 1887. Oil on canvas, 48¾ x 36¼ in. Wadsworth Atheneum Museum of Art; Gift of Mrs. Austin Cheney 1975.92. Photograph courtesy Art Resource, NY

Fig. 31. William Henry Lippincott, *Childish Thoughts,* 1895. Oil on canvas, 32¼ x 45¹¹⁄₁₆ in. Pennsylvania Academy of the Fine Arts; Gift of Mary H. Rice 1976.3

the charming and carefree child is one of the focal points of the composition, underscored by the painting's title and the fact that mother and grandmother gaze intently at her.

Lippincott's interest in depicting family interactions and stereotypic characterizations is also evident in *Infantry in Arms,* 1887 (fig. 32), a humorous vignette situated in a lavishly decorated Victorian home. This engaging narrative painting contrasts the personalities and behaviors of little boys and girls. In the foreground is a young girl dressed in white who clutches her mother in terror. The source of her dismay is her tiny brother, the subject of the painting's title, who is gaily playing soldier. While she holds a pretty blond doll with a serene face, he brandishes a toy sword. Even though the boy is considerably younger than his sister, he is depicted as the forceful and extroverted sibling. Throughout the nineteenth century, when brothers and sisters were shown together in the same picture, the boys had active and commanding poses indicating assertive personalities that would enable them to succeed in the world, while passive and submissive demeanors defined their sisters, who were groomed to be supportive wives and mothers.

When Cecilia Beaux painted the double portrait of Harold and Mildred Colton, 1886–1887 (fig. 33), she differentiated the male and female sitters, but her portrait is unusual since both children appear as strong personalities, suggested by their penetrating gazes. Although Harold is the elder and male, he is not the dominant figure; each child possesses an equally powerful physical and psychological presence—the space on the huge Chippendale corner chair is shared and their heads occupy similar elevations. Brother and sister are shown as equals, which was atypical for the period, eliciting a number of intriguing speculations. Was Beaux, as a woman

Fig. 32. William Henry Lippincott, *Infantry in Arms,* 1887. Oil on canvas, 32 x 53¼ in. Pennsylvania Academy of the Fine Arts; Gift of Homer F. Emens and Francis C. Jones 1922.10

Fig. 33. Cecilia Beaux, *Portrait of Harold and Mildred Colton,* 1886–1887. Oil on canvas, 55⅞ x 42 in. Pennsylvania Academy of the Fine Arts; Partial gift of Captain and Mrs. J. Ferrell Colton, Partial purchase, Academy Purchase Fund 1998.7

painter, disinclined to marginalize or trivialize her female sitter? Was Mildred, who grew up to be a militant social activist, already a forceful personality? Perhaps, but Beaux did resort to traditional gendered attributes for each sitter, as Harold holds a whip and Mildred is placed near a large vase, one of the oldest female symbols.[46]

At the end of the century, dolls continued to be girlhood attributes, but Charles Dana Gibson provided an unusually subversive interpretation of the traditional pairing of girl and doll, humorously responding to concerns about the new, emancipated woman. *The Nursery*, 1906 (fig. 34), portrays a girl with a doll in her lap, looking directly at the viewer. At first glance, she appears to be angelic—pretty and sweet—but her actions are anything but benevolent. She gently holds two leads attached to an older boy, who is on his hands and knees in a subservient, bestial position with his face averted. Since the action takes place in the nursery, the implication is that the scene portrayed is just juvenile fun and games. In the context of the period, however, the scene has unsettling undertones, which resonated with Gibson's audience, many of whom were apprehensive that women were becoming too assertive and confident—even overbearing and aggressive. Gibson, who popularized the image of the New Woman through his well-known prints of the Gibson Girl, suggests that the origins of bold, confident, and strong women began in the nursery, where in this instance the female dominates her male playmate. For one so young, the girl's composure is uncommon and even unnerving. She is calm and calculating, her effortless control indicated by her gentle grasp of the reins. Her forthright gaze, directed at the implied male viewer, radiates a sense of command and self-confidence. In previous art, female dominance was often physical and sexual, embodied in the sinister femme fatale, but at the end of the nineteenth century, a new generation of American women began to aspire to positions of authority through their focused, strong intellect.

The stereotyping of young girls in art, literature, and popular culture through such feminine attributes as flowers, pets, and dolls continued into the twentieth century and is still prevalent today. Toys continue to have gender associations: girls play with dolls, and boys amuse themselves with toy trucks and soldiers. But today American girls have a much greater variety of role models than they did in the nineteenth century, when they were encouraged and expected to remain in the domestic sphere. When twenty-first-century girls become adults, they also will have increased professional and personal opportunities not available to earlier generations of women.

Fig. 34. Charles Dana Gibson, *The Nursery,* 1906. From Charles Dana Gibson, *The Gibson Book,* I (New York: Charles Scribner's Sons, 1906). Photomechancial print on paper; 9½ x 6½ in. Newark Museum; Purchase 2005, Helen McMahon Brady Cutting Fund 2005.23.1 205 B

1. Louisa May Alcott, *Little Women* (New York: Modern Library, 2000), 20.
2. For more information on childhood innocence and androgyny, see Anne Higonnet, *Pictures of Innocence: The History and Crisis of Ideal Childhood* (New York: Thames and Hudson, 1998), 15–71; Steven Mintz, *Huck's Raft: A History of American Childhood* (Cambridge, MA: Harvard University Press, 2004), 76–81.
3. Deborah Gorham, *The Victorian Girl and the Feminine Ideal* (Bloomington: Indiana University Press, 1982), 67–72. England and America had similar child-raising practices during the nineteenth century.
4. Marion Harland, *Eve's Daughters; or, Common Sense for Maid, Wife, and Mother* (New York: John R. Anderson and Henry S. Allen, 1882), 46.
5. Colleen R. Callahan, *Is It a Girl or a Boy? Gender Identity and Children's Clothing* (Richmond, VA: Valentine Museum, 1999), [1–2].
6. Mintz, *Huck's Raft,* 16, 79; Rosamond Olmsted Humm, *Children in America: A Study of Images and Attitudes,* exhibition catalogue (Atlanta, GA: High Museum of Art, 1979), 11–15. Humm notes that colonial children were depicted as miniature adults and that baby boys and girls were attired in similar clothing. Karin Calvert, "Cradle to Crib: The Revolution in Nineteenth-Century Children's Furniture," in *A Century of Childhood, 1820–1920,* ed. Mary Lynn Stevens Heininger (Rochester, NY: Margaret Woodbury Strong Museum, 1984), 33–35. Calvert mentions the significance of an upright posture for young children.
7. Henry Francis du Pont Winterthur Museum, *Kids! 200 Years of Childhood* (Winterthur, DE: Henry Francis du Pont Winterthur Museum, 1999), 4, 9.
8. Joseph E. Illick, *American Childhoods* (Philadelphia: University of Pennsylvania Press, 2002), 26. For an in-depth discussion of seventeenth- and eighteenth-century depictions of children, see Karin Calvert, "Children in American Family Portraiture, 1670 to 1810," *William and Mary Quarterly,* Third Series, 39, no. 1 (1982): 87–113.
9. For more information on the Romantic child, see Higonnet, *Pictures of Innocence,* 15–71.
10. I am indebted to Kimberly Fisher for identifying the flower and its symbolism. For a discussion of the pansy's various meanings, see Marina Heilmeyer, *The Language of Flowers: Symbols and Myths* (Munich: Prestel, 2001), 80. The religious upbringing of the two boys played a role in their future careers, as William became the first Episcopal bishop of the diocese of Albany, NY, and George—after converting to the Catholic faith—became Monsignor Doane of Newark. See *American Art in the Newark Museum: Paintings, Drawings, and Sculpture* (Newark, NJ: Newark Museum, 1981), 335.
11. Jennifer A. Yunginger, *Is She or Isn't He? Identifying Gender in Folk Portraits of Children,* exhibition catalogue (Sandwich, MA: Heritage Plantation of Sandwich, 1985). In the folk portraits that she examined: 67 percent of the girls have center parts, while only 5 percent of the boys do; 35 percent of the boys have their hair parted on the right side, while only 6 percent of the girls do; 43 percent of the girls wear jewelry, while only 3 percent of the boys do. Although Yunginger's extensive research focused on folk portraits, her general findings can be applied to academic portraits, since they reflect nineteenth-century social practices. For similar observations on children's hairstyles, see James M. Volo and Dorothy Denneen Volo, *Family Life in Nineteenth-Century America* (Westport, CT: Greenwood, 2007), 262.
12. The four portraits described here were included in the exhibition *The Seduction of Light: Ammi Phillips / Mark Rothko Compositions in Pink, Green and Red* at the American Folk Art Museum from October 7, 2008, to March 29, 2009. See Stacy C. Hollander, *The Seduction of Light,* exhibition catalogue (New York: American Folk Art Museum, 2008), 27. While these portraits were shown together as a group, no mention was made in the exhibition label copy or the catalogue that the little boy is wearing the same dress as the three little girls.
13. According to Mary Black, "*Andrew Jackson Ten Broeck* is, so far, the only known Phillips portrait set into a landscape." See Black, "Ammi Phillips: The Country Painter's Method," *The Clarion* 11, no. 1 (1986): 37. This complicates an analysis of the setting, which was probably inspired by the sitter's namesake, President Andrew Jackson, whose nickname was Old Hickory.
14. Lucy Larcom, *A New England Girlhood, Outlined from Memory* (Boston: Northeastern University Press, 1986), 166.
15. For an insightful discussion of late nineteenth-century paintings in which women are associated with floral imagery, see Annette Stott, "Floral Femininity: A Pictorial Definition," *American Art* 6, no. 2 (1992): 61–77.
16. Alcott, *Little Women,* 84.
17. Lydia Maria Francis Child, *The Little Girl's Own Book* (Boston: Carter, Hendee, 1835), 13–15. In the game called "The Butterfly and the Flowers," girls assumed the role of flowers and boys played insects.
18. Heilmeyer, *Language of Flowers,* 50, 74.
19. See Beverly Seaton, *The Language of Flowers: A History* (Charlottesville and London: University Press of Virginia), 168-197.
20. Among the numerous other nineteenth-century novels featuring young girls as protagonists are Susan Warner's *The Wide, Wide World* (1850), Maria Susanna Cummins's *The Lamplighter* (1854), Henry James's *Watch and Ward* (1871) and *What Maisie Knew* (1897), and Louisa May Alcott's *Moods* (1864), *Little Women* (1868–1869), and *An Old-Fashioned Girl* (1870).
21. Henry James, *The Turn of the Screw and Other Short Fiction* (New York: Bantam, 1981), 85.
22. Henry James, *The Portrait of a Lady* (Harmondsworth: Penguin, 1986), 307.
23. Mrs. Phelps, *The Female Student; or, Lectures to Young Ladies on Female Education* (New York: Leavitt, Lord, and Co., 1836), 70.

24. "American Treasures at the Fenimore Art Museum," website of the Fenimore Art Museum, www.fenimoremuseum.org/files/fenimore/collections/fine_folk_art/exhibit1/e10/17/2008.
25. Stott, "Floral Femininity," 62–63.
26. Judith Walsh, "The Language of Flowers and Other Floral Symbolism Used by Winslow Homer," *The Magazine Antiques,* November 1999, 708–717.
27. For more information on this painting, see *American Paintings in the Detroit Institute of Arts,* vol. 2 (New York: Hudson Hills Press, 1997), 124.
28. Fanny Travis Cochran's handwritten note in the curatorial files of the Pennsylvania Academy of the Fine Arts states that Beaux made the sash.
29. The thoughtful Fanny grew up to be a well-educated social activist. She graduated from Bryn Mawr College and was committed to improving labor conditions. See Sylvia Yount, "Family Pictures," in *Cecilia Beaux: American Figure Painter,* exhibition catalogue (Atlanta: High Museum of Art, 2007), 24.
30. Sargent painted a second portrait of Katherine, as Katherine's father felt that "S. did not try to have a good likeness" in his first portrait. See Richard Ormond and Elaine Kilmurray, *Complete Paintings of John Singer Sargent,* vol. 2, *John Singer Sargent: Portraits of the 1890s* (New Haven: Yale University Press, 2002), 39.
31. "Blue hydrangeas became popular in the 1880s and were the Symbolist flower *par excellence* because of their oriental origin, unnatural color, and drained appearance." Quote from Alison Syme, *A Touch of Blossom: John Singer Sargent and the Queer Flora of Fin-de-Siecle Art* (University Park, PA: The Pennsylvania State University Press, 2010), 180.
32. Heritage Plantation of Sandwich, *Canines and Felines: Dogs and Cats in American Art* (Sandwich, MA: Heritage Plantation, 1988), 5, 10. For cats as symbols of lust, see E. de Jongh, *Questions of Meaning: Theme and Motif in Dutch Seventeenth-Century Painting,* trans. and ed. Michael Hoyle (Leiden: Primavera, 2000), 43.
33. For a description of the game, see Child, *The Little Girl's Own Book,* 28.
34. Bailey Van Hook made connections between passive women in late nineteenth-century art and their powerless status in "Decorative Images of American Women: The Aristocratic Aesthetic of the Late Nineteenth Century," *Smithsonian Studies in American Art* 4, no. 1 (1990): 59–61.
35. For an especially thoughtful and extensive examination of *Home Scene,* see Debra William Hanson, "Thomas Eakins' Home Scenes of the 1870s" (Ph.D. dissertation, Virginia Commonwealth University, 2005), 24–112. Eakins's awareness of the sexual symbolism of the pairing of cats with girls and women is particularly evident in his portrait of Kathrin Crowell (1872; Yale University Art Gallery, New Haven, CT), in which Eakins provocatively placed a furry brown cat in Kathrin's lap.
36. Guy began his career in England and immigrated to the United States in 1854. For the most recent information on Guy, see Bruce Weber, "Seymour Joseph Guy: 'Little Master' of American Genre Painting," *The Magazine Antiques,* November 2008, 140–149.
37. Examples include Krimmel's *The Quilting Frolic,* 1813 (Plate 4), Sargent's *Beatrice Goelet,* 1890 (private collection), and Chase's *The Pet Canary,* c. 1886 (private collection). For a discussion of women with birdcages in seventeenth-century Dutch art, see De Jongh, *Questions of Meaning,* 43.
38. Gary Cross, *Kids' Stuff: Toys and the Changing World of American Childhood* (Cambridge, MA: Harvard University Press, 1997), 67–68.
39. Harland, *Eve's Daughters,* 50.
40. Child, *The Little Girl's Own Book,* 78. An entire section of Child's book is devoted to dolls.
41. Henry Francis du Pont Winterthur Museum, *Kids! 200 Years of Childhood,* 27.
42. Eleanor often posed for her father, see Nancy Dustin Wall Moure, *Partners in Illusion—Alberta Binford and William J. McCloskey,* exhibition catalogue (Santa Ana, CA: The Bowers Museum of Cultural Art, 1996), 21, 23.
43. In numerous children's stories, dolls come to life. See for example, Louisa May Alcott, "The Dolls' Journey from Minnesota to Maine," in *Louisa May Alcott's Fairy Tales and Fantasy Stories,* ed. Daniel Shealy (Knoxville: University of Tennessee Press, 1992), 242–254.
44. On the connection between girls and dolls in French Impressionist paintings, see Greg M. Thomas, "Impressionist Dolls: On the Commodification of Girlhood in Impressionist Painting," in *Picturing Children: Constructions of Childhood Between Rousseau and Freud,* ed. Marilyn R. Brown (Hants: Ashgate, 2002), 103–125.
45. For a detailed analysis of the symbolism of the hearth, see Sarah Burns, *Pastoral Inventions: Rural Life in Nineteenth-Century American Art and Culture* (Philadelphia: Temple University Press, 1989), 265–275.
46. For an insightful analysis of this portrait, which proposes a connection between the Colton children and the children in "The Turn of the Screw," see Sylvia Yount, "The Delicious Character of Youth: Harold and Mildred Colton," *The Pennsylvania Magazine of History and Biography* 124, no. 3 (2000): 375–380.

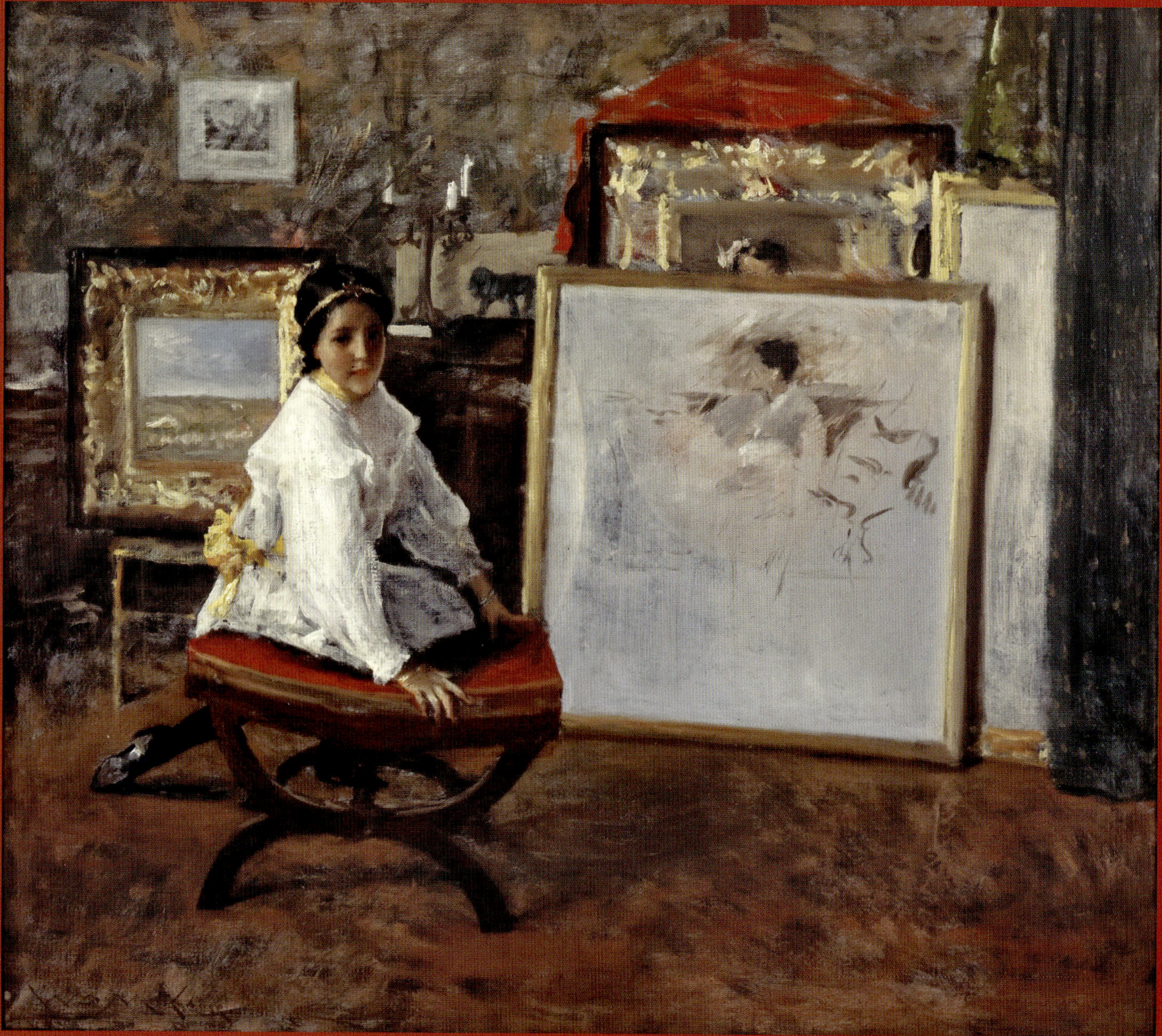

Family Matters

Artists and Their Model Girls

BARBARA DAYER GALLATI

In her 1917 biography of the recently deceased William Merritt Chase, Katherine Metcalf Roof wrote, "Of course, it was the natural destiny of all the children, especially the girls, to pose for their father."[1] Chase's well-known custom of using his daughters as models is plainly revealed in *Did You Speak to Me?* circa 1897 (fig. 35). Here, the artist's eldest child, Alice Dieudonnée (born 1887 and known as Cosy), acts as a charming reminder of the thematic construct that was not only a blend of portraiture and genre but also a prime mechanism for defining Chase's public persona as a creative force. Many nineteenth-century artists routinely used their own children as models. The sweetly comic presence of youngsters in artists' studios entered the domain of popular imagery, as witnessed by a drawing after Joseph Henry Hatfield's *Helping Papa* (fig. 36) that was reproduced in an 1894 article. Described as "the most intimate of human interests," the child was identified as the artist's daughter Dot, who had featured in paintings by her father exhibited at the Paris Salon of 1891 and the World's Columbian Exposition of 1893.[2] It stood to reason that artists' children would be pressed into modeling for their parents; although there were professional child models available for hire in various European cities, few American children seem to have entered that sphere, most likely because of the business's unsavory associations.[3] Then, too, recruiting a son or daughter to pose in the studio was convenient, incurred no fees, and, one would assume, held the promise of obedience to parental instructions to remain still.

These practicalities notwithstanding, there remains to be explored the iconography of girlhood as it may have been inflected by familial relationships between various artists and the children they painted. Such an investigation encompasses a broad range of factors, including generational and gender differences, as well as the cultural heritage and academic training of the artists under consideration. Much can be gleaned from the thematic complexities manifested in Lilly Martin Spencer's *War Spirit at Home (Celebrating the Victory at Vicksburg)*, 1866 (fig. 70, page 96), a work that qualifies as a conversation piece, because it is believed to show the artist and some of her children in their own household. Rather than focusing on girlhood *per se,* Spencer created an image that was more a meditation on her life as a working mother. And, as literal extensions of the parent-artist, Spencer's children (she and her chronically

Fig. 36. Joseph Henry Hatfield, *Helping Papa,* n.d. From George Parsons Lathrop, "My Favorite Model," *The Quarterly Illustrator* 2, no. 5 (1894): 72. General Research Division, New York Public Library, Astor, Lenox and Tilden Foundations

Fig. 35. (opposite) William Merritt Chase, *Did You Speak to Me?,* c. 1897. Oil on canvas, 38 x 43 in. The Butler Institute of American Art, Youngstown, OH; Museum purchase, 1921

unemployed husband had thirteen children, seven of whom survived childhood) are components of a visual declaration of selfhood that illuminates the artist's private and professional milieus.[4]

Although Spencer was arguably the most successful woman artist of her time in America, her visibility on the art market relied largely on the sales of print reproductions after her works (e.g., *The Young Teacher,* 1858, fig. 5, page 14), a commercial enterprise that paid relatively little. *War Spirit at Home,* one of Spencer's most notable paintings, has prompted a number of eminently plausible interpretations; most of these center on Spencer's marginalized position in a male-dominated profession and the conflicts arising from her responsibilities as mother, wife, and principal breadwinner.[5] Additional interpretative possibilities arise out of an analysis of the painting's unusually intricate composition. On the surface, it appears that we are dealing with an indifferent mother who absentmindedly supports an infant on her lap while she reads the *New York Times,* which, according to the painting's subtitle, reports the 1863 Union victory at Vicksburg. The newspaper acts as a barrier separating the mother from the youngsters, who enact their own raucous victory parade in the disorderly, claustrophobic space. All of this takes place under the eye of a haggard maidservant whose glance in the direction of Spencer might either be read as one of disapproval or of empathy. By placing herself at the edge of the composition, Spencer stressed her doubly marginalized position as an artist and as a parent; her limited interaction with the external sphere is signaled by the newspaper—a commonly understood symbol of the greater world—to which she assiduously devotes her attention and which also denotes her unwillingness to concentrate fully on household duties. Essentially, then, Spencer portrayed herself as being neither completely part of the family circle (which is literally represented in the circular arrangement of the figures) nor able to function entirely outside the parameters of domestic activity.[6]

What has not been entirely explored is how the children's victory celebration affects the painting's meaning. The playful procession was a childish but relevant reaction to the Civil War played out in homes throughout the North and South, and determined by the environmental tensions wrought by the war's effects and youngsters' innate tendencies to imitate what they see and hear.[7] But what of the little girl? The child, who is likely Spencer's daughter Angélique Caroline (born 1859), happily participates in the impromptu parade, hitting her makeshift drum (a metal cooking pot) with a spoon. Her red dress coordinates with the blue and white of her mother's clothing, echoing the colors of the Stars and Stripes as if to underscore the patriotic nature of the occasion and possibly to establish a special connection between mother and daughter. She is dressed as well as any proper, middle-class child, this despite the impression of disarray given by her dress as it slips from her shoulder and the ribbon at her waist that hangs loosely, dragging on the floor to be preyed upon by the cat that lurks beneath the tablecloth. The conceit of the predatory feline imparts a negative touch to the image of the jubilant child, suggesting that external influences might interfere with her progress in the world. What is more, Angélique wears a Union cap, a sign of masculinity that may suggest Spencer's own ambivalence concerning her identity as housewife and professional artist in the male arena. Additionally, the young girl embodies the contradictions of her mother's life by altering the purpose of kitchen utensils—turning them into an aggressively noisy musical instrument—a playful conversion that reiterates Spencer's ironic transformation of common domestic objects into the stuff of her art.

During Spencer's lifetime, her paintings were recognized for their humorous and satirical treatments of female behavior. One critic lauded her especially for her "'Hogarthian' turn of mind," and continued, "Mrs. Spencer sustains her reputation as a satirist."[8] In part, the satire detected by contemporary writers depended on the often grotesque facial expressions worn by Spencer's figures, a characteristic that sometimes led critics to assume that she was unable to draw accurately. This, however, was not the case, as shown by other more traditionally (or academically) proficient works from her hand. It is most likely that the perceived division between what can be called the "grotesque" and "naturalistic" modes manifested in her art reflects her ironic (and subversive) acknowledgment of the necessity of catering to market expectations. Such an attitude may have had its origins in Spencer's familiarity with nascent feminism, ideas that colored her ways of depicting women, at times imbuing her imagery with a wryly perverse tone. Thus, the almost manic faces of some of Spencer's happy homemakers may indicate her resentment of the general popularity of such works on the market and her corresponding need to accommodate those market desires at the expense of more elevated aesthetic goals. Her family background lends itself to the conclusion that she knowingly suppressed her ambitions to create high art, inasmuch as her French émigré parents were highly politicized intellectuals who subscribed to the socialist tenets of Charles Fourier, which included an early form of feminism.[9] The Martins may also have been attuned to the "cult of childhood" that permeated British culture (Spencer spent her first eight years in England), much of it informed by the thinking of Jean-Jacques Rousseau. In this sense it is possible to view Spencer's imagery, which alternated between good and mischievous girls, as ironic commentary on her own conflicted situation.

Fi Fo Fum of 1858 (fig. 37), which was praised for its depiction of sweet girlhood, conformed to notions of appealingly malleable children.[10] Yet Spencer could also turn to the playfully subversive portrayal of her pot-banging daughter in *War Spirit at Home* to derive satisfaction from defying gendered expectations.[11] Like *War Spirit at Home*, *Fi Fo Fum*—whose stereotypically fearful children are in the thrall of their father's fearsome histrionics—contains a delicious irony, inasmuch as Spencer again plays the part of the distant mother, an observer of family interaction rather than a participant.

Spencer's integration of elements from her personal life with her art—a consequence of financial hardship and the limitations placed on her due to her sex—met the expectations of an audience that perceived her in gendered terms. Such

Fig. 37. Lilly Martin Spencer, *Fi Fo Fum,* 1858. Oil on canvas, 35⅞ x 28⅝ in. Location unknown. Photograph courtesy of David Lubin

gendered assumptions did not affect the reception of the English expatriates John George Brown and Seymour Joseph Guy, whose productions suggest a genuine commitment to picturing children. Both men had tried unsuccessfully to establish careers in the fiercely competitive London portrait market before sailing for the United States—Brown arrived in 1853 and Guy in 1854. The two left England just as the vogue for child imagery was taking firm hold there, and they surely would have known the works of such early contributors to the subgenre as William Mulready and Thomas Webster, in addition to the many child-oriented paintings by the Pre-Raphaelites. Together, Brown and Guy imported an English taste for childhood, fashioning it for an American audience primed and eager, in the decades after the Civil War, for optimistic views of a coming generation that promised to heal the nation.[12]

Although Brown's reputation eventually relied on his paintings of impoverished urban street boys, his American career began with paintings of country boys and girls.[13] Around late 1862 or early 1863, Brown moved to Fort Lee, New Jersey, a rural community within easy commuting distance of New York City, where he maintained a studio in the Tenth Street Studio Building. The art that he produced throughout the roughly eight years of his residence in Fort Lee reveals a tangential relationship with Pre-Raphaelitism; a fine example is *Watching the Woodpecker*, 1866 (fig. 38), a painting that captures a girl's sympathetic connection with nature, reflecting a well-established idea that childhood was, like nature, an unspoiled state.[14]

Brown had married in 1855 and his first children, daughters Charlotte (Lottie) and Isabelle (Belle), were born in 1860 and 1863, respectively.[15] It is thought that Lottie and Belle are pictured in *Fishing—Fort Lee, New Jersey,* circa 1870 (fig. 39), in which two little girls are shown at the edge of a stream flowing through a bucolic meadowland. The

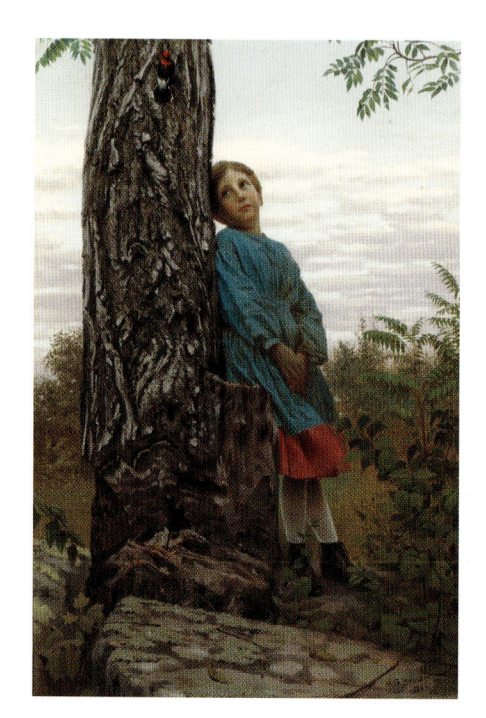

Fig. 38. (left) John George Brown, *Watching the Woodpecker,* 1866. Oil on canvas, 18 x 12 in. Private collection
Fig. 39. (right) John George Brown, *Fishing—Fort Lee, New Jersey,* c. 1870. Oil on canvas, 17 x 22 in. Private collection

FAMILY MATTERS

almost horizonless landscape encloses the children, gently implying that this countryside is a realm of childhood exploration and play. Here, however, Brown injected an atypical, slightly melancholy air: the girls are contemplative rather than playful, apparently lost in their own thoughts. It is tempting to attribute this sense of isolation and quietude (aptly reinforced by the pastime of fishing) to a personal loss experienced by Brown—his wife Mary Ann had died at Fort Lee in September 1867 at the age of thirty-two. Lottie and Belle may also have modeled for *We Can't Be Caught,* circa 1876 (fig. 40), in which the closely entwined, identically dressed figures imply the inseparability of the two girls, who by this time are adolescents, yet, perhaps in keeping with a father's hopes, resistant to romance.[16]

By the end of the 1870s, Brown's interest in painting rural children was fading. One of his last country subjects, *The Cider Mill,* 1880 (fig. 41), portrays five little girls greedily consuming apples. The painting subtly merges an idealized vision of childhood health and well-being with moral

Fig. 40. John George Brown, *We Can't Be Caught,* c. 1876. Oil on canvas, 25 x 30 in. Location unknown. Photograph © 2012 Bonhams & Butterfields Auctioneers Corp.

Fig. 41. John George Brown, *The Cider Mill*, 1880. Oil on canvas, 30 x 24 in. Terra Foundation for American Art, Chicago; Daniel J. Terra Collection 1992.19. Photograph courtesy of Art Resource, NY

undertones rooted in contemporary reform movements. Here the artist fused the notions of childhood innocence and the debilitating effects of alcohol consumption to construct teasingly light-hearted associations founded on Eve's part in the fall of man with her offer of the apple.[17] It is doubtful that any of Brown's daughters modeled for these little "Eves," who were probably the local children he is known to have sketched during his summer sojourns in the Catskills and the Adirondacks.[18] And, in contrast to the comparatively subdued moods established in the paintings for which his daughters are known to have posed, the carefree girls of *The Cider Mill* recall the charming 1889 autobiographical accounts of Lucy Larcom, which highlighted the freedom enjoyed by girls who were allowed to "romp and run wild" with minimal parental supervision.[19] Indeed, in light of such works as *Golden Locks,* 1880 (fig. 42), which portrays a petulant child securely identified as Mabel Brown, it appears that Brown invested images of his daughters with a heightened degree of emotional intensity.[20] Yet to search for firm distinctions between the ways in which Brown portrayed his own little girls and others is ultimately impracticable, for, as the artist put it, "I want people a hundred years from now to know how the children that I paint looked."[21]

Like his friend and colleague Brown, Seymour Joseph Guy had a large family and, to judge from the recurrence of faces that visibly mature in his art over the years, he must have used some of his nine children as models. Brown is usually credited with stimulating Guy's interest in painting children in the out-of-doors, having introduced him to the rural delights of Fort Lee, where the Guy family relocated in the mid-1860s.[22] Guy occasionally depicted a poor child of the streets, in works like *The Crossing Sweeper,* circa 1863 (fig. 43), but he generally portrayed childhood as a period during which youngsters spent their days playing in the sun or in the security of homey interiors.

By 1875 it was noted that "Mr. Guy's subjects mostly relate to scenes and incidents drawn from child-life, and in their composition and treatment he has no superior in American art."[23]

One of the most popular of Guy's early paintings, *Unconscious of Danger when Thinking of the Future,* 1865 (now known simply as *Unconscious of Danger,* fig. 44), prompted narratives that followed familiar stereotypes. One critic described the painting in the following terms: "The figure of a boy stands on an eminence gazing at the sea below, wholly unconscious of danger. The figure of a girl stretches forth her hand to take hold of the boy, and is meant to

Fig. 42. John George Brown, *Golden Locks,* 1880. Oil on canvas, 23 x 14¾ in. Private collection. Photograph courtesy of Spanierman Gallery, LLC, New York

Fig. 43. Seymour Joseph Guy, *The Crossing Sweeper*, c. 1863. Oil on canvas, 12⅛ x 8½ in. Metropolitan Museum of Art; Bequest of Collis P. Huntington, 1900 25.110.50. Photograph courtesy of Art Resource, NY

FAMILY MATTERS

embody the fear or timidity of the female sex, whilst the boy conveys the boldness of man."[24] Another writer complained that the boy's dreamy thoughts of the future were "far-fetched" since boys that age rarely contemplated anything but "candy and the grim necessity of going to school." The same writer judged that the little girl (most likely Guy's daughter Anna), who "leans half timidly, all affectionately forward to pull him out of danger," was far more successfully rendered than the boy.[25] These readings, which pit the girl's reticence against the boy's bold contemplation of his future, may not have been Guy's intention. In general, he portrayed boys as hapless, comic little characters, whereas the girls he pictured possessed self-control and good sense, and often wielded the upper hand in their relationships with boys. Thus, it is the girl who takes center stage in *Children in Candlelight,* 1869 (fig. 45, probably originally titled *Who's There?*), looking inquiringly into the darkness while a younger brother hovers expectantly at the doorway and their mother holds an infant in the shadowy background.[26] Using his signature combination of highly finished surfaces and dramatic chiaroscuro effects, Guy placed the girl just outside the threshold that separates the familiar comforts of home from the mysterious velvet darkness. In doing so, he articulated a palpable moment of suspense that metaphorically anticipated the girl's passage from childhood to adolescence.

Guy reveled in constructing compositional and narrative tensions to delineate common childhood dramas that unfold in such works as *A Bedtime Story,* 1878 (fig. 46); *Making a Train,* 1867 (fig. 90, page 117); and *Dressing for the Rehearsal,* circa 1890 (fig. 47, page 68). The first offered such a sensitive interpretation of the world of a child that it caused one reviewer to declare, "Nobody but a father could have made such a painting as this."[27] Focusing on girls on the verge of sexual maturity, these works explore the notion of expectation, each in its own way. While the narrative suspense of *A Bedtime Story* rests on the outcome of an alarming tale read to two wide-eyed boys by an older sister, *Making a Train* uses similar formal means to convey an expectant moment when a girl rehearses her future as a woman. Here the fanciful mood evoked by the girl's makeshift costume is countered by the looming shadows and the ragged, torn print of the biblical Samuel hanging askew on the wall behind her, which have been interpreted as cautionary symbols of the loss of innocence.[28] Again, the very notion of preparation for adult life is foregrounded in *Dressing for the Rehearsal,* as a woman assists a girl with her costume for a theatrical performance. The uneasy girl steadies herself, placing a hand on the woman's

Fig. 44. Seymour Joseph Guy, *Unconscious of Danger,* 1865. Oil on canvas, 20 x 16 in. Iris and B. Gerald Cantor Center for Visual Arts, Stanford University; Anonymous gift in memory of George F. Getty II 2007.11

Fig. 45. Seymour Joseph Guy, *Children in Candlelight,* 1869. Oil on canvas, 24⅛ x 18⅛ in. Newark Museum; Purchase 1957, C. Suydam Cutting Special Gift Fund 57.74

Fig. 46. Seymour Joseph Guy, *A Bedtime Story,* 1878. Oil on canvas, 34 x 27½ in. Private collection

Fig. 47. Seymour Joseph Guy, *Dressing for the Rehearsal,* c. 1890. Oil on canvas, 34⅛ x 27⅜ in. Smithsonian American Art Museum, Washington, D.C.; Gift of Jennie Anita Guy 1936.12.5

shoulder as she is about to step into the dance leotard that will transform her into a butterfly, a role that acts as a metaphor for her own transformation from girl to woman. The impression of the girl's anxiety is intensified by the placement of the woman's head, which simultaneously obscures and calls attention to the child's genital area, as if to relocate the source of the girl's stress to her dawning sexuality.

Adolescence is especially pertinent to the discussion of fathers' images of daughters, and it is useful in this connection to consider some basic anthropological approaches. In her study of daughter-father relationships, Lynda Boose points out that in "the anthropological narration of family, the father is the figure who controls the exogamous [marriage] exchange of women" and that the "exchangeable figure is the daughter."[29] Without relying too heavily on psychoanalytic complexities, it is nonetheless possible to borrow the essential dynamic stressed by Boose to construct a conceptual transaction that takes place when, by means of the image, artist-fathers virtually enacted the exchange of the daughter, taking her out of the private home sphere and exhibiting her in painted form in the public arena. There can be no question about Guy's awareness of the transitional phase his daughter-models were entering when he painted the works mentioned here, and it is helpful to remember that the legal age of consent for females in New York State was ten in 1885.[30] Thus, the images of girls on the verge of puberty may have tacitly communicated a sense of urgency derived from the artist's own feelings or those of the viewers. Guy indirectly asserted his patronymic status through the public exhibition of these and similar works bearing his signature, as if to underscore his paternal authority. Yet his portrayals of his daughters in situations that underscored this liminal phase of life were depersonalized through rich narrative schemes that gently drew attention to female adolescence—a tactic that cloaked a sometimes difficult subject with an aura of fairy-tale enchantment. No doubt it was the absence of such anecdotal devices that discomfited viewers of some of William Sergeant Kendall's paintings of his own daughters (e.g., fig. 48) in the next century.

It is probable that most nineteenth-century viewers assumed that Spencer, Brown, and Guy pictured their own children, but contemporaneous commentators made only the rare, oblique reference to the possibility. Occasionally, however, an artist would appear to court recognition of the connection. This seems to have been the case with Eastman Johnson's 1879 *Winter, Portrait of Child* (fig. 49), a work that shows the artist's only child, Ethel (born 1870), who occasionally featured, albeit anonymously, in the artist's genre paintings (e.g., *Child with a Rabbit*, 1879, Joslyn Art Museum, Omaha, Nebraska).

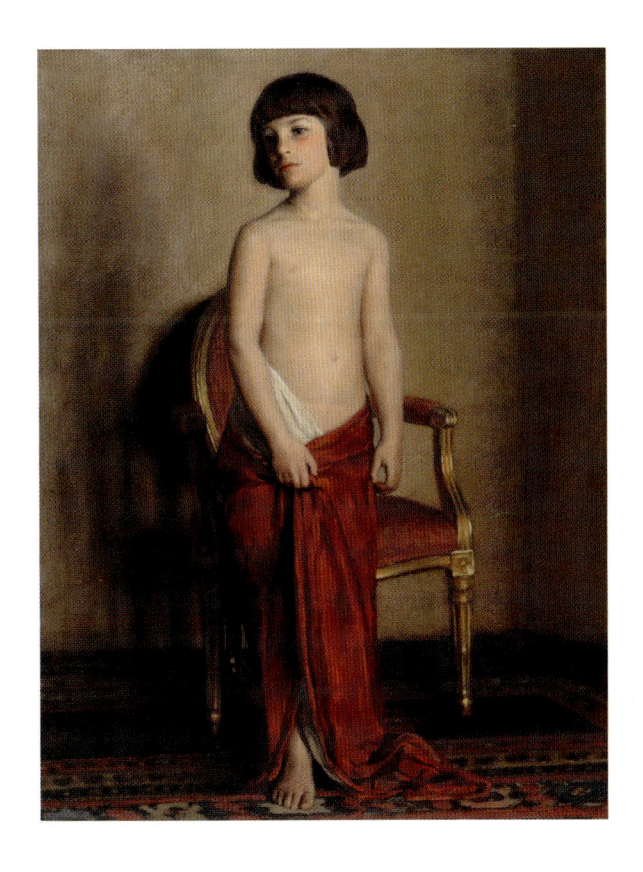

Fig. 48. William Sergeant Kendall, *A Statuette*, c. 1914. Oil on canvas, 54 x 42 3/16 in. Brooklyn Museum; Gift of Mrs. William Sergeant Kendall 45.165

Fig. 49. Eastman Johnson, *Winter, Portrait of Child*, 1879. Oil on canvas, 50^{15}⁄$_{16}$ x 32 in. Brooklyn Museum; Gift of the Charles M. Kurtz Trust 1992.108

The painting debuted at the Century Association in 1879 under the present title, but by 1881, when it was shown at the Society of American Artists, it was listed simply as *A Portrait*.[31] Certainly the scale of the sturdy child—the figure is nearly life-size—signaled a departure for Johnson. Moreover, the title indicated that this was a particular little girl, placing the painting into a realm where genre and formal portraiture overlapped. As one critic observed, the painting was "an honest, straightforward portrait of a real child."[32] Although the viewer is not expressly privy to the model's identity, the conclusion that she is the artist's daughter is almost unavoidable. Indeed, it was common practice not to name sitters whose portraits were publicly exhibited, a custom that stemmed from social codes that deemed it unrefined to publicize or draw attention to oneself or one's family. However, Johnson forced the issue of identity by determinedly directing the viewer's gaze to the girl's rosy countenance, the painting's only bright spot of color. The eye is drawn upward, along the roughly triangular shape of her dark, silhouetted form, to her face, which is anchored at the center of the v-shape of the snowy crevices. Johnson's unconventional portrait registers as a monumentalizing, albeit casual, snapshot of a child at play. Yet it possesses an intimacy by virtue of the figure's proximity to the picture plane. Through these devices, which separate the image from formal portraiture, Johnson relayed his paternal connection, portraying the beloved features of an obedient daughter who doubtless posed in the artist's top-floor studio in the family home, rather than in the chill air of winter.

Just as Johnson's large portrait of Ethel is a relative rarity in his art, so too are Thomas Eakins's paintings of girls enveloped in the Victorian gloom of domestic interiors, a thematic strain that occupied him only in the years immediately after his return to Philadelphia from study in Europe in 1870. For these Eakins focused primarily on his sisters, Frances, Margaret, and Caroline ("Caddie"), and occasionally on Kathrin and Elizabeth Crowell, the sisters of his best friend, William Crowell, who would essentially become family through his marriage to Frances in 1872, followed two years later by Eakins's engagement to Kathrin (the engagement ended with her death in 1879). While Johnson offered a glimpse of his private sphere by publicly exhibiting an uncharacteristic portrait of his daughter, Eakins apparently guarded this aspect of his life and art by withholding all but one of these works from public display.[33]

Home Scene, circa 1871 (fig. 50), the earliest of Eakins's intimate examinations of his sisters in the family's Chestnut Street residence, shows his favorite sister, Margaret, at the piano, looking over her shoulder at Caddie, who is sprawled on the floor, busy with chalk and slate. Much has been written about this claustrophobic image, mostly comparisons of Caddie's activity, whether writing or drawing, with Eakins's own artistic pursuits, and assessments of the role of the piano (characterized by Elizabeth Johns as "a moral and entertainment center of the home") in fostering the intellectual discipline and cultural refinement of young women.[34] These theories notwithstanding, the painting is strangely disquieting, mainly through the tensions introduced by the contorted poses of both figures and Margaret's enigmatic gaze. It is the opacity of Margaret's expression that proves most problematic. Although Johns interprets it as a "maternal look [that] conveys the sweet affection that the presence of the piano in the home was felt to promise," such a reading ignores what can also be perceived as worried concern or anxiety, an impression amplified by the fact that Margaret appears to be far older than her seventeen or eighteen years.[35]

What is more (and as Marc Simpson has observed), the maternal relationship suggested by

Fig. 50. Thomas Eakins, *Home Scene,* c. 1871. Oil on canvas, 21 7/16 x 18 in. Brooklyn Museum; Gift of George A. Hearn and Charles A. Schieren, by exchange; Frederick Loeser Art Fund and Dick S. Ramsay Fund 50.115

the composition—and metaphorically echoed by the kitten on Margaret's shoulder and the cat on the left—is a fiction that underscores the emotional absence of the girls' (and the artist's) mother, whose insanity (and eventual death in 1872) impressed its sad effects on the entire Eakins household.[36] While Eakins's interest in music and drawing may have influenced the making of *Home Scene,* his casting of Margaret in an ambiguous role that permits her to be seen as either sister or mother may betray his own apprehension about the futures of both sisters and, indeed, his own fate.

The same oppressive sensibility infuses Eakins's slightly later work of 1871, *Elizabeth Crowell with a Dog* (fig. 51), in which the schoolgirl, who has apparently just returned home (the Eakins residence is recognizable; Elizabeth lived there after her brother married Frances Eakins), has dropped her books and draped her coat on the covered piano to train or play with Eakins's dog, Lizard. Here, as in *Home Scene,* Eakins merged the opposing notions of work and play, building on a theme that would come to dominate his art, in which well-honed physical and intellectual skills had equal weight. Added to this is an incipient sense of female authority conveyed by Elizabeth's ability to control the dog, part of a discourse that saw women restraining and refining unruly males through patient resolve.[37]

Eakins's hushed interiors—sites of intense mental and physical tension—are, indeed, private, not only because they were not exhibited during his lifetime, but also because they portray girls in his family circle as emotionally isolated, consumed by their own thoughts, and presumably unaware of the artist's presence. What meaning they ultimately held for him can only be imagined; here, as always, the famously inscrutable Eakins constructed psychologically riveting imagery from the stuff of his everyday life. It may be that creating these scenes was a cathartic process through which his unease about his mother's absence (emotional and eventually physical) was continually reenacted on canvas by

Fig. 51. Thomas Eakins, *Elizabeth Crowell with a Dog,* c. 1871. Oil on canvas, 13¾ in. x 17 in.
The San Diego Museum of Art; Museum purchase and gift from Mr. and Mrs. Edwin S. Larsen 1969.76

Fig 52. Abbott Handerson Thayer, *Angel,* 1887. Oil on canvas, 36¼ x 28⅛ in. Smithsonian American Art Museum; Gift of John Gellatly 1929.6.112

his sisters and the female members of his extended family, onto whom he projected his own anxieties.

While such a therapeutic reading is pure speculation, a similar interpretation of Abbott Handerson Thayer's depictions of girls in the guise of sacred femininity rests on surer ground. Thayer's 1887 *Angel* (fig. 52), for which his daughter Mary posed, marks the inception of the iconography of the winged figure in his art. Like Eakins, who repeatedly painted his sisters at a time of family crisis, Thayer began this painting not long before his wife Kate was institutionalized for severe depression (then called "melancholia"). Originally called *Mignon* (a French word meaning darling, sweet, or favorite), the painting initially depicted Mary (born in Paris in 1876) holding a lily and a mandolin, objects usually associated with Christian iconography.[38] However, by 1888, when the work was displayed as *Angel* in Boston and New York, all traces of the flower and musical instrument had been erased and her arms abruptly cropped at the wrists, rendering the young winged female open and receptive, yet also bereft of physical agency.

A scholarly consensus links Kate Thayer's illness and the artist's transformation of Mary into a purifying, angelic being. She symbolizes her absent mother, representing not only the idealizing, transcendent love Thayer had for his wife, but also the "angel of death," then a colloquial term for the tuberculosis that hastened Kate's death in May 1891.[39] Extrapolating from these family circumstances and the pallid, almost consumptive look of the winged figure, Elizabeth Lee has concluded that Thayer fused his feelings about his adored wife and child, saying: "Mary/Kate thus binds the contradictory tensions in Thayer's art, vacillating between healthy daughter and sickly mother in a liminal space that collapses the promise of wholesome youth with the horror of bodily disintegration."[40]

Lee's hypothesis is borne out in an 1888 review, which noted the painting's "theme of suggestive and speculative interest." The critic added, "I am told that Mr. Thayer's wife and daughter were his models and that the face is a blending of the two—a flattering and pleasant conceit, if it were no more than that."[41] Others did, indeed, find more in the image. William Howe Downes, for instance, dwelt on its striking duality: "Our childish notions of angels must be modified to accept such a sad creation . . . Yet we would not have Mr. Thayer's angel otherwise than as she is, because the great worth of his work is bound up in the web of its personal peculiarities, and it exists as art only in the integrity of the original conception. In the grave brown eyes and pinched mouth of this delicate child is an uncanny charm, not altogether agreeable, but extraordinary in its force and persistency . . . In his pictures of children he reveals a sentiment of downright paternal love for them which is assuredly as near to be divine as any passion of which man is capable."[42]

Thayer's despair over his wife and the joy he derived from his children coexisted in life and in his art. Mary functioned as the point of convergence for these emotions, as Thayer's idiosyncratic iconography cast her as both mother and child. This scheme is most overtly presented in *Virgin Enthroned*, 1891 (fig. 53), a composition modeled on Venetian Renaissance altarpieces: the girl occupies the space ordinarily given to the Virgin Mary; flanking her are her younger sister (Gladys) and brother (Gerald). Although no doubt calculated to conjure orthodox religious meaning, the painting's content veers away from Christian doctrine by paying homage to the artist's children and memorializing his wife, who died not long before the painting was completed.[43] Products of the artist's complex fears about physical contamination and his belief in the transcendence of the spirit, such paintings are not only undisguised paeans to his children (e.g., fig. 54), they are also testaments to the spiritual love—*caritas*—which absorbed his thoughts.[44] For Thayer, his daughter embodied the nurturing ideal of motherhood while retaining her virginal purity.

The conceptual synthesis of mother and daughter was not unusual at a time when little girls were popularly seen as "mothers-in-waiting," whose play with dolls prepared them for adulthood. The issue takes on an added dimension when considering how men portrayed father-daughter relationships, whether in literature or the visual arts. This subject has been addressed with respect to fiction by Lynda Zwinger, who characterized major examples of fictional fathers and daughters in terms of the "sentimental romance of heterosexuality," taking as examples Paul Dombey and his long-suffering Florence, and William Dorrit and his dutiful "Little Dorrit" (from Charles Dickens's *Dombey and Son*, 1846–1848, and *Little Dorrit*, 1855–1857). Zwinger asserted that the "father-daughter story lays the foundation of culturally sanctioned heterosexual desire—the one in the father's place looking to defeat death, love, sexual relation; the one in the daughter's place looking to him for love, attention, approval . . . Insofar as sentimentalizing her [i.e., the daughter] masks that value [desire], it serves to protect her desiring father from himself, as desiring what he should not take; from her, as presumptively desiring what he can not or will not provide; and from desire itself, as an amorphously threatening and finally mortal condition."[45] For the most

Fig. 53. (left) Abbott Handerson Thayer, *Virgin Enthroned*, 1891. Oil on canvas, 72½ x 52½ in. Smithsonian American Art Museum; Gift of John Gellatly 1929.6.131.   **Fig. 54.** (right) Abbott Handerson Thayer, *My Children (Mary, Gerald, Gladys Thayer)*, c. 1897. Oil on canvas, 86¼ x 61⅛ in. Smithsonian American Art Museum; Gift of John Gellatly 1929.6.122

part, the father-daughter narratives that Zwinger explored involve the loss of the wife-mother figure and resolve the father-daughter relationship with the daughter's maturation and departure from home.

The mixture of promise and loss that governs father-daughter connections occasionally surfaces in the works of William Merritt Chase. His *Young Girl in Black: The Artist's Daughter in Mother's Dress,* circa 1897–1898 (fig. 55), is a fine example, for it portrays his first child, Alice Dieudonnée (named after her mother and called Cosy), attired in her mother's gown; this maternal masquerade took place when she was approximately the same age as her mother when Chase first met her.[46] This somewhat anomalous image in Chase's oeuvre embodies the "sentimental daughter" and betrays tensions attendant to adolescence that seem to stem from Chase's awareness of his daughter's imminent entry into womanhood and the concomitant disappearance of the child that she once was. What is more, the air of sadness that suffuses the painting—Cosy's sober expression, the generally subdued palette, and the dark clothing—may relate to other, more painful losses: by the end of 1895 three Chase children had died in close succession.[47] Another portrait of Cosy, executed around 1895, shows an unsmiling, impassive girl (fig. 56), but it lacks the psychological intensity of *Young Girl in Black.*

From the start of his career, Chase had painted children's portraits on commission and had occasionally used his younger sister Hattie as a model for genre subjects. However, Cosy's birth in 1887 heralded a new "domesticated" subject matter for Chase, whose work had undergone harsh criticism in the early 1880s because of his adherence to the dark realism associated with his Munich training. Themes of family harmony, often expressed in portraits of Alice and Cosy (e.g., fig. 57), aided in relieving the severity of this dark style and, when Chase turned to a brighter, Impressionist manner, he courted critical acceptance of this radical stylistic move by inserting white-clad women and girls into his landscape compositions, as emblems of gentility as well as moral and physical health (e.g., fig. 58).[48]

The great majority of the works he produced had autobiographical references, calling viewers' attention to Chase's public persona as innovative artist and to his role as dedicated family man. And, in the case

Fig. 55. William Merritt Chase, *Young Girl in Black: The Artist's Daughter in Mother's Dress,* c. 1897–1898. Oil on canvas, 60⅛ x 36³⁄₁₆ in. Hirshhorn Museum and Sculpture Garden, Smithsonian Institution; Gift of Joseph H. Hirshhorn Foundation 1966.66.87

Fig. 56. William Merritt Chase, *Portrait of the Artist's Daughter,* c. 1895. Oil on canvas, 32⅜ x 25⅝ in. Hirshhorn Museum and Sculpture Garden, Smithsonian Institution; Gift of Joseph H. Hirshhorn 1966.66.879

Fig. 57. William Merritt Chase, *Mrs. Chase and Cosy,* c. 1895. Oil on canvas, 55¼ x 26¼ in. Sheldon Memorial Art Gallery, University of Nebraska–Lincoln; UNL–F. M. Hall Collection. Photograph © Sheldon Memorial Art Gallery

Fig. 58. William Merritt Chase, *Idle Hours,* c. 1894. Oil on canvas, 25½ x 35½ in. Amon Carter Museum of American Art, Fort Worth, TX

of *Idle Hours,* circa 1894 (fig. 58), and other sunlit scenes, viewers were no doubt reminded of Chase's reputation as the head of the Shinnecock Summer School of Art for Men and Women. This intersection of public and private identities in which art and life were one and the same was purposefully established in the press, as demonstrated by a photograph of the artist's famous Tenth Street studio in which his recently completed painting *My Little Daughter Dorothy* (circa 1894, Detroit Institute of Arts) is prominently displayed (fig. 59).[49] Like Cosy in *Did You Speak to Me?* (fig. 35, page 57), little Dorothy is portrayed in the studio in front of one of her father's paintings, but she is accorded center stage, reminding us that she, too, is her father's creation.

The works under discussion in this essay represent threads of reality intertwined with aesthetic intentions that the viewer is invited to unravel but cannot ultimately separate. What may be said with certainty, however, is that girlhood was (and is) a multivalent site whose meaning alternates between moral and physical contagion or virtue and health, emotional anxiety or reassurance, or as a souvenir of the past or a harbinger of the future. Drawing on familiar iconographic stereotypes and reacting to shifting social concepts about childhood itself, artists of disparate experience, talents, and intentions created intensely personal works of art whose content remains tantalizingly familiar yet ultimately impenetrable.

Fig. 59. Photograph of east end of William Merritt Chase's middle studio, showing Chase's painting *My Little Daughter Dorothy* (c. 1894), published in Wendy Cooper, "Artists in Their Studios," *Godey's Magazine* 130, no. 777 (March 1895): 292. General Research Division, New York Public Library, Astor, Lenox and Tilden Foundations

1. Katherine Metcalf Roof, *The Life and Art of William Merritt Chase* (1917; repr., New York: Hacker Art Books, 1975), 273.
2. George Parsons Lathrop, "My Favorite Model," *The Quarterly Illustrator* 2, no. 5 (January–March 1894): 69–83. Canadian-born Joseph Henry Hatfield trained in Paris at the Académie Julian and spent most of his career in the Boston area, where he specialized in child subjects.
3. See, for instance, "Artists' Models in New York," *The Century Magazine*, n.s., 25, no. 3 (February 1883): 573. There the author stated: "Advertisements for pretty little children to serve as models are often seen in the morning papers, and are doubtless viewed by the unenlightened and ignorant as the device of some hideous ogre, some Croquemitaine of the metropolis, seeking what he may devour in the shape of tender nurselings." Scant information is available on professional child models in the United States. In general it appears that the children who posed professionally were introduced to artists by parents who were themselves already established models. See also Gustav Kobbé, "The Artist and His Model," *The Cosmopolitan* 31, no. 2 (June 1901): 115.
4. For the standard survey of Spencer's life and career, see Robin Bolton-Smith and William H. Truettner, *Lilly Martin Spencer, 1822–1902: The Joys of Sentiment*, exhibition catalogue (Washington, D.C.: Smithsonian Institution, 1973).
5. See, e.g., Jochen Wierich, "'War Spirit at Home': Lilly Martin Spencer, Domestic Painting, and Artistic Hierarchy," *Winterthur Portfolio* 37, no. 1 (Spring 2002): 23–42; David M. Lubin, *Picturing a Nation: Art and Social Change in Nineteenth-Century America* (New Haven, CT: Yale University Press, 1994), 159–203; Elizabeth L. O'Leary, *At Beck and Call: The Representation of Domestic Servants in Nineteenth-Century American Painting* (Washington, D.C.: Smithsonian Institution Press, 1996), 105–107.
6. This is not to say that Spencer was an indifferent mother, for her letters confirm that she was an affectionate and concerned parent. See Lilly Martin Spencer Papers, Archives of American Art, reel 131.
7. For an account of the effects of the Civil War on children, see James Marten, *The Children's Civil War* (Chapel Hill: University of North Carolina Press, 1998).
8. "The National Academy of Design," *Emerson's Magazine and Putnam's Monthly* 7, no. 49 (July 1858): 104.
9. Spencer's mother, Angélique Martin, was actively engaged in promoting women's rights. Although Spencer declined her mother's invitations to participate in the women's rights movement, it does not necessarily follow that she was unsympathetic. In fact, Spencer begged off, because the responsibilities of home and career left her no time for such pursuits. See Elsie F. Freivogel, "Lilly Martin Spencer," *Archives of American Art Journal* 12, no. 4 (1972): 9–14.
10. The painting was shown at the 1858 annual exhibition of the National Academy of Design and purchased by the Cosmopolitan Art Association later that year, when prints after it were offered as a premium to subscribers; the association advertised the image as an example of Spencer's power "in portraying passion and emotion." "Catalogue of Premiums," *Cosmopolitan Art Journal*, vol. 3, no. 1 (December 1858), 55.
11. Josephine Withers noted Spencer's regret at not having given closer study to landscape painting, citing the artist's comment that landscapes "sell quicker than any other kind of painting." See Withers, "Artistic Women and Women Artists," *Art Journal* 35, no. 4 (Summer 1976): 334. By inference, Spencer's choice of subject matter was governed by her perception of market demand and personal circumstances, and not necessarily personal preference.
12. Writing about the American concept of childhood in the last quarter of the nineteenth century, Harvey Green observed, "Childhood and youth were thus often characterized as opposite to the present circumstances of life in America, and the positive metaphor of the healthy, unbridled child took hold of the populations, expressing itself in a variety of forms." See Green, "Scientific Thought and the Nature of Children in America, 1820–1920," in *A Century of Childhood, 1820–1920*, ed. Mary Lynn Stevens Heininger, exhibition catalogue (Rochester, NY: Margaret Woodbury Strong Museum, 1984), 133. This viewpoint has persisted in American culture, as witnessed by Heininger's assertion that even today the idea of childhood purity is "an indispensable element of American optimism . . . It is precisely because the young are untainted that the nation can willingly vest in them its best hopes. No matter what the difficulty, then, it is possible to 'begin again' with 'new blood.'" See Heininger, "Children, Childhood, and Change in America, 1820–1920," in *Century of Childhood*, 31.
13. The principal publication devoted to Brown is Martha Hoppin, *The World of J. G. Brown* (Chesterfield, MA: Chameleon, 2010).
14. For a discussion of the painting in this context, see Linda S. Ferber and William H. Gerdts, *The New Path: Ruskin and the American Pre-Raphaelites* (New York: Brooklyn Museum, 1985), 243–244.
15. I am indebted to Martha Hoppin for providing the names of Brown's children and their life dates: Charlotte (1860–1936), Isabelle (1863–1942), George (1872–1925), Oscar (1874–before 1938), Mabel (1876–1939), Homer Guy (1878–1882), and Florence (1883–1972).
16. Hoppin proposes that the girls are sisters, based on their identical dresses and resemblance to known images of Lottie and Belle. See *World of J. G. Brown*, 97.
17. This idea is presented in the Terra Foundation for American Art's online interpretation of the painting. See http://terraamericanart.org/collections.
18. Hoppin has determined that Brown's family did not always accompany him on his summer trips. Email message from Martha Hoppin to the author, August 4, 2010.
19. Lucy Larcom, *A New England Girlhood, Outlined from Memory* (Boston: Houghton, Mifflin, 1889), 30.

20. G. W. Sheldon, *Hours with Art and Artists* (New York: D. Appleton, 1882), 151.

21. Hoppin, *World of J. G. Brown,* 99.

22. The most comprehensive published source on Guy is Bruce Weber, "Seymour Joseph Guy: 'Little Master' of American Genre Painting," *The Magazine Antiques* (November 2008): 140–149.

23. "American Painters. Seymour Joseph Guy, N.A., Lemuel Wilmarth, N.A.," *Art Journal,* n.s., 1 (September 1875): 277.

24. "The Studios," *American Art Journal* 5, no. 16 (August 9, 1866): 244.

25. "Brooklyn Art Association. Second Exhibition of the Season," *Brooklyn Eagle,* March 21, 1866, 2. Relying on the 1880 census, which gives Anna's age as twenty-two, Stephen Edidin has identified her as the child in this painting. See John Wilmerding et al., *An American Perspective: Nineteenth-Century Art in the Collection of Jo Ann and Julian Ganz, Jr.,* exhibition catalogue (Washington, D.C.: National Gallery of Art, 1981), 135–136.

26. Bruce Weber has suggested that *Who's There?* was the original title. See Weber, "Seymour Joseph Guy," 147.

27. "The Academy Exhibition," *The Art Journal,* n.s., 5 (1879): 159.

28. For a detailed analysis of the possible meanings the painting carried for nineteenth-century viewers, see Lubin, *Picturing a Nation,* 204–271.

29. Lynda E. Boose, "The Father's House and the Daughter in It: The Structures of Western Culture's Daughter-Father Relationship," in *Daughters and Fathers,* ed. Lynda E. Boose and Betty S. Flowers (Baltimore: Johns Hopkins University Press, 1989), 19.

30. Mary E. Odem, "Delinquent Daughters: The Age-of-Consent Campaign," in *Childhood in America,* ed. Paula S. Fass and Mary Ann Mason (New York: New York University Press, 2000), 496.

31. Teresa A. Carbone, ed., *American Paintings in the Brooklyn Museum: Artists Born by 1876* (New York: Brooklyn Museum, 2006), 713–714.

32. "Some American Artists," *New York Times,* April 15, 1881, 5.

33. Marc Simpson, "The 1870s," in *Thomas Eakins,* organized by Darrel Sewell (Philadelphia: Philadelphia Museum of Art, 2001), 31.

34. Michael Fried, "Realism, Writing, and Disfiguration in Thomas Eakins's 'Gross Clinic,'" *Representations* 9 (Winter 1985), 33–104; Elizabeth Johns, *Thomas Eakins: The Heroism of Modern Life* (Princeton, NJ: Princeton University Press, 1983), 117.

35. Johns, *Thomas Eakins,* 117.

36. Eakins's mother, who required constant care, remained at home during her illness. Her death on June 4, 1872, was attributed to "exhaustion from mania." See Simpson, "The 1870s," 31.

37. Claire Perry, *Young America: Childhood in Nineteenth-Century Art and Culture* (New Haven, CT: Yale University Press, 2006), 67. Perry also observes that images of girls taming or training pets "communicated the idea of the taming and domestication girls underwent as part of their transition to womanhood." Ibid.

38. Nelson C. White, *Abbott H. Thayer: Painter and Naturalist* (Hartford, CT: Connecticut Printers, 1951), 51–52.

39. Elizabeth Lee, "Therapeutic Beauty: Abbott Thayer, Antimodernism, and the Fear of Disease," *American Art* 18, no. 3 (2004): 32–5l; Richard Murray, "Abbott Thayer's 'Stevenson Memorial,'" *American Art* 13, no. 2 (Summer 1999): 2–25.

40. Lee, "Therapeutic Beauty," 42.

41. "Gallery and Studio," *Brooklyn Eagle,* June 17, 1888, 11.

42. William Howe Downes, "Fine Arts: American and French Pictures in the Fifth Gallery of the Museum of Fine Arts," unidentified newspaper clipping, 1888, from Mrs. Thayer's scrapbook, Archives of American Art, Nelson White Papers. Cited in Murray, "Abbott Thayer's 'Stevenson Memorial,'" 8.

43. Ross Anderson, *Abbott Handerson Thayer,* exhibition catalogue (Syracuse, NY: Everson Museum, 1982), 53.

44. Lee, "Therapeutic Beauty." Thayer included the word *caritas* in the titles of several of his paintings.

45. Lynda Zwinger, *Daughters, Fathers, and the Novel: The Sentimental Romance of Heterosexuality* (Madison, WI: University of Wisconsin Press, 1991), 9.

46. The date to which this painting may be assigned is open to question. There appears to be no reliable evidence for the date of circa 1895 provided in Ronald G. Pisano, completed by Carolyn K. Lane and D. Frederick Baker, *The Complete Catalogue of Known and Documented Work by William Merritt Chase (1849–1916),* vol. 2, *Portraits in Oil* (New Haven, CT: Yale University Press, 2007), 130. In references to the painting that were published earlier, Pisano assigned the work to the later years of the decade.

47. Chase's son John Rudolf died just short of his first birthday on August 10, 1895. Twin girls Mabel and Sarah were born on September 20, 1895; Mabel died that day, while Sarah died less than two weeks later, on October 1. Chase family births and deaths were recorded in a family bible (consulted by author in 2000, at which time it was held by a private dealer). The particularly solemn depiction of Cosy may reflect recent family tragedies.

48. For an expanded treatment of these ideas, see Barbara Dayer Gallati, *William Merritt Chase: Modern American Landscapes, 1886–1890* (Brooklyn: Brooklyn Museum, 2000).

49. The photograph was reproduced in W. A. Cooper, "Artists in Their Studios," *Godey's Magazine* 130, no. 777 (March 1895): 292.

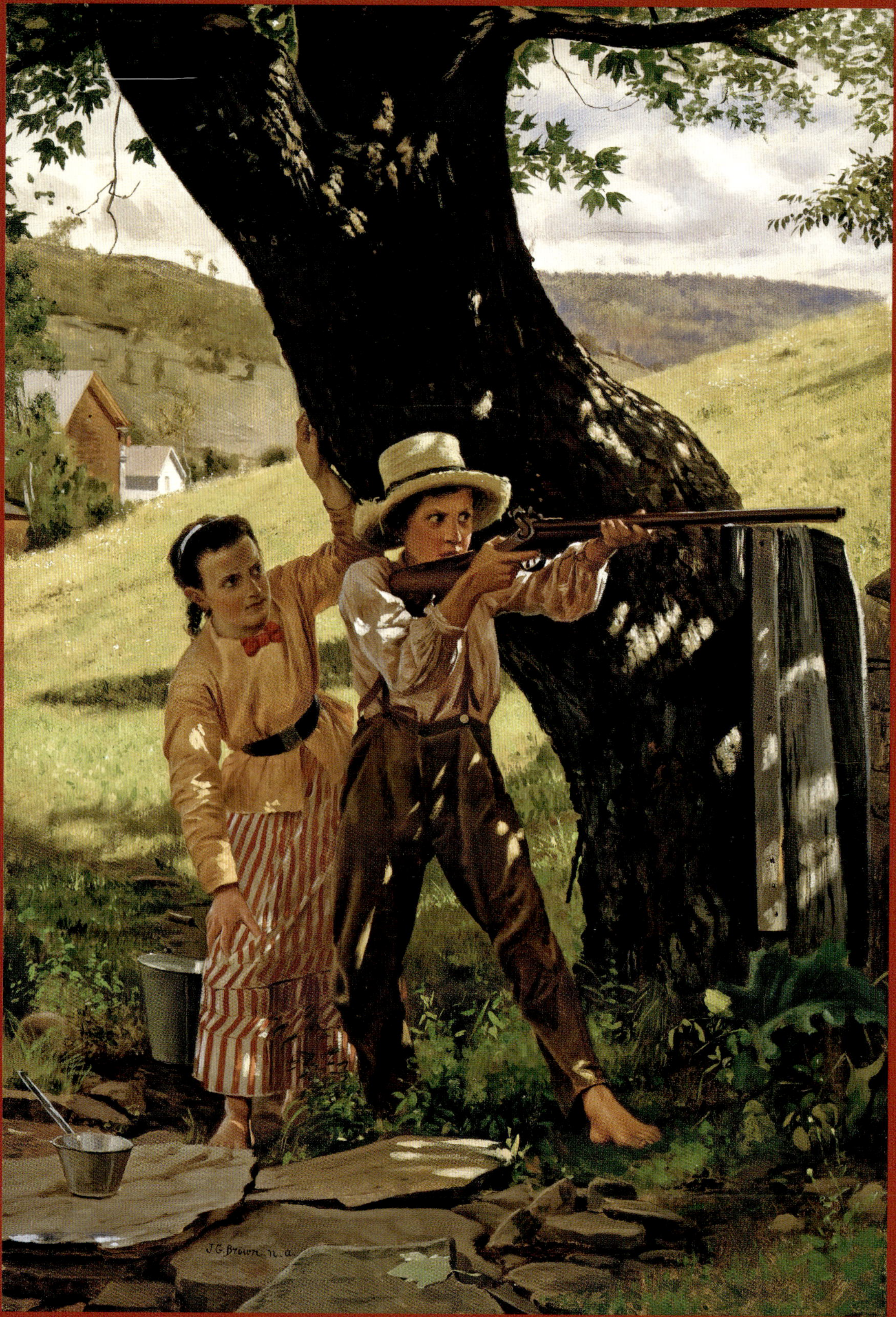
J.G. Brown. n.a.

Making Mischief

Tomboys Acting Up and Out of Bounds

SARAH BURNS

At first glance, Eastman Johnson's *In the Hayloft*, circa 1877–1878 (fig. 61), seems a charming, if conventional, genre painting typical of the nostalgic country scenes that made this painter so hugely popular in the decades following the Civil War. A dozen or so children of varying age are playing in the hayloft of a dark and cavernous barn. Four are poised on the massive beam; several frolic in the high-piled hay, and one boy shinnies up an angle brace to higher ground. Dominating the group is the figure of a young girl in short skirts and boldly striped stockings. Standing on the beam like a gymnast, dusty sunlight burnishing the loose folds of her dress and the frilly hem of her sagging petticoat, she is the dynamic focal point of the composition.

On visits to his sister's summer home in Kennebunkport, Maine, Johnson painted other hayloft scenes, including *Barn Swallows*, 1878 (fig. 62), in which several little girls and boys chatter with each other while perched on the same beam, their feet dangling over the heaped green hay. Far more sedate, this painting nonetheless prompted critic Raymond Westbrook to imagine an active narrative in which "the question evidently is, supremely contented as they all are, what shall be done next? The leader, the roguish one of nine, with blue sleeves, and a ribbon in her hair, and her round cheek visible only in profile, will decide it in a moment, I know, by plunging down with a wild shriek, and the rest will follow after as best they can."[1]

Fig. 61. Eastman Johnson, *In the Hayloft*, c. 1877–1878. Oil on canvas, 26½ x 33 in. The San Diego Museum of Art; Gift of Mrs. Herbert S. Darlington 1935.54

Fig. 60. (opposite) John George Brown, *A Sure Shot*, c. 1875. Oil on canvas, 20⅞ x 14¹³⁄₁₆ in. Brooklyn Museum; Dick S. Ramsay Fund 48.139

literature—into two paths. Along one, we find girls like the beam-balancer in Johnson's hayloft scene. Along the second, we discover not the boundary-busting tomboy in drag, as in *The Hidden Hand,* but another type, equally disconcerting in her own way: the mischief-making girl. Together, these two and their literary counterparts make up what we might think of as a counterculture of nineteenth-century American girlhood. But whereas heroines like Rosa Lee and Katy Carr enjoy a state of temporary tomboy grace before maturing into proper, good young women, the unregenerate bad girls hold out the possibility of some radical and redemptive alternative.

Eastman Johnson's 1879 paintings *Ice Skater* (fig. 63) and *Winter, Portrait of Child,* 1879 (fig. 49, page 70), represent good tomboys, as does Winslow Homer's wood-engraved illustration *"Winter"—A Skating Scene,* which appeared in *Harper's Weekly* on January 25, 1868 (fig. 64). *Ice Skater* depicts a schoolgirl who sits warming her hands by a glowing pot-bellied stove in a rustic interior. She perches on an upended packing case with feet propped up on the stove's platform and elbows on knees as she reaches toward the heat. The ice skates lying on the floor tell us that the child has just come in from active exercise out in the cold winter air. In *Winter, Portrait of Child* Johnson portrayed his daughter, Ethel, bundled up in a dark coat, sturdy boots, cap, and scarf, standing in an urban park with her sled in front of a towering heap of shoveled snow. Cheeks glowing pink and brown eyes sparkling, the girl is the picture of health. So too, albeit in black and white, are Homer's skaters, linked by a rope as they cut vigorously across the ice, hair and ribbons streaming behind.

These young girls so exuberantly enjoying winter sports might conceivably be the products of the urgent and constant calls for the improvement of female health that had since the 1850s been a major rallying point of reform. Media pundits deplored what they perceived as a disastrous decline in women and men alike. Wrote one: "The females are almost universally sickly, and unfit for the duties and pains of maternity, and the males devoid of muscle, spirit, and energy." Exercise was the best and indeed the only way to reverse the trend: "It is on behalf of those who have the good fortune not to belong to this emasculated generation that we plead for skating and all muscular exercise. We plead for the boys, young men, and young girls of the American cities."[11] Skating, which by the 1860s had become a hugely popular sport, was of particular benefit to girls. As one of the new skating manuals put it, "The practice of skating is peculiarly adapted to give our females that outdoor recreation they so much need. It expands the chest, strengthens the hips, and invigorates the entire system. If young ladies would become good skaters, they would be much better fitted to become mothers of American children."[12]

Fig. 63. Eastman Johnson, *Ice Skater,* 1879. Oil on canvas, 24¼ x 20 in. Collection of Spanierman Gallery, LLC, New York

This was exactly the sort of tomboy activity that reformers endorsed and urged on American girls. Dio Lewis—a medical man and a feminist despite his gender—was among the most vocal proponents of this sensible and healthy lifestyle. Lewis regarded the tomboy stage as an essential part of growing up. It was even intrinsic to patriotism: "The noblest women I have personally known, were 'regular tomboys' in their girlhood. I have made many inquiries about the women who figured conspicuously in the 'Sanitary Commission,' the 'Christian Commission,' and in the hospitals, and so far as I have been able to learn from them, and their friends, not one began with being a *'proper' young lady!*" If a girl were "prim and nice and proper," he went on, one could "write out the story of her life in five lines; and without waiting for her to live it." A strong woman began as the girl who "breaks through the trammels of propriety, rides the saddle astride, climbs fences and trees . . . or acquires distinction in any roystering game which demands pluck and endurance."[13]

The skaters depicted in Homer's illustration and Johnson's painting are hardly rebellious and far from threatening. They stay well within the bounds of conventional femininity while at the same time participating in wholesome and energetic sports that will make robust women out of them. Not one of them wears any article of clothing that suggests boyishness. In this, they mirror the tomboys of popular fiction. The state of tomboy grace enjoyed by Rosa, Katy, and many other rambunctious heroines is temporary. Eventually—through various trials—they evolve into good and sensible young women, modern yet unequivocally feminine. We can assume, therefore, that the little ice skater in Johnson's painting will in time learn to sit like a lady rather than perch boyishly with elbows on knees.[14] Even Johnson's daughter Ethel, portrayed

Fig. 64. Winslow Homer, *"Winter"—A Skating Scene*, 1868, published in *Harper's Weekly,* January 25, 1868. Woodcut, 9⅛ x 13½ in. Private collection

so unconventionally with a sled instead of a doll or other girlish attribute, was destined to follow that path. In later portraits by her father, she is every inch the figure of elegant, feminine fashion.

Homer's *Winter* can serve as a visual metaphor for the transition from tomboy freedom to the condition of a proper young lady. Three of the figures in Homer's scene are still girls. With their long, flowing locks and short skirts, they exercise actively and without restraint, even while sporting frippery such as zigzag bobble fringe and cunning little hats. Leading the energetic procession on the left is an older girl, whose longer skirt suggests that she is on the threshold of womanhood. Finally, there is the fifth figure in a stylish winter outfit, hair done up under her smartly tilted headgear. The only uninvolved member of the group, she has tucked her hands into her muff and remains stationary on the ice. It is as if, having passed through that liminal stage of unfettered boyish activity, she has now assumed the trappings, and the bearing, of womanhood. Her parents, and society, have reined her in.

Did such a pattern allow for variation? Did the tomboy ineluctably become the good wife? Certain biographies suggest that the path to marriage and motherhood was not the only option. The Wisconsin childhood of Frances E. Willard—later a suffragist and a fierce activist in the Women's Christian Temperance Union—was adventurous and rowdy. Willard was a tomboy, in fact, well before it became the new model for American girls. Her mother recalled that "she was very fond of playing outdoors, indoor amusements seeming irksome to her always. Her brother was her favorite comrade, and his sturdy little playmates among the boys would sometimes call her 'Tomboy,' which she resented very much."[15] Resentful or not, Willard provided rich details in her autobiography about her tomboy adventures with older brother, Oliver, recalling, "When he went hunting I often insisted on going along, and he never made fun of me but would even let me load the gun, and I can also testify that he made not the slightest objection to my carrying the game!"[16] "A needle and a dishcloth I could not abide," she wrote, declaring that she was "bound to live out-of-doors."[17] With Oliver and her sister Mary, Willard walked on stilts, spun tops, climbed trees, trapped quail, and even practiced target shooting. True, she had broad-minded parents who believed in the importance of outdoor exercise and healthy romps. And at a time when higher education for women was still almost unheard of, she attended Northwestern Female College (later to merge with today's Northwestern University). Never to become a strong and capable wife and mother, she preferred to share her life with other women.

Whether being a tomboy had anything to do with Willard's life course is impossible to say with any certainty. It is interesting, nonetheless, to note that other highly unconventional women had similar childhood experiences. There is the well-known life history of author Louisa May Alcott, whose alter ego was the character Jo in *Little Women*. Unlike Willard, Alcott did not detest the needle, but she too reveled in the freedom of the outdoors, recalling, "I must have been a deer or a horse in some former state, because it was such a joy to run. No boy could be my friend till I had beaten him in a race, and no girl if she refused to climb a tree, leap fences and be a tomboy."[18]

But where can we find such out-and-out tomboys in art, tomboys that go beyond haylofts and ice skates? John George Brown's *A Sure Shot*, circa 1875 (fig. 60), seems at first glance to be in the Frances Willard mold. Is this the sort of girl who plays with boys as an equal? Does she shelter from danger behind him, or is she urging him on? While her body language suggests active engagement, and her face bespeaks an alert and serious concentration, other signs assert her feminine identity and role. Behind her is a milking pail, and on the flat stone to the left is her dipper. A country girl, she has been occupied with chores conventionally coded female. A likely narrative here is that she has stopped to offer a drink of fresh milk to the farm boy—her brother, perhaps—when suddenly he spies a target and snatches up the rifle.

Although Brown later went on to specialize in street urchins, he painted a considerable number of country genre scenes in the 1860s and 1870s, nearly all of them featuring girls in demure and feminine roles. He ventured into tomboy territory with a handful of paintings in which girls play boisterously on swings or swing on gates, but not one of them ever threatens to trespass on masculine territory.[19] Even Homer, fascinated by the impact of modernity on gender roles, refrained from depicting young women as border-crossing or obstreperous tomboys, however independent their behavior.

Given the power of conventions defining gender-appropriate behavior—and even considering the latitude tomboys enjoyed—it may not after all be surprising that male artists chose to stay in safer territory. Mass culture to be sure did tread on edgier ground. During the resurgence of suffrage activism that followed the Civil War, there were cartoons aplenty of mannish activists and so-called "Girls of the Period" brazenly appropriating male roles.[20] But those depicted had left childhood and the tomboy years behind, and for the most part the cartoons reflected a masculine and highly critical point of view.

Where, then, do we find girls out of bounds? In the world of painting, one of the only exceptions to the rule is the art of Lilly Martin Spencer, whose heyday in the 1850s and 1860s coincided with the emergence of the tomboy in life and literature. Alone among her peers, Spencer gave at least a handful of pictured girls the liberty to cross borders—and, perhaps, not to return. Like Frances Willard, Spencer enjoyed an unusual childhood. Born Angélique Marie Martin, she was the eldest offspring of French parents who espoused a Utopian doctrine of communal living and equal rights for women. Spencer lived her first eight years in England and then immigrated with her family to New York. Three years later, the Martins moved to Marietta, Ohio, where, she later recollected, the eldest child lived the classic tomboy existence. Enjoying perfect liberty, she roamed "at will through woods and fields . . . Her time was passed in working in her garden, playing and racing with other children, hunting for insects, shells, and minerals."[21] Certain episodes in this idyllic life conjure up startling images, as when Spencer, then thirteen, and wanting a "pet," tackled a deer: "As he sprang over the fence she caught his hind legs and clung to them, while her father's dog throttled the captive. Some men came up directly, and, seeing the girl with her face covered with blood, killed the deer, not withstanding her entreaties."[22]

Spencer's career was even more unconventional than her girlhood. After training and beginning her career in Cincinnati, she moved in 1848 with her husband Benjamin Spencer to New York and—while bearing a staggering total of thirteen children (of which seven survived)—took on the role of breadwinner. Seeking a market for her pictures, Spencer found a rich lode in the sentimental and often humorous representation of middle-class domestic life. For a time, she enjoyed modest success as a purveyor of popular, familiar subjects, but she never prospered. Beset by financial worries and torn between family demands and professional pressures, she had to perform a difficult and never-ending balancing act, yet she never lost her sense of humor or her relish for the absurd. Importantly, humor permitted Spencer to scatter clues to the subversive potential of girlish behavior in many of her works of art while seeming to adhere to middle-class norms of decorum and propriety in the domestic realm.[23]

The focus of Spencer's *Fruit of Temptation,* circa 1857 (fig. 65), is a mischievous little girl raiding an overturned sugar bowl on a dining room table heaped with baskets and bowls of luscious fruit. On the floor is her brother, looking out at us while gobbling a slice of watermelon. Everything is out of control: the servant, ignoring the children, preens before a mirror, her discarded feather duster lying next to the girl's cast-off doll. Standing on the rumpled rug, the family dog devours a piece of cake that has somehow ended up on the seat of a chair, while up on the table the family cat laps cream from a pitcher. The plot hinges on the open door to the rear, from which the well-dressed lady of the house—her face a mask of dismay—beholds the awful scene. It is not difficult to guess what is supposed to happen next: Mother will restore order; the miscreants will be punished and reform their errant ways.[24]

But does the implied moral dénouement impose such an ironclad meaning on Spencer's vision of domestic disarray? Not necessarily. Regarding Spencer's *Don't Touch,* her sponsor, the *Cosmopolitan Art Journal,* commented: "A mischievous little beauty, of some four or five summers, is forbidden to touch a basket of fruit on the table. Seizing an opportunity, when her mother is not looking, she reaches up her hand and touches the very tempting contents of the basket, looking back to notice if anyone detects the act. The expression on her face is that mingling of mischief and willful indulgence,

Fig. 65. (left) Jean Baptiste Adolphe Lafosse, after Lilly Martin Spencer, *Fruit of Temptation,* 1857. Lithograph, 24½ x 20⅛ in. Published by Goupil. Courtesy of the Ohio Historical Society.   **Fig. 66.** (right) Unknown artist, *The Mischief-Maker Discovered,* print illustration from *The Little Mischief-Maker, and Other Stories,* by Uncle Frank (Francis Channing Woodworth), 1852, p. 47. General Research Division, The New York Public Library, Astor, Lenox and Tilden Foundations

which only the true artist can catch . . . To loving mothers and fathers, this picture will have nameless charms." Clearly related to *Fruit of Temptation* and exactly contemporary with it, *Don't Touch* celebrated roguish disobedience and mischief.[25]

Here it is instructive to compare Spencer's visual narratives with those in popular children's books that presented the misdeeds of the trouble-making child as moral counterexamples. Such was the tale told by "Uncle Frank" about little Clara Redwood who, no matter what the punishment, obdurately refuses to mend her evil ways, "because she loved mischief so well."[26] Left alone in the parlor one day, she reduces the room to utter confusion. When her mother and her aunt Sophia return, they find that, "to crown all, Clara had made a huge ink-blot on one of the beautiful books which was lying on the centre-table."[27] Clara never does become good. As "Uncle Frank" explains, he has told her story so that his young readers may "see what mischief costs."[28] An illustration to the story (fig. 66) shows the discovery of Clara's parlor mischief by her mother and her aunt. Even given the anonymous illustrator's meager skills, we can readily perceive that the unrepentant Clara—caught in the act—is far from a role model.

But is that the message of the mischievous little girl in *Fruit of Temptation?* There is nothing furtive about her actions: she reaches for the forbidden sweets as if they were rightfully hers. She indulges herself, satisfies her desires. It is difficult even to imagine that there might be serious consequences. Rather than view this as a scene of imminent retribution, we might rather consider it a celebration of carnivalesque excess, one woman's subversive vision of the domestic world upside down, all rules suspended, allowing a "good" girl to go "bad," if only in fantasy. By breaking the rules, Spencer's self-absorbed plunderer has gained full possession of herself, has flouted the rules of feminine deportment.[29] We might even imagine her a girlish Eve, helping herself to forbidden fruits—without risk of expulsion. Spencer's humorous edge made it possible for contemporaries—like the writer for the *Cosmopolitan Art Journal*—to understand *her* scenes of mayhem as comedies rather than homilies. That same journal praised Spencer time and again for "her inimitable delineations of the humorous side of life and character."[30]

Such sugarcoating presumably made it possible for admirers to ignore or misread the undercurrent of seditious meaning in Spencer's now lost *Grandpa's Prodigies*, which the *Cosmopolitan Art Journal* reproduced in its September 1860 issue (fig. 67). In this cozy tableau, the old man's "prodigies" engage in a highly unconventional game. On hands and knees, a boy with an improvised bit in his mouth plays "horse" to his little sister's "rider." The girl

Fig. 67. T. Rogers, after Lilly Martin Spencer, *Grandpa's Prodigies*, 1860. Engraving. Published in *Cosmopolitan Art Journal* (New York: Cosmopolitan Art Association, 1856–1861). Courtesy of American Antiquarian Society

exuberantly straddles her brother's back and pulls hard at the reins while brandishing a whip fashioned from a knobbed cane (perhaps Grandpa's walking stick) and a length of ribbon. Both appear to be enjoying themselves immensely, and the *Journal* gaily noted the "exquisite apprehension of the humors of the little folks," praising the "richness of coloring, strength of characterizations, force of delivery," all "quite in the artist's best vein."[31]

Far more than in *Fruit of Temptation*, Spencer shows us a world radically upside down, the little woman on top, mastering the little man, who shows no inclination to buck her off. Though costumed in the innocence of childhood, the world is topsy-turvy, the gender hierarchy reversed—more explicitly than in *Fruit of Temptation*. Are we to understand that after the brief interlude of childish freedom, the hierarchy will right itself, the boy will reclaim his place on top, the girl will be tamed? Will absent parents reappear to rein in this willful girl, to train her for wifehood and motherhood? Or did Spencer encode a dangerously subversive message for those with the eyes to see it? After all, she herself had enjoyed a childhood of unfettered freedom only to find herself hobbled in adulthood when domestic demands and sexism threatened her professional aspirations. Did humor allow the artist to give vent to frustrations and hopes that she could never express overtly without alienating the market she struggled so hard to win?[32]

Of course, not every image of mischief was necessarily subversive. There was innocuous misbehavior, too, displayed in a thriving genre of harmless childhood fun, exemplified by the 1857 Currier and Ives print (after Louis Maurer) titled *Into Mischief* (fig. 68). Although the German-born Maurer specialized in images of champion racing trotters and fire brigades, in the 1850s he turned his hand to sentimental or sprightly childhood scenes which tapped into a popular middle-class market. The lithograph shows a small girl who has single-handedly turned her world upside down in an all-out parody of domesticity. Pretending to be a cook, she has upended her father's top hat and filled it with inedible ingredients, including a lace collar, presumably Mama's, hanging over the brim. Pouring some sort of liquid from a teacup and stirring the whole mess with an umbrella, she engages the viewer with a merry smile. At her feet are a woman's fan and a bottle of ink, spilled over a piece of notepaper and an envelope. Her doll, stuffed head first into a tall pitcher, is a graphic emblem of inversion.

Art historian Laura Napolitano has suggested that such prints were designed to decorate the

Fig. 68. Currier and Ives, publishers, after Louis Maurer, *Into Mischief*, c. 1857. Lithograph, 16½ x 12⅝ in. The Old Print Shop

middle-class nursery.³³ Currier and Ives's *The First Step: "Come to Mama,"* circa 1859 (fig. 69), actually gives prominent place to a framed, large-format version of *Into Mischief* hung above the teetering baby and the mother with protective arms outstretched. Napolitano relates this to changing attitudes toward childish misbehavior: over the mid-century decades older disciplinary patterns relaxed and mischief was treated—up to a point—as harmless and natural. The inclusion of Maurer's print in *The First Step* suggests that the nursery is the province of naughtiness, where it is both tolerated and contained. As Napolitano points out, the lithographs Spencer designed for her agent, William Schaus, also represented children—boys and girls alike—being playfully but winningly wayward.³⁴ Parents who performed in the new loving and tolerant key, Spencer and her husband found their children an endless source of amusement rather than miscreants in need of punishment. In her letters, Spencer often referred to their easygoing parental style. On one occasion, she wrote to "dearest dearest Mother" how much she longed for a visit: "Charley our little funny Charley is a baby for I think he would amuse you both so much. Our little Ben reads pretty well, and our Angelo begins to read his A B C and he is so funny at it." Other letters express the same affectionate amusement.³⁵

The girl on top in *Grandpa's Prodigies* may be funny, but she is also purposeful. A similar tableau drawn by the immensely popular cartoonist Charles Dana Gibson at century's end (fig. 34, page 53) is significantly different. *The Nursery* (the first installment in Gibson's "Seven Ages of Woman") appears at first to be a revival of *Grandpa's Prodigies,* differing only in that the boy is now roped to his younger playmate's chair as if he were pulling her along in a buggy. Unlike Spencer's rider, Gibson's girl holds the "reins" loosely, and her hands curve round to support the doll on her lap. She looks out at us not with manic glee but with somewhat vacant sweetness. Member of a gender, and a class, unsettled by the rise of the New Woman in the 1890s, Gibson used humor to defuse the threat while commenting with tongue in cheek on everything that men stood to lose. But *his* girl rehearses her designated role as a mother who will reproduce and perpetuate the class to which she belongs. She may grow up to play golf, but she will never invade male territory. By contrast, Spencer's humor bites: *her* triumphant rider cherishes no doll but wields her whip as if in training for an Amazonian future.

Fig. 69. Currier and Ives, publishers, after Louis Maurer, *The First Step: "Come to Mama,"* c. 1859. Lithograph. Library of Congress, Prints and Photographs

Fig. 70. Lilly Martin Spencer, *War Spirit at Home (Celebrating the Victory at Vicksburg),* 1866. Oil on canvas, 30 x 32¾ in. Newark Museum; Purchase 1944, Wallace M. Scudder Bequest Fund 44.177

MAKING MISCHIEF

Spencer delivered an equally pointed message of young female empowerment in *War Spirit at Home,* 1866 (fig. 70), yet another topsy-turvy and very untidy domestic scene. A mother reads war news in the *New York Times,* ignoring both the baby about to tumble from her lap and her other children running amok in an impromptu procession, while a dour servant dries dishes in the background. The painting must certainly be Spencer's ironic comment on the contemporaneous Currier and Ives print *Training Day* (fig. 71), in which we see nearly the identical scene—with the difference that the household is sunny, clean, and neat. Here, not a newspaper in sight, the mother embraces her baby securely, and the servant looks on cheerfully as the children enjoy their patriotic parade. So well ordered is this household that even the tiny tea set on the seat of a chair behind the youngest child is neatly laid, as if to suggest that "training" also connotes practice in domestic skills. Beyond inverting the pristine neatness of the print, Spencer also—significantly—reversed the two older children's roles. In the lithograph, big brother in his paper hat leads the way, banging on a tin pan with a tablespoon, while his sister, in a kepi, blows a pretend trumpet that is really a funnel. But in Spencer's parody, the daughter steps into the limelight. Wearing a jaunty soldier's forage cap and a red dress, she has taken over the post of drummer. Her brother, in drab gray, toots his little horn in the dim background. Although a half-naked toddler with a paper bag on his head leads the procession, the girl insistently claims our attention: she sounds the brightest note of color and is making the most noise. By no coincidence did the postwar years see a strong resurgence of women's rights activism, along with new freedoms that girls increasingly demanded and enjoyed. Emblematic of that social sea change, Spencer's girl in red, unrestrained, marches happily out of bounds.[36]

Spencer couched her messages in visual terms. It was up to viewers to decide whether the artist's images of girls acting up, and out, were cautionary or celebratory. At the very least, they suggested that a little girl might add snips and snails to "sugar and spice and all things nice" for a dash of zest and grit—and get away with it. Art critics might embroider moral messages and concoct narratives for genre paintings like Spencer's, but in the end they could not control meaning and its making. In visual culture more generally, illustrations of mischief-making girls did the same work. That is, while the tales or verses they accompanied more often than not drove home some moral point, the pictures themselves—almost invariably funny or ludicrous—allowed greater interpretive latitude.

In certain cases, that latitude could expand almost to infinity, most extravagantly in Heinrich Hoffmann's *Slovenly Peter* (*Struwwelpeter* in German) a little book of nursery rhymes and funny pictures published in German in 1845 and in English in 1848. Hoffmann had originally penned the stories

Fig. 71. Currier and Ives, publishers, *Training Day,* 1866. Handcolored lithograph, 11¾ x 15¾ in. The Old Print Shop

and drawn the pictures for his three-year-old son as an antidote to the sanctimoniously didactic tales that then dominated the market. The first *Slovenly Peter* featured only egregiously naughty boys, but the second edition introduced "The Dreadful Story of Pauline and the Matches." Phenomenally popular, *Slovenly Peter* generated an entire industry of clones and imitators; altogether, hundreds of editions appeared.[37] In nearly every case, the illustrations added as much fun as instruction, if not more. Hoffmann's own simple drawings traded so blithely in ludicrous excess and grotesquely horrific humor as to transcend, and transgress, any moral message altogether.

In "The Dreadful Story of Pauline and the Matches," for example, a child who disobeys her mother by playing with matches ends up burning herself to a crisp. Granted, there is nothing funny about such a subject in real life. But Hoffmann's illustrations (fig. 72), which tell the story like a comic book, push the tale to laughable extremes. However gruesome the pictures and their accompanying jingles, many children found them hilarious, since they so impudently parodied the sort of solemn moral tale exemplified by the account "Uncle Frank" offered of the unregenerate Clara Redwood.[38] The American spin-offs, like those published by McLoughlin Brothers, often added moralizing tag ends, but even they did not altogether snuff out the possibility of interpretation along more subversive lines, especially since the illustrations, following Hoffmann's lead, were so often comical and even cartoonish in style.

The lively vignettes accompanying the later spin-off *Slovenly Kate,* for example, depict a girl known as "Tomboy Kate" engaging in all manner of rowdy romps with boys (fig. 73). She climbs a tree, runs a race (and wins it), expertly catches a ball, and kicks her schoolbooks into the air, while her brother— "by far more ladylike"—watches in dismay.[39] The

Fig. 72. Heinrich Hoffmann, *Pauline and the Matches,* 1851. From "The Dreadful Story of Pauline and the Matches," in Heinrich Hoffmann, *Slovenly Peter; or, Cheerful Stories and Funny Pictures, for Good Little Folks* (Philadelphia: Henry T. Coates, c. 1900). Harvard College Library, Widener Library KG1019

TOMBOY KATE.

Kate's a tomboy, sure enough,
Fond of games, so very rough,
Other girls declare that they
With Miss Katy will not play.
Running races, climbing trees,
Playing ball, in sports like these
Katy finds her great delight,
Keeps them up from morn till night.
Seldom does she care to look
At a picture, or a book;
Such a restless thing as she
On the go must always be.
Papa chides her with a frown;
Mamma whispers "Kate, sit down!"
And her younger brother, Ike,
Is by far more ladylike.
It is nice to romp and run;
Girls should have their share of fun;
But they ought to know enough
Not to be too rude and rough.

Fig. 73. *Tomboy Kate.* From Josephine Pollard, *Freaks and Frolics of Little Girls and Boys* (New York: McLoughlin Brothers, 1887), YC-f1887. Collection of New-York Historical Society 85443d

message is emphatic: "It is nice to romp and run; / Girls should have their share of fun; / But they ought to know enough / Not to be too rude or rough."[40] And yet by showing an exuberantly active tomboy, confident and self-possessed, the illustrations not-so-subtly undermine the explicit moral and sneakily extol girlish liberation.

Slovenly Peter may have set the standard, but anomalous and disruptive images cropped up elsewhere as well. "Little Mischief," a series of tales and pictures that ran briefly in *The Nursery: A Monthly Magazine for Youngest Readers,* followed the exploits of Bessie Allen, a chronic but comical troublemaker who washes (and ruins) her father's top hat, inks her dog's face, gives her wax doll a hot bath (with predictable results), and—most outrageously— paints a big blue handlebar moustache on a portrait she finds on the easel in her artist uncle's studio (fig. 74).[41]

That implicit suggestion of role reversal gets serendipitous reinforcement in the very next story in that issue, which presents a solemn little boy on Christmas morning, surrounded by masculine playthings, including a cannon, a rifle, and a toy soldier (fig. 75).[42] He has rejected them all, instead clutching a female doll to his chest. The boy is in petticoats, suggesting that he is between babyhood and properly panted boyhood and thus in a fluid or liminal stage of becoming. Yet together with the picture of Bessie—a graffiti artist in the making—this image highlights the arbitrary nature of socially prescribed gender roles—and the possibility (however remote at that time) of a world beyond them.

Some, at least, were beginning to recognize and reckon with such questions during that turbulent post–Civil War decade when a new generation of girls claimed new liberties and privileges. Seeking advice from the editor of *Arthur's Home Magazine,* one young mother wanted to know whether she ought to curb her daughters' "strong propensities to be 'Tomboys'" and their delight in "rough, boyish sports," to which they took as if "born boys." Rather than nurse their dolls, these tomboys took naturally to boys' toys: "It is no uncommon sight to see the three girls in procession, with their little brother bringing up the rear, 'playing soldier,' with childish substitutes for uniforms, flag, drum, trumpet, guns, and swords, and making *nearly* as much din as the same number of boys could do." At the same time, she added, "my little boy wanted a doll," a desire his "old-fashioned" grandmother squelched by "telling him he wouldn't be a *man* if he played with dolls." The editor's response was reassuring and openminded. Girls, like boys, possessed an "instinct for

Fig. 74. *Little Mischief.* From *The Nursery: A Monthly Magazine for Youngest Readers* 13, no. 2 (Boston: John L. Shorey, 1873), p. 59. Rare Books, Special Collections and Preservation Department, Rush Rhees Library, University of Rochester, Rochester, NY

noise and dirt that need not be reined in. It was far more important that boys and girls alike learn values that would teach them to be "generous and just, kind and considerate." Why should they not play with each other "as much as they will"? "Your boys will be all the more surely gentlemen for this companionship with their sisters, and your girls will . . . prove none the less ladies, because you have given them the chance to be women with strong nerves, healthy bodies, and whole souls."[43]

That editor's message may have fallen short of a call for revolution, but it was nonetheless a sign of the times. Many other stories and occasional pieces from the 1870s on assumed an increasingly permissive and even supportive stance toward the tomboy and the mischief-maker. Being a tomboy was almost a prerequisite for success outside the domestic sphere. The inventor Margaret Knight, for example, very early in life "mortified" her parents and friends by being "that childish feminine monstrosity called a 'Tomboy.'" Rather than play with dolls or learn to sew, she "wanted gimlets and augurs, and saws and hatchets, and nails, and lumber," which she used to make sleds and wagons and kites for her "lazy numbskull brothers." She went on to become the inventor of the flat-bottomed paper bag, in the process winning a legal battle for the patent rights against a male coworker who claimed her designs as his own. As one reporter put it, "Several attempts had previously been made by men of 'mechanical genius,' and all had failed. This 'Tomboy' has now done it, and made a success."[44]

Tomboyism also functioned as harbinger of women's eventual victory in the battle for equal rights. Debby Ann, the titular doughty and self-reliant septuagenarian in Sarah Hallowell's story, exemplifies a new view of women's mission that "will be known perhaps at that great day when women shall cast in their votes." Asked about her girlhood, Debby Ann recounts her young days as a tomboy who played with the boys "just as rough" and had an ongoing battle with her mother over a sewing sampler, which the rebellious child refused to complete and regularly hid, finally concealing it in the "big dictionary, and it lay there safe for years."[45] Noteworthy in the stories of the real Margaret Knight and the fictional Debby Ann is the matter-of-fact acceptance of the tomboy as a model rather than a maverick. Whereas individuals like Frances Willard and Lilly Martin Spencer embarked on radical paths to nonconformity, the mainstream tomboy or trouble-maker evolved into a less disruptive figure. But did that evolution necessarily weaken her?

In late-nineteenth-century visual culture, there were still very many more images of good girls,

Fig. 75. *Too Many Presents*. From *The Nursery: A Monthly Magazine for Youngest Readers* 13, no. 2 (Boston: John L. Shorey, 1873), p. 61. Rare Books, Special Collections and Preservation Department, Rush Rhees Library, University of Rochester, Rochester, NY

angelic little misses with their dolls, pets, and flowers. Most tomboys did indeed put aside their rough-and-ready ways when they lengthened their skirts and put up their hair.[46] However, there remains that scattered trail of bad girls and boy-girls leading—bit by bit—to the era of the New Woman and to the even greater changes that would take place in the twentieth century. We can measure the magnitude of that transformation by comparing two images separated by some forty years.

A vignette in *Dolly and I,* 1863 (fig. 76), a moralizing tale ascribed to "Oliver Optic," shows a little girl looking furtively about as she plunges the points of her scissors into the eyes of the doll on her lap. There is nothing funny about the image, nor is there meant to be. In the story, wicked, envious Katy savagely attacks her sister's doll, to ensure that *her* doll will be the best. But soon she discovers her fatal mistake: confusing the two dolls in the dark, she has spoiled her own instead. The author humorlessly asks, "Don't you think it served her right?"[47] Katy is an evil and destructive child who must pay for her crime.

Her counterpart in the 1907 stereograph *Private Investigations Lead to —* (fig. 77), however, seems to be getting away with murder. A more sophisticated sister of Louis Maurer's merry mischief-maker with doll upended in pitcher, this little girl, so demurely dressed, stands alone and unsupervised in an overstuffed stage set of a parlor complete with potted palms and, on the wall behind her, a tasteful Japanese fan. She cradles her doll, but hardly to play Mommy. Holding a formidable pair of scissors, she cuts open its stomach—in a symbolic act as flagrantly bad as anything in the *Slovenly Peter* books. And like those books, this scene, with its deadpan presentation of extreme violence, is meant to be funny and open-ended. Is this "baby killer" a Medea in the making? Does this act of dissection foreshadow the little

Fig. 76. *What Katy Did.* From Oliver Optic (William Taylor Adams), *Dolly and I: A Story for Little Folks* (Boston: Lee and Shepard, 1862), p. 74. Courtesy of the Lilly Library, Indiana University, Bloomington, IN

investigator's future medical career? Or will this "private investigation" lead only to discovery and chastisement? It is up to the viewer to decide.

Private Investigations adds one more to that small but mighty tribe of bad girls created by Lilly Spencer and others, children who acted out, breaking the mold meant to contain them. Such images succeeded because they used humor to soften and disguise the threat of girlish misbehavior. These visual jokes cut both ways. By making light of badness and boyish behavior, they whittled transgression down to manageable size and kept it within bounds. At the same time, they opened up loopholes, or knotholes, through which beholders, not least little girls, might glimpse new and powerful roles for women. Unmoored from whatever moralizing text anchored them, comic pictures of bad girls having fun engaged in a sort of cultural guerrilla action, launching random but relentless attacks on long-standing conventions. Their humor reproduced or duplicated the tension, the push-pull between liberation and constraint that over the latter decades of the nineteenth century constituted the core of the debate about the American girl and what she might become.

Fig. 77. *Private Investigations Lead to —,* 1907. Photographic print on stereo card. H. C. White Co. Library of Congress, Prints and Photographs

1. Raymond Westbrook, "Open Letters from New York, V," *Atlantic Monthly* 41 (June 1878), 787. On Johnson, see Teresa A. Carbone and Patricia Hills, *Eastman Johnson: Painting America,* exhibition catalogue (New York: Rizzoli for Brooklyn Museum of Art, 1999).

2. Mary J. Holmes, *Meadow Brook* (New York: Carleton, 1869), 11, 23.

3. Susan Coolidge, *What Katy Did* (Boston: Roberts Brothers, 1890), 11, 13. This tale was enormously popular; at least seventeen editions or reprints appeared from 1872 to 1900.

4. Louisa May Alcott, *Little Women; or, Meg, Jo, Beth, and Amy* (Boston: Roberts Bros., 1868), 10.

5. L. G. Abell, *Woman in Her Various Relations; Containing Practical Rules for American Females . . .* (New York: J. M. Fairchild, 1855), 152–171.

6. *The Tiny Picture Book* (Charlestown, MA: George W. Hobbs, n.d.), 10.

7. Frances B. Cogan, *All-American Girl: The Ideal of Real Womanhood in Mid-Nineteenth-Century America* (Athens: University of Georgia Press, 1989), 3–26.

8. Michelle Ann Abate, *Tomboys: A Literary and Cultural History* (Philadelphia: Temple University Press, 2008), ix–xxix.

9. Jane Hunter, *How Young Ladies Became Girls: The Victorian Origins of American Girlhood* (New Haven, CT: Yale University Press, 2002), 140.

10. Abate, *Tomboys,* xxx, 22. Abate also describes "tomboy taming" (41, 47) as a ritual designed to ensure that girls would grow up to produce the next generation of the ruling Anglo-American class. Although dating back to the English Renaissance, the term "tomboy" did not come into wide use in the United States until the middle of the nineteenth century, when it supplanted its precursor, "hoyden." See Abate, *Tomboys,* xiv. Southworth's *The Hidden Hand; or, Capitola, the Mad-Cap* was serialized in the *New York Ledger* in 1859 and twice thereafter, in 1868–1869 and 1883, finally published in book form in 1888. It was also available as a drama in five acts, which went through numerous printings in its own right. *The Hidden Hand* is the subject of Abate's first chapter.

11. "The Athletic Revival," *Harper's Weekly,* January 28, 1860, 50.

12. Edward L. Gill, *The Skater's Manual: A Complete Guide to the Art of Skating,* rev. ed. (New York: A. Peck, 1867), 13. For a useful overview, see Luna Lambert, *The American Skating Mania: Ice Skating in the Nineteenth Century,* exhibition catalogue (Washington, D.C.: National Museum of History and Technology, 1978).

13. Dio Lewis, *Our Girls* (New York: Harper and Brothers, 1871), 337–338. Lewis did have reservations about skating, since like dancing and walking it exercised only the lower limbs and hips; in this and other works, he urged readers to take up home gymnastics to train and strengthen the upper body.

14. Etiquette books advised against balancing on the edge of the chair, bending forward, or extending one's feet onto andirons; see, for example, Emily Thornwell, *The Lady's Guide to Perfect Gentility* (New York: Derby and Jackson, 1856), 87.

15. Frances E. Willard, *Glimpses of Fifty Years: The Autobiography of an American Woman* (Toronto: Rose Publishing for Woman's Temperance Publication Association, 1889), 3:5.

16. Ibid., 3:17–18.

17. Ibid., 3:25.

18. Lousia M. Alcott, "Recollections of My Childhood," *Youth's Companion,* May 24, 1888, 261.

19. On Brown, see Martha Hoppin, *Country Paths and City Sidewalks: The Art of J. G. Brown,* exhibition catalogue (Springfield, MA: George Walter Vincent Smith Art Museum, 1989). The tomboy paintings include *Swinging on the Gate,* c. 1878–1879 (Plate 8; Taubman Museum of Art, Roanoke, VA), *Three Girls on a Swing,* 1868, and *The Tomboy,* 1873 (the last two are both in private collections).

20. Christine Boufis, "'Of Home Birth and Breeding': Eliza Lynn Linton and the Girl of the Period," in *The Girl's Own: Cultural Histories of the Anglo-American Girl, 1830–1915,* ed. Claudia Nelson and Lynne Vallone (Athens: University of Georgia Press, 1994), 98–123.

21. Mrs. Ellet, *Women Artists in All Ages and Countries* (New York: Harper and Brothers, 1859), 319. The standard source on Spencer is still Robin Bolton-Smith and William H. Truettner, *Lilly Martin Spencer, 1822–1902: The Joys of Sentiment,* exhibition catalogue (Washington, D.C.: Smithsonian Institution Press, 1973).

22. Ellet, *Women Artists,* 319.

23. The assumption that in her art Spencer replicated and reified middle-class standards of propriety has by and large shaped recent scholarship on the artist. See Wendy Jean Katz, "Lilly Martin Spencer and the Art of Refinement," *American Studies* 42, no. 1 (spring 2001); Wendy Jean Katz, *Regionalism and Reform: Art and Class Formation in Antebellum Cincinnati* (Columbus: Ohio State University Press, 2002). David M. Lubin and Elizabeth Johns have read more subversive or even deviant connotations (respectively) into Spencer's images of impudent housewives and sexualized children; see Lubin, *Picturing a Nation: Art and Social Change in Nineteenth-Century America* (New Haven, CT: Yale University Press, 1994), 159–203; Johns, *American Genre Painting: The Politics of Everyday Life* (New Haven, CT: Yale University Press, 1991), 173. Spencer was ambivalent about the women's rights movement that was emerging in the 1850s. That, however, does not preclude the subversive potential of her pictured mischief-makers.

24. Claire Perry, *Young America: Childhood in Nineteenth-Century Art and Culture,* exhibition catalogue (New Haven, CT: Yale University Press, 2006), 64–67. Perry discusses *Fruit of Temptation* as a moralizing painting and suggests that viewers would construe the children's imminent punishment as well-deserved indigestion.

25. "Mrs. Lilly M. Spencer's Paintings," *Cosmopolitan Art Journal* 1, no. 5 (September 1857): 65.

26. Uncle Frank [Francis Channing Woodworth], *The Little Mischief-Maker, and Other Stories* (New York: Charles Scribner, 1852), 10.

27. Ibid., 49.

28. Ibid., 51. Woodworth, also a minister, edited the didactic periodical *Youth's Cabinet*.

29. G. Raymond Babineau, "Compulsive Border Crosser," *Psychiatry* 35, no. 3 (1972). Mikhail Bakhtin presented the the medieval carnival as quite literally a topsy-turvy and chaotic world capable of generating rebellious, liberating energies. See Bakhtin, *Rabelais and His World,* trans. Hélène Iswolsky (Bloomington: Indiana University Press, 1984). In *Picturing a Nation,* Lubin contends that much of Spencer's work could be described as carnivalesque (191).

30. "Our Artists and Their Whereabouts," *Cosmopolitan Art Journal* 2, no. 4 (1858): 209.

31. "Catalogue of Premiums," *Cosmopolitan Art Journal* 4, no. 4 (1860): 191.

32. Spencer also did her share of naughty-boy paintings, but given the codes of conduct in force at that time, her images of girls have a more subversive edge. Spencer herself declined to take an active role in the emerging feminist movement. As she told her mother, her babies and her business were her highest priorities, and she had neither time nor the resources to travel to women's rights meetings. See Lilly Martin Spencer to Angélique Martin, October 11, 1850, Lilly Martin Spencer Papers, microfilm roll no. 131, Archives of American Art, Smithsonian Institution.

33. Laura Napolitano, "Nurturing Change: Lilly Martin Spencer's Images of Children" (Ph.D. dissertation, University of Maryland, 2008), 133.

34. Ibid., 120, 132–134.

35. Lilly Martin Spencer to Angélique Martin, August 11, 1852, Lilly Martin Spencer Papers, microfilm roll no. 131, Archives of American Art, Smithsonian Institution.

36. While women have never been permitted to hold combat roles in the armed forces of the United States, many did go to war, and many more dreamt of going without leaving their home towns. See, for example, Elizabeth D. Leonard, *All the Daring of a Soldier: Women of the Civil War Armies* (New York: Norton, 1999).

37. On *Slovenly Peter* in America, see Walter Sauer, "'Struwwelpeter' Naturalized: McLoughlin Imprints of 'Slovenly Peter' and Related Books," and J. D. Stahl, "'Struwwelpeter' and the Development of American Children's Books," both in *Princeton University Library Chronicle* 62, no. 1 (2000).

38. Heinrich Hoffmann, "The Dreadful Story of Pauline and the Matches," in *Slovenly Peter; or, Cheerful Stories and Funny Pictures, for Good Little Folks* (Philadelphia: Henry T. Coates, c. 1900), 6–7. David Blamires stresses that the "conclusion to every story is so over the top" that it is "meant to provoke laughter and be understood as a satire at the expense of the traditional moral tale." See Blamires, *Telling Tales: The Impact of Germany on English Children's Books, 1780–1918* (Cambridge, UK: Open Books, 2009), 332. Also see Barbara Smith Chalou, *Struwwelpeter: Humor or Horror? 160 Years Later* (Lanham, UK: Lexington, 2007).

39. Josephine Pollard, *Freaks and Follies of Little Girls and Boys* (New York: McLoughlin Brothers, 1887), 15.

40. Ibid., 15.

41. "Little Mischief," *The Nursery,* February 1873, 57–60. Subsequent to this installment, the Bessie stories bowed to convention, always concluding with the little girl's expressions of remorse. This suggests that the stories may have been too open-ended for comfort. *The Nursery* credited no author for the "Little Mischief" chronicles.

42. "Too Many Presents," *The Nursery,* February 1873, 61.

43. "The Management of Girls," *Arthur's Home Magazine,* October 1870, 226–227.

44. "What Came of a Tomboy," *Boston Investigator,* December 25, 1872. Autumn Stanley notes that contemporaries recounted Knight's childhood from the "amazing-tomboy perspective," reminiscent of the untaught genius myth of the artist. It is significant that there *was* an amazing-tomboy perspective. See Stanley, *Mothers and Daughters of Invention: Notes for a Revised History of Technology* (Metuchen, NJ: Scarecrow, 1993), 356.

45. Sarah C. Hallowell, "Debby Ann," *Harper's New Monthly Magazine,* April 1878, 777.

46. On the lengthening of skirts as a rite of passage into womanhood, see Hunter, *How Young Ladies Became Girls,* 140–145.

47. Oliver Optic [William Taylor Adams], *Dolly and I: A Story for Little Folks* (Boston: Lee and Shepard, 1864), 94.

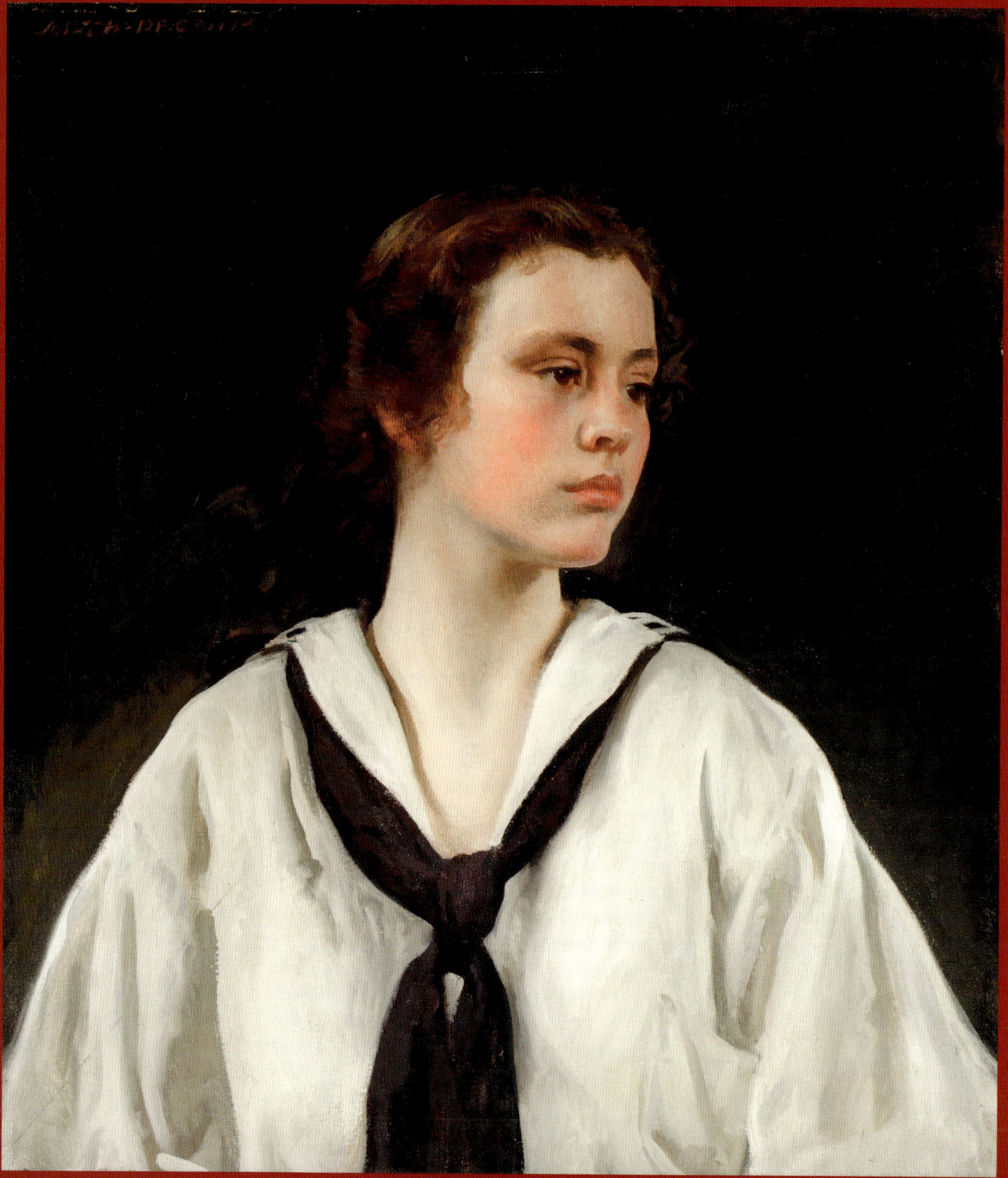

Roses in Bloom
American Images of Adolescent Girlhood

LAUREN LESSING

In December 1841, Henry Wadsworth Longfellow sent a draft of his poem "Maidenhood" to his friend Samuel Ward Jr., who responded that he and his family admired the work "excessively."[1] The poem (which was published the following year) describes a representative girl on the cusp of womanhood, her "meek brown eyes" shadowed by trouble. It reads in part:

> Standing, with reluctant feet,
> Where the brook and river meet,
> Womanhood and childhood fleet!
>
> Gazing, with a timid glance,
> On the brooklet's swift advance,
> On the river's broad expanse!
>
> Deep and still, that gliding stream
> Beautiful to thee must seem,
> As the river of a dream.
>
> Then why pause with indecision,
> When bright angels in thy vision
> Beckon thee to fields Elysian?

Longfellow's poem was almost certainly influenced by Thomas Cole's series of allegorical paintings "The Voyage of Life," 1839–1840 (Munson-Williams-Proctor Art Institute), which the Ward family owned. As a frequent visitor to the Wards's Manhattan home, Longfellow undoubtedly knew the four paintings well. They depict a metaphorical river journey symbolizing a man's progress from infancy to old age. In particular, "Maidenhood" can be read as a response to the second painting in the series, *Youth* (fig. 79). In both *Youth* and "Maidenhood," a young person in transition to adulthood is transfixed by a bright, distant vision at the spot where a gentle brook becomes a broad river. The differing reactions of the youth and the maiden reflect mid-nineteenth-century gender roles and expectations. Driven by ambition, Cole's young man steers his small boat away from the safety of the riverbank and straight toward the gleaming palace he sees in the clouds, ignoring the warnings of his guardian angel gesturing to him from the shore. Longfellow's maiden, on the other hand, hesitates. Although she, too, longs to go forward, she fears the dangers before her. In the next painting in Cole's series, his protagonist is swept toward a rocky precipice. Longfellow confirms that trouble also lies in the maiden's path. He warns:

> O, thou child of many prayers!
> Life hath quicksands,—Life hath snares
> Care and age come unawares![2]

Fig. 78. (opposite) Joseph Rodefer DeCamp, *Sally*, c. 1907. Oil on canvas, 26 x 23 in. Worcester Art Museum, Worcester, MA; Museum purchase. Fig. 79. (right) Thomas Cole, *Voyage of Life: Youth*, 1840. Oil on canvas, 52½ x 78½ in. Munson-Williams-Proctor Arts Institute, Museum of Art, Utica, NY 55.106

All four paintings of "The Voyage of Life" were sold as engravings, but the printed version of *Youth*, produced in 1849, was engraved first, and it was the only print from the series that the American Art-Union distributed as an annual membership gift to its subscribers.[3] Longfellow's "Maidenhood" was even more popular. It was reprinted hundreds of times, frequently illustrated, and throughout the remainder of the century writers commenting on female adolescence made frequent reference to it. Daniel Huntington, who illustrated the poem for an 1845 edition of Longfellow's poetry, depicted a girl romantically clothed in Renaissance garb, leaning on an outcrop and gazing timidly down and to the left where lies, presumably, the river's edge (fig. 80). Emphasizing the importance of her religious faith, the crucifix she wears is at the exact center of the picture. Behind her, under a cloudy sky, a brook threads its way toward the place where she stands. Whereas Cole placed his diminutive young man in a vast landscape, Huntington made the maiden herself—with her developing figure, childish face, and hesitant expression—the largest part of his picture. In this way, he invited viewers to ponder the internal currents moving her during what one reviewer of Longfellow's poem referred to as "a mysterious phase, and a charmed stage" of a girl's life.[4]

Sixty years later, the American Impressionist Joseph DeCamp painted a portrait of his fifteen-year-old daughter, Sally, that, like Longfellow's "Maidenhood," struck a chord with its audience (fig. 78). The picture bears a superficial resemblance to Huntington's, but rather than look shyly down at her feet, Sally gazes confidently to her left. Wavy brown locks frame a face that is flushed by sun and exercise. In her loose, masculine sailor's top with its correctly knotted scarf, she appears both ready and able to navigate any river that flows in her path. Critics praised DeCamp's technique using language that seems equally descriptive of his subject. "He mixes vigor in his paint," wrote one, "and lays on with definite, outspoken grip."[5] Another critic described Sally as "the fresh, fearless, intelligent type so characteristic of our young American."[6] Indeed, Sally resembles innumerable contemporaneous images of American girls in their teens, including the members of the 1905 Lowell High School girl's basketball team, who appear in their championship portrait photograph with rolled-up sleeves and no-nonsense expressions (fig. 81). This essay examines images that both reflected and transformed American conceptions of adolescent girlhood over the course of the nineteenth century.

Although the term "adolescence" did not emerge in popular parlance until the early twentieth century, well before that Americans began to view the transition from childhood to adulthood as a distinct phase of life with its own particular qualities and problems. In 1840, half of the nation's citizens were sixteen years of age and under. By 1900,

Fig. 80. John Cheney and J. I. Pease, after a painting by Daniel Huntington. Illustration for the Henry Wadsworth Longfellow poem "Maidenhood." From *Poems by Henry Wadsworth Longfellow* (Philadelphia: Carey and Hart, 1845). Courtesy of the Bowdoin College Library, Brunswick, ME

the median age of the population—which had more than quadrupled in the intervening sixty years—was just twenty-two.[7] Coinciding with this swell in the number of young Americans, a new understanding of childhood as a period of Edenic innocence emerged—a view that made the end of childhood seem to many like an expulsion from paradise. Unlike young children, whose place in heaven was assured, Protestant teenagers felt compelled to seek their own salvation. Millions joined the early nineteenth-century evangelical movement known as the Second Great Awakening, in which young women and girls were particularly prominent.[8] This youth movement forced established Christian denominations to pay greater attention to the needs of their young parishioners. For instance, an 1839 manual for Sunday school teachers published in Philadelphia describes the years between fourteen and eighteen as a period of temporal and spiritual crisis for boys and girls alike, characterized by ardent affections, self-consciousness, and impressionability. The author warned that during this "eventful and critical period . . . the character usually becomes fixed for life, and for the most part for eternity."[9]

American girls became emblems of both the hopes and the fears associated with progress in the nineteenth century. As their numbers grew, white girls' horizons broadened. Before the Civil War, factory work, domestic service, and participation in evangelical movements afforded them new opportunities to move beyond their parents' protection and control. For middle-class girls, opportunities continued to expand after the war. They enjoyed greater freedom from housework, more mobility in public spaces, and more years of schooling, often in coeducational settings. The new liberty that girls enjoyed was, however, a source of great anxiety for many Americans who feared that their future roles as wives and mothers would be compromised by the corrosive influence of modern life. Until the turn of the

Fig. 81. *The Lowell High School Girls' Basketball Team—New England Champions,* c. 1905. Photograph. Library of Congress, Prints and Photographs

Fig. 82. John George Brown, *Crossing the Brook,* 1874. Oil on canvas, 23 x 14½ in. George Walter Vincent Smith Art Museum, Springfield, MA; George Walter Vincent Smith Collection. Photograph by David Stansbury

century, the period between puberty and marriage was commonly presented as a perilous crossroads for girls, with one path leading to spiritual, moral, and physical well-being, and the other—strewn with the quicksands and snares of worldly temptations—to ruin. This is evident in John George Brown's 1874 painting *Crossing the Brook,* where a girl stepping gingerly across a stream looks around as if searching for the safest route to womanhood (fig. 82).

Throughout the nineteenth century, artists also used the metaphor of the garden to convey an ideal of adolescent girlhood. In his 1816 painting *The May Queen,* Jacob Marling depicted a group of girls from the Raleigh Academy in North Carolina, where he and his wife taught drawing (fig. 83). In an idyllic park near the school, under the watchful eyes of their teachers, the teenagers celebrate the arrival of spring by crowning one of their peers as Flora, the goddess of flowers. Describing this annual ritual in 1821, a Raleigh journalist wrote, "It is delightful to recall, by such scenes, the pleasures of our Spring of Life, and to observe in others the same buoyancy of spirit, the same happy susceptibility to pleasurable emotion, and ardor in the pursuit of objects, which we ourselves have known, but which seem to us now as the shadowy beauties of a dream."[10] In Marling's

Fig. 83. Jacob Marling, *The May Queen (The Crowning of Flora),* 1816. Oil on canvas, 30⅛ x 39⅛ in. Chrysler Museum of Art; Gift of Edgar William and Bernice Chrysler Garbisch 80.181.20

painting, the Raleigh Academy appears as a garden of blossoming adolescent girls. Nearly thirty years later, in 1845, mill workers in Lowell, Massachusetts, chose as the frontispiece of their literary journal an engraving that similarly compares a girl to cultivated plants (fig. 84). During his 1842 visit to the United States, Charles Dickens observed that the privilege of being a young lady—reserved in Britain for the wealthy—was claimed in the United States by a broad cross section of the population, including thousands of farmers' daughters employed in Lowell's textile mills. Expecting to amaze his English readers, he described the educational and literary pursuits of these young women, most of whom were between the ages of sixteen and twenty-five:

> Firstly, there is a joint-stock piano in a great many of the boarding-houses. Secondly, nearly all these young ladies subscribe to circulating libraries. Thirdly, they have got up among themselves a periodical called *The Lowell Offering,* "A repository of original articles, written exclusively by females actively employed in the mills,"—which is duly printed, published, and sold . . . The large class of readers, startled by these facts, will exclaim, with one voice, "How very preposterous!" On my deferentially inquiring why, they will answer, "These things are above their station." In reply to that objection, I would beg to ask what their station is.[11]

Although mill laborers worked indoors from dawn to dusk six days a week, the representative factory girl depicted in the *Offering*'s frontispiece strolls in the sunshine along a country lane. To her right, a beehive can be seen under the laden branches of a fruit tree. Bees and fruit are long-standing symbols of female industry and productivity, but the girl herself is not currently at work. She walks away from the town with its prominent mill, schoolhouse, and church, along a path that symbolizes her movement into the future. The open book in her hand suggests study, and the biblical caption below—"Is Saul also among the Prophets?"—refers to religious conversion. Like the healthy vine growing on a trellis to her left, she is maturing in a manner that is both natural and controlled.[12]

Many Americans shared Dickens's belief that American girls had no fixed station, and this provoked both pride and anxiety. On the one hand, through diligence and education they might improve

Fig. 84. Frontispiece from the *Lowell Offering: A Repository of Original Articles, Written by "Factory Girls,"* December 1845. Courtesy of the American Textile History Museum

themselves beyond their parents' sphere. On the other, worldly temptation and their own unregulated desires could lead them astray. Dozens of crime pamphlets and melodramas produced from the 1830s through the 1870s dramatizing the tragic seductions and violent deaths of young factory girls reveal anxieties surrounding adolescence, a moment when nature might overwhelm the constraints of culture.[13]

Not only were a girl's class, status, and religious convictions in play during this pivotal period, so was her racial identity. In his best-known sculpture, *The White Captive,* 1857–1858 (fig. 85), Erastus Dow Palmer articulated fears about the safety and identity of young girls. The statue depicting a white girl kidnapped by American Indians is a pendant to his earlier depiction of an Indian maiden gazing thoughtfully at a crucifix, *Indian Girl,* 1853–1856 (Metropolitan Museum of Art, New York). Palmer told his friend John Durand that he intended *Indian Girl* "to show the influence of Christianity upon the savage" and *The White Captive* to show "the influence of the savage upon Christianity."[14] Together these sculptures comment on the fraught relationship between white and Native Americans in the mid-nineteenth century, while presenting adolescence as a pivot point upon which a girl's future identity rests.

The nude, pubescent subject of *The White Captive* stands in a strained and awkward contrapposto pose. Her left arm is pulled behind her back by a bark thong, which binds both of her wrists to the tree stump at her right side. Her right hand, which is the most visible, clutches fearfully at the stump. Although the captive's smooth marble body is flawlessly white and lacks both body hair and genitalia, her face is realistic in both its proportions and its expression of shock and dread.

Palmer displayed the sculpture at Schaus's Art Gallery in Manhattan, and later in Boston. From the beginning, it was controversial. Even the most favorable responses to *The White Captive* betray anxiety about the girl it depicts, who has neither the idealized physiognomy nor the perfect poise of Hiram Powers's celebrated and similarly themed *The Greek Slave,* 1847 (Newark Museum, Newark, New Jersey). A scathing review in *The Crayon* lambasted Palmer for being "void of moral delicacy and sensibility."[15] Another critic found *The White Captive*'s ordinary face and terrified expression "ignoble and common."[16] As cultural historian Joy Kasson has noted, the sculpture provoked anxiety because it raised an unspoken question: what would

Fig. 85. Erastus Dow Palmer, *The White Captive,* 1857–1858, carved 1858–1859. Marble, 65 x 20¼ x 17 in. Metropolitan Museum of Art; Bequest of Hamilton Fish, 1894 94.9.3. Photograph by Jerry L. Thompson; courtesy of Art Resource, NY

the girl represented hope for the future.[22] In *Sunday Morning in Virginia*, 1877, Winslow Homer depicted another educated African American girl, described by one reviewer as "a sable girl of twelve summers or so," teaching the children of a former slave to read the Bible (fig. 89).[23] Unlike the feckless boy in Rogers's statuette, who has abandoned his books to mischievously tickle the older man's foot, the boy in Homer's painting leans forward to absorb his lesson, pressing his cheek into the girl's sleeve. Homer's young teacher embodies the educational and professional aspirations of both African Americans and young women following the Civil War; still, her behavior—selflessly helping others while remaining gentle and loving—conforms to antebellum conventions of femininity.[24]

In scores of genre paintings and wood engravings made for popular magazines and newspapers, Homer also depicted a new sort of girl that emerged after the Civil War. In *"Winter"—A Skating Scene*, 1868 (fig. 64, page 89), for instance, girls ranging in age from about six to sixteen skate exuberantly on a frozen pond. As Sarah Burns has noted, this scene and others by Homer present a type of modern American female often referred to as the "Girl of the Period," a label denoting "the spoiled, overdecorated, boisterous young misses who seemed to have overthrown the domestic angels of an earlier day."[25] The social historian Jane H. Hunter has described the real middle-class American girls who inspired this type. Largely free from domestic duties, they read novels and socialized with peers. They attended school through their teen years, often side-by-side with boys their own age. They walked unescorted in public and also skated, swam, played croquet, and—eventually—rode bicycles. They frequented shops, concerts, and the theater, and they flirted with boys.[26]

Fig. 89. Winslow Homer, *Sunday Morning in Virginia*, 1877. Oil on canvas, 18 7/16 x 24 in. Cincinnati Art Museum; John J. Emery Fund 1924.247

As Elizabeth Johns has observed, paintings featuring adolescent girls became far more common in the years following the Civil War.[27] The greater freedom girls enjoyed and their increased public visibility contributed to this trend. Furthermore, during this period of rapid urbanization, immigration, geographic growth, and technological innovation, the already fraught transition from girlhood to womanhood became a lightning rod for fears about the future. In particular, disquiet about the dramatic social changes taking place in the United States contributed to new fears about the effects of puberty on girls' bodies.[28] As writers, educators, and physicians debated the question of what would become of American girls, artists used images of adolescents to comment on the disorienting changes taking place in American society.

In his moralizing genre painting *Making a Train* (1867), Seymour Joseph Guy addressed a little girl's desire to be both fashionable and adult (fig. 90). Originally titled *The Votary* (or *Votaress*) *of Fashion*, the painting presents a little girl playing dress-up by lamplight in her attic bedroom. She has lowered her dress to mimic the latest Parisian fashion, a décolleté gown with a sweeping train. Guy (who received his artistic education in London) employed the symbol-laden vocabulary of Victorian social realism to criticize the child's precociousness and materialism.

Fig. 90. Seymour Joseph Guy, *Making a Train*, 1867. Oil on canvas, 18⅛ x 24⅛ in. Philadelphia Museum of Art; The George W. Elkins Collection, 1924 E1924.4.14

Fig. 91. Eastman Johnson, *The Party Dress (The Finishing Touch)*, 1872. Oil on composition board, 20⅝ x 16¹¹⁄₁₆ in. Wadsworth Atheneum Museum of Art. Photograph courtesy of Art Resource, NY

Absorbed in her narcissistic fantasy, she has neglected her possessions. Her abandoned dolls symbolize the end of childhood, while her rumpled quilt, cast-off clothing, and open drawer suggest moral laxity and the disarray she will bring to married life. Most significantly, an engraving after Sir Joshua Reynolds's iconic depiction of childish piety, *The Infant Samuel*, circa 1776, pinned to the wall, has torn loose at one corner. It hangs lopsidedly and precariously over the bed at precisely the same angle as the girl's head as she turns to admire herself. While Samuel gazes up to heaven, she looks down at her dress.[29] Relying on these various markers, Guy not only condemned the girl's vanity as idolatrous, he also commented sardonically on a shift in American visual culture. Although religious and moralizing pictures like *The Infant Samuel* continued to be popular as domestic decorations, Guy implied that fashion plates in periodicals like *Harper's Bazaar* (which began publication in 1867) had a far greater impact on modern girls' behavior.

Throughout the nineteenth century, skirt length was a key indicator of maturity in girls. While the subject of *Making a Train* seems eager to dress like a grown woman, real girls often expressed ambivalence about the transition to long skirts, which impeded their movements and forced them to behave like ladies. Reflecting on her girlhood working in the mills at Lowell in the 1840s, the poet Lucy Larcom recalled her misery when her family lengthened her skirts: "I felt injured and almost outraged because my protestations against this treatment were unheeded; and when the transformation in my visible appearance was effected, I went away by myself and had a good cry . . . And the greatest pity about it was that I too soon became accustomed to the situation. I felt like a child, but considered it my duty to think and behave like a woman. I began to look upon it as a very serious thing to live."[30]

Eastman Johnson's 1872 painting *The Party Dress* (fig. 91; originally titled *The Finishing Touch*), which depicts a girl of about thirteen experiencing a moment of anxious reverie as she prepares for a social engagement, echoes Larcom's ambivalence about growing up.[31] The abandoned doll lying on an outgrown child-sized chair beneath the window, and the girl's nearly floor-length skirt, communicate her new maturity. Her gay, fashionable attire contrasts with the dim, rustic, old-fashioned interior of her New England home, reminding viewers that by the 1870s railroads were distributing fashion plates and patterns, as well as fine fabrics, to the remotest recesses of the country, making it possible even for rustic mothers to dress their daughters in "glorious apparel."[32] Unlike Guy's "votary of fashion," however, this girl appears reluctant to leave the safe haven of her childhood. As her younger sister fastens the collar of her jacket, she gazes through a window at the rolling green landscape beyond as if contemplating a perilous journey.

Thomas Eakins presented a girl stubbornly holding on to childhood freedoms in *Elizabeth Crowell with a Dog*, circa 1871 (fig. 51, page 73). The painting depicts Elizabeth Crowell, the fourteen-year-old sister of the artist's brother-in-law, seated on the floor of the Eakins family parlor, commanding a terrier to perform a trick. Having apparently just come from school, she has carelessly dropped her possessions. Elizabeth's stern expression, unselfconscious pose, and air of command as she leans forward to point a warning finger at the dog are starkly at odds with both her frilly, fashionable attire and the requirements of decorum which—like long skirts and corsets—constrained grown women's bodies. In her *Ladies' Book of Etiquette, and Manual of Politeness* (1872), for instance, Florence Hartley advised: "To sit with the knees or feet crossed or doubled up, is awkward and unlady-like . . . When seated, if you are not sewing or knitting, keep your hands perfectly quiet . . . Never gesticulate when conversing; it looks theatrical, and is ill-bred; so are all contortions of the features, shrugging of the shoulders, raising of the eyebrows, or hands."[33] By creating a visual parallel between Elizabeth's ruffled black skirt and bright red blouse and the dog's fur and collar, Eakins suggests that the girl too may soon be compelled to sit up straight. Yet, for the moment, she resists behaving like a young lady. The fact that Eakins later used a slight variation of Elizabeth's pose for the centrally placed, kneeling figure in *The Swimming Hole*, 1884–1885 (Amon Carter Museum of American Art, Fort Worth, Texas), in which the artist and five other nude men throw off the constraints of culture to enjoy themselves freely in nature, suggests that he empathized with her reluctance to accept the yoke of civilized adult behavior.

While parents allowed their daughters unprecedented freedom in the latter part of the nineteenth century, they also worried about them. Added to earlier anxieties about girls' moral and spiritual well-being were new fears about the onset of puberty. Childhood was commonly viewed as a state of precious innocence to be savored and enjoyed as long as possible, so as it became clear that white middle-class American girls, for reasons unknown (almost certainly better nutrition and generally improved health), were crossing the threshold from childhood to adolescence earlier than had their parents, adults

Fig. 92. William Merritt Chase, *At Her Ease (The Young Orphan, Study of a Young Girl)*, c. 1884. Oil on canvas, 44 x 42 in. National Academy of Design

grew alarmed. If, as they believed, a girl's body revealed her character, the declining average age of puberty suggested that some corrupting influence was at work on girls' morals.[34] Reactionary physicians theorized that all manner of stimulants, whether fashion, coffee, spicy food, novels, hot baths, lack of fresh air, or the pace of modern life itself were to blame, and they devised cures to delay (and even reverse) the onset of adolescence, which they had come to view as an extended, physically draining crisis. At the heart of this new conception of puberty was the belief that a girl's body was a closed system with a finite amount of energy. According to Dr. Edward H. Clarke, whose influential 1873 book, *Sex in Education; or, A Fair Chance for the Girls,* went through seventeen printings in thirteen years, activities such as studying, reading, and even walking could divert needed resources away from the developing reproductive organs. Mental and physical rest was paramount for adolescent girls, Clarke argued, particularly during menstruation. Failure to observe this rule could lead to a host of ailments, including hysteria and infertility.

In his painting *At Her Ease* (originally titled *The Young Orphan*), circa 1884 (fig. 92), William Merritt Chase seems to embrace Clarke's view of adolescent girls' energy as finite. The teenager shown, who was most likely one of the fatherless children at the Half-Orphan Asylum next door to Chase's Manhattan studio, also embodies a new conception of adolescents as subject to self-absorption and melancholy.[35] Dressed in black mourning garb and holding a handkerchief, Chase's young subject slumps into a plush armchair as if her head and arms were too heavy to lift. Like the girls suffering from the nervous and hysterical disorders of puberty described by Dr. Thomas More Madden in 1889, who exhaust themselves with "morbid fancies and exaggerated sensations," her sadness seems to have depleted her limited resources and she gazes helplessly at the viewer.[36]

By the late nineteenth century, many Americans feared that adolescent girls' bodies were being assailed, not only from within but also from without. As reformers campaigned to raise the legal age of consent to eighteen, stories of young innocents lured into prostitution began appearing in the popular press. An 1885 editorial in the New York magazine *The Philanthropist* raged, "It will doubtless astonish many of our readers, who have hitherto avoided the subject as indelicate, or painful, to be told that the young girl of the Empire State is held by its criminal laws to be capable of giving 'consent' to her own corruption at the tender age of TEN YEARS!"[37] In his 1869 exposé, *The Women of New York,* George Ellington accused wealthy urban parents of putting their daughters at risk by prematurely sexualizing them and displaying them in public:

> The New York fashionable girls! If they haven't beaux, and are not well versed in the art of coquetry at ten years of age, then they are stupid; that is all. It seems as if American parents were not satisfied with the natural stimulus which life in a great city gives, but resort to artificial, hot-house processes to develop their children . . . Silks, satins, velvets, laces, jewels—things costly enough for a princess. These little wretches are then taken out on to the public parks and exhibited, or they come down the west side of Broadway in shoals. We tremble for their future health and morals.[38]

Gretchen Sinnett has insightfully explored how, by the 1880s, images of schoolgirls misbehaving in public frequently appeared in *The National Police Gazette,* reflecting the new freedom accorded adolescents while presenting them as rebellious.[39] Titillating images like *Beauty and the Beer* (fig. 93), in which a barelegged teenager with whip in hand races through the city streets in her father's beer wagon as men look on admiringly, also presented girls as potentially sexually available. Writers in the first half of the nineteenth century had stressed the importance of self-control and good judgment for young women's future happiness. In particular, the French traveler Alexis de Tocqueville lauded American girls' management of their own sexuality. Noting that the American girl was not sheltered from the "vices and dangers of society," he remarked that "she braves them without fear; for she is full of reliance on her own strength, and her reliance seems to be shared by all who are about her."[40] By the last third of the century, physicians, writers, and artists were describing girls as helpless to resist the temptations modern life offered and holding parents responsible for protecting their daughters' health and virtue.

Seymour Joseph Guy expressed this idea in his 1870 painting *A Knot in the Skein* (fig. 94), which a critic described as follows: "The scene is in a parlor, by gas-light, and a young girl and her brother are winding silk or yarn. Behind the girl her father is standing, and looking rather fiercely at a young man who is just entering the room. Evidently, the relations between the girl, the father, and the youth form the real knot—harder to untie than the one the girl has in her fingers."[41] The adolescent female, wearing a startlingly bright red evening dress, sits between her father and younger brother, a position that symbolizes her liminal place between the worlds of children and adults. Although she appears at first

Fig. 93. (left) *Beauty and the Beer.* Wood engraving. From Edward Van Emery, *The Sins of New York, as "Exposed" by the Police Gazette* (New York: Frederick A. Stokes Company, 1930; illustration originally published in *The National Police Gazette,* July 9, 1881)
Fig. 94. (right) Seymour Joseph Guy, *A Knot in the Skein,* 1870. Oil on wood, 30 x 24½ in. Wadsworth Atheneum Museum of Art; Mary Catlin Summer fund, 1986.27. Photograph courtesy of Art Resource, NY

glance to be looking down modestly at the yarn she is untangling, her eyes beneath their heavy lids have actually slipped to the side in an attempt to observe the scene taking place behind her.

A similar confrontation takes place in Louisa May Alcott's 1870 novel, *An Old-Fashioned Girl,* when fourteen-year-old Fanny Shaw's father discovers that she has been surreptitiously keeping company with a young man. "Mr. Shaw stood on the rug, looking rather grim; the bouquet lay on the table, and beside it a note, directed to 'Frank Moore, Esq.' . . . Pointing to this impressive epistle, Mr. Shaw said, knitting his black eyebrows as he looked at Fanny, 'I'm going to put a stop to this nonsense at once; and if I see any more of it, I'll send you to school in a Canadian convent.'"[42] Like many of her contemporaries, Alcott attributed modern girls' precocious interest in romance to the pace of urban life—a stimulus that she believed also caused early puberty—and she idealized the countryside as a place where girls could mature naturally. Her views are perfectly in line with those of Dr. John D. West, who advised the following in an 1887 childrearing manual: "A regular life, with hygienic habits of eating and drinking, healthful exercise and labor, with no social dissipation, will allow the girl to pass to the full natural time of puberty. On the other hand, idleness, dissipation in diet, especially in richness of quality, drink, stimulants and social dissipation tend to prematurity in this epoch."[43]

Fourteen-year-old Rose Campbell, the heroine of Alcott's 1875 novel, *Eight Cousins,* is moody, sickly, and precocious as the story begins.[44] By transplanting her to the country and taking away her fashionable clothes, coffee, hot food, and novels, the girl's reform-minded Uncle Alec halts the process of puberty. Rose does not mature until she is considerably older—the title of the sequel (set six years after *Eight Cousins*) is *Rose in Bloom.*[45] As Holly Pyne Connor notes in her essay in this volume, Alcott was not alone in using floral metaphors to describe adolescent girls. Physicians writing about female puberty in the second half of the nineteenth century used the term "budding girls" to express their view of human development as an organic process governed by natural laws. In order to ensure that girls bloomed properly, doctors and advice writers urged adults to act as careful gardeners, providing appropriate nourishment and support while removing harmful environmental influences.[46]

Winslow Homer, too, used horticultural symbolism in a number of genre scenes featuring adolescent girls that he painted during the 1870s. In two paintings titled *Peach Blossoms,* he positioned a girl on or near a fence beside the blossoming branches of a young fruit tree. Describing the 1878 version on view at the Mathews Gallery in New York in 1880 (fig. 95), a critic for the *New York Tribune* wrote: "A gray stone fence runs across the front of the canvas, upon which is sitting a maiden of sixteen or so draped in white, and herself in the bloom of the springtime of womanhood." A reviewer for *The Evening Post* called the girl "a peach blossom

Fig. 95. Winslow Homer, *Peach Blossoms,* 1878. Oil on canvas, 13¼ x 19⅝ in. The Art Institute of Chicago; Gift of George B. Harrington 1946.338

Fig. 96. Winslow Homer, *Girl and Laurel,* 1879. Oil on canvas, 22⅝ x 15¾ in. Detroit Institute of Arts. Image courtesy of The Bridgeman Art Library

herself."[47] *Girl and Laurel,* 1879, similarly depicts a young girl standing in front of a fence and near blossoming plants (fig. 96). Here, a pink tinge in the sky echoes the delicate hue of the flowers, conveying that it is early morning. The rude fence suggests a walled garden—a longstanding symbol of virginity in Western art. Unlike her more fashionable and exuberant urban counterparts in *"Winter"—A Skating Scene,* the rustic subject of *Girl and Laurel* is modest and restrained.

Homer's paintings of country girls were generally well received; however, Henry James sounded a dissenting note in 1875. Declaring that he detested Homer's rustic subject matter, James criticized the artist's "flat-breasted maidens, suggestive of a dish of rural doughnuts and pie."[48] Homer's rural maidens are indeed often flat-breasted. As the art historian Henry Adams has noted, the artist used two adolescent boys from Belmont, Massachusetts, as the models for some of these girls.[49] A letter in the curatorial files of the Detroit Institute of Arts suggests that a third boy may have posed for *Girl and Laurel.*[50] Although scholars have attributed Homer's odd choice of models to his shyness, his reasons may well have been more practical. Dressing boys as teenaged girls allowed the artist to fabricate the tall, healthy, but sexless ideal that many Americans associated with natural girlhood in the late nineteenth century.

During the last two decades of the nineteenth century, erudite Americans favored depictions of young women as otherworldly beings. This predilection had its roots in the popularity of Aestheticism and French Symbolist art, and also in widespread anxiety about girls' bodies, which were perceived to be not only fragile and besieged by the forces of modernity, but also dangerously unconstrained and alluring.[51] As Sinnett has shown, Abbott Handerson Thayer's exaltation of virginal innocence in paintings like *Angel,* 1887 (fig. 52, page 74) was directly related to pervasive fears about adolescent sexuality and the artist's perception of modern girls as easily corruptible.[52] "Never was there such a premium on chastity as now," Thayer wrote.[53] Arguing that artists should paint girls as "dewy fragrant beings" endowed with "ultra-virgin purities," Thayer transported them to a heavenly realm beyond worldly action or contamination.[54] He repeatedly painted his daughters Mary and Gladys and their friend Elise Pumpelly as angels and holy virgins. *Angel,* which is the earliest of these paintings, depicts eleven-year-old Mary from the hips up, clothed in a spotless white tunic with blue sky behind her. Enormous snowy wings spread upward from her back, framing her slim body and delicate head. Thayer's angel is depicted at the far edge of childhood but, unlike a mortal girl, she will remain forever innocent. *Angel*'s elaborate Renaissance Revival frame, which resembles an altarpiece, marks its subject as an object of veneration. "They do not make Welsh rabbits or go skating, those virgins of Thayer," wrote Samuel Isham, "They are set up frankly for our adoration, and it goes to them at once without reserve, they are so strong and beautiful and pure."[55] The art critic Leila Mechlin described Thayer's ideal maidens as images of "the American girl at her best."[56]

In a series of genre paintings of the 1870s and 1880s, George Fuller painted adolescent girls enveloped in dreamlike haze, wearing old-fashioned clothes, and bearing old-fashioned names. These paintings appealed directly to the antimodernist nostalgia of American elites, who longed for a supposedly simpler agrarian past. Elisabeth Luther Cary wrote of Fuller's 1879 painting *Hannah* (fig. 97): "The face is of the demure New England type with the intimate mystic beauty belonging to a reticent and vision-seeing race."[57] *Hannah* is a girl in the early stages of puberty, wearing a dress and apron of homespun cloth. Placed close to the picture plane with her arms demurely at her sides, she confronts the viewer with a grave, steady gaze. Like the French painters Jean-François Millet and Jules Breton, who clearly influenced him, Fuller romanticized preindustrial rural labor. In *Hannah,* the central figure's homemade clothing and the antiquated scythe used by the reaper in the field behind her dislodge viewers from the present and transport them to the "Old New England" studied by Roger Stein–a symbolic landscape representing a lost way of life.[58] Fuller's pairing of a reaper and an adolescent girl also recalls the time-honored allegory of Death and the Maiden, reminding viewers that even the young and fair must one day fall beneath the inexorable scythe of death. By scraping through dense layers of oil paint with the handle of his brush, Fuller imposed a screen of atmosphere between the viewer and the figure, rendering Hannah's body nearly as insubstantial as the spirits he said he encountered during séances the previous year.[59]

After Fuller's death in 1884, John Greenleaf Whittier compared the artist to a magician, "haunted of beauty . . . who from commonest elements / Called up divine ideals, clothed upon / By mystic lights soft blending into one / Womanly grace and child-like innocence."[60] Though one critic wrote that Fuller, in his paintings, "has given us a refined and sweet country maiden, full of health and youthful vigor, and rich in the promise of perfect womanhood," Hannah's melancholy mood of foreboding reflects pervasive fears about the well-being of adolescent girls and the future of the New England "race."[61]

During this same period, declining birthrates among middle- and upper-class Americans and an influx of Catholic and Jewish immigrants spawned new anxieties about the moral and physical health of white Protestant American girls.[62] In an 1869 cartoon for *Harper's Bazaar* (fig. 98), Thomas Nast articulated fears that the liberated, materialistic "girl of the period" might grow into the "Wife of the Period"—a woman more concerned with flirtation and entertainment than children. While his self-indulgent spouse declares, "Suffer no little children to come unto me," a horrified man is transfixed by a vision of his never-to-be-born progeny. A stern angel points to an inscription that ominously declares, "The American race is dying out!" Equally dangerous to the future of the "American race" were girls who—through careless, unregulated behavior during adolescence—rendered themselves nervous invalids, incapable of bearing healthy children. In an

Fig. 97. George Fuller, *Hannah,* 1879. Oil on canvas, 50⅛ x 40⅜ in. The Nelson-Atkins Museum of Art, Kansas City, MO; Purchase, William Rockhill Nelson Trust 33-15/1. Photograph by Jamison Miller

1897 address to the Mothers' Congress of the City of New York titled "The Care of the Adolescent Girl," the feminist physician Mary Putnam Jacobi advocated proper diet, long walks, fresh air, and sunshine to ensure girls' health, and advised her audience of elite mothers that their daughters' "individual lives are attached to the main life of the race as branches are attached to a tree."[63]

The same year that Jacobi addressed the Mothers' Congress, Cecilia Beaux painted the fifteen-year-old daughter of her close friends Richard Watson Gilder and Helena de Kay Gilder in the woods near the Gilders' Berkshire Mountains summer retreat (fig. 99). Like Jacobi (another friend of the Gilders'), Beaux was a successful, professional New Woman who frequently extolled her elite ancestry and celebrated good breeding in her portraits of upper-class American girls.[64] When she exhibited *Dorothea in the Woods* at the American Art Galleries in New York, a critic acidly described its subject as "a young girl . . . whose love for trees and grass is evidently an important element in her character."[65] Indeed, Dorothea sits directly on the ground. Her interlaced fingers, the stripes of her blouse, and her long, wavy hair echo the shapes of the tree against which she leans so that she appears almost to be an extension of its trunk and curving roots. As both Gretchen Sinnett and Barbara Dayer Gallati

Fig. 98. Thomas Nast, *The Wife of the Period*. From *Harper's Bazaar,* April 17, 1871. New-York Historical Society, TT500.H3 Oversize; Negative no. 85442d

Fig. 99. Cecilia Beaux, *Dorothea in the Woods,* 1897. Oil on canvas, 53¼ x 40 in. Whitney Museum of American Art; Gift of Mr. and Mrs. Raymond J. Horowitz 70.1587

have noted, Dorothea's proximity to nature and withdrawn, thoughtful persona reflect the late nineteenth-century conception of adolescent girls as timid and prone to reverie.[66] These qualities also reflect contemporary beliefs about race. Describing critical reactions to Beaux's work the same year that she painted *Dorothea in the Woods,* William Walton noted that the traits of "self-concentration, introspection, and silence" expressed in so many of her portraits had been recognized by French critics as qualities that rendered "the English-speaking race the 'élite' of contemporary humanity." He went on to quote a French writer on Beaux's portraits of girls:

> This is, then, what [Beaux] has to tell us—that all the American girls have not the assurance—I would not venture to say the impudence—to thrust themselves before the world that they might laugh in its face . . . No, they do not all chatter like a flock of parrakeets; the bicycle and the tandem . . . are not their sole delights. Madame Cecilia Beaux demonstrates to us that they have, among themselves, thoughtful moments—the most natural and the most graceful, something almost like timidity, even when they are not before the world . . . Pretty as plums on the tree, Madame Cecilia Beaux presents them to us as "fruits of the garden."[67]

Dorothea appears in Beaux's portrait as a naturally refined and vital offshoot of a tree firmly rooted in New England soil.

In the decades surrounding the turn of the century, popular writers and illustrators, journalists, and realist artists challenged the idealized, elite vision of the American girl as passive, innocent, and ethereal. They were aided by girls themselves, who rebelled against the constraints of decorum that governed previous generation, and who—with the aid of Kodak cameras—began fashioning images of (and for) themselves. Following the trend that began after the Civil War, the adolescent girls that pervaded American popular culture around the turn-of-the-century were plucky, flirtatious, athletic.

1. Ward to Longfellow, December 17, 1841, in *The Letters of Henry Wadsworth Longfellow,* ed. Andrew Hilden (Cambridge, MA: Harvard University Press, 1972), 2:364n2.

2. Henry Wadsworth Longfellow, "Maidenhood," in Longfellow, *Ballads and Other Poems* (Cambridge, MA: John Owen, 1842), 125–128.

3. After purchasing the entire series from the Ward family, the Art-Union selected *Youth* as the subject of an engraving to be distributed to its members in 1849. See Mary Bartlett Cowdrey, ed., *American Academy of Fine Arts and American Art-Union,* vol. 1, *Introduction, 1816–1852* (New York: New-York Historical Society, 1953), 289.

4. "Longfellow," *The National Magazine,* July 1853: 6. Huntington's illustration, engraved by John Cheney, appeared in Henry Wadsworth Longfellow, *Poems* (Philadelphia: Carey and Hart, 1845), facing 73. When Longfellow saw the engraving, he pronounced it "lovely." See Longfellow to Abraham Hart, November 24, 1845, in Hilden, *Letters of Henry Wadsworth Longfellow,* 3:91.

5. David Lloyd, "The Exhibition of the Ten American Painters," *The International Studio,* May 1907, xciv.

6. Philip L. Hale, "The Best Pictures of the Year," *Boston Sunday Herald,* February 23, 1908, 5. See also W[illiam] H[owe] Downes, "Mr. DeCamp's Portraits," *Boston Evening Transcript,* December 29, 1915, 25; William R. Lester, "Figure Paintings and Portraits at Art Academy Exhibition Overshadow Landscape Pictures in Public Interest," *North American* (Philadelphia), January 26, 1908, sect. 3, 9; Laurene Buckley, *Joseph DeCamp: Master Painter of the Boston School* (Munich: Prestel, 1995), 81.

7. William C. Reavis, ed., *Significant Aspects of American Life and Postwar Education* (Chicago: University of Chicago Press, 1944), 145; Michael R. Haines and Richard H. Steckel, ed., *A Population History of North America* (Cambridge, UK: Cambridge University Press, 2000), 306.

8. Nancy F. Cott, "Young Women in the Second Great Awakening in New England," *Feminist Studies* 3, no. 1/2 (Fall 1975): 15–29.

9. [Frederick A. Packard], *The Teacher Taught: An Humble Attempt to Make the Path of the Sunday-School Teacher Straight and Plain* (Philadelphia: American Sunday-School Union, 1839), 87.

10. *Raleigh Register,* May 4, 1821, quoted in Charles L. Coon, *North Carolina Schools and Academies, 1790–1840: A Documentary History* (Raleigh, NC: Edwards and Broughton, 1915), 458–459.

11. Charles Dickens, *American Notes for General Circulation* (London: Chapman and Hall, 1842), 159–160.

12. As Claire Perry has noted, this "Arcadian idyll" served as effective propaganda, reassuring readers of "the erudition and cultivated sensibilities of the mill maidens," while also idealizing factory labor. See Perry, *Young America: Childhood in Nineteenth-Century Art and Culture,* exhibition catalogue (New Haven, CT: Yale University Press, 2006), 55.

13. Judith A. Ranta, "Blighted and Deceived: Dangerous Desires and Women's Wrongs," *Women and Children of the Mills: An Annotated Guide to Nineteenth-Century American Textile Factory Literature* (Westport, CT: Greenwood, 1999), 106–132.

14. Palmer to Durand, January 11, 1858, in J. Carson Webster, *Erastus D. Palmer* (Newark: University of Delaware Press, 1983), 183.

15. "Naked Art," *The Crayon* 6, December 1859, 877.

16. James Jackson Jarves, *Art Thoughts: The Experiences and Observations of an American Amateur in Europe* (New York: Garland, 1976), 309.

17. Joy S. Kasson, *Marble Queens and Captives: Women in Nineteenth-Century American Sculpture* (New Haven, CT: Yale University Press, 1990), 73–100.

18. J. A. F., "Recovery of Miss Olive Oatman from the Mohave Indians," *Saturday Evening Post,* April 26, 1856, 7. Oatman was actually nineteen when she was ransomed.

19. "Palmer's White Captive," *New York Times,* December 30, 1859, 2. This letter prompted an outraged response from gallery owner William Schaus, who called the writer "the hero of a blunder as indelicate as it is stupid." See "Palmer's White Captive," *New York Times,* January 2, 1860, 4.

20. For instance, writing of the "much needed" school for Oneida Indian girls that the federal government opened in 1838, the superintendent of schools for the Oneidas and Menomonies noted: "The education of females is certainly all-important to the progress of civilization among the tribe." See *Annual Report of the Commissioner of Indian Affairs, Transmitted with the Message of the President at the Opening of the Second Session of the Twenty-Sixth Congress, 1840–1841* (Washington, D.C.: J. Gideon Jr., 1840), 158.

21. John Mix Stanley, *Portraits of North American Indians, with Sketches of Scenery* (Washington, D.C.: Smithsonian Institution, 1852), 14. Julie Schimmel has argued that Stanley intended this painting "to convince whites of [Eleanora's] capacity to absorb the gentle arts of reading, writing, and drawing." See Schimmel, "Inventing 'the Indian,'" in *The West as America: Reinterpreting Images of the Frontier, 1820–1920,* ed. William H. Truettner, exhibition catalogue (Washington, D.C.: Smithsonian Institution Press, 1991), 181–182.

22. Freeman Henry Morris Murray, *Emancipation and the Freed in American Sculpture: A Study in Interpretation* (Washington, D.C.: privately published, 1916), 158–160.

23. "Pictures for the Paris Exhibition," *New York Evening Post,* January 26, 1878, 2.

24. For an interpretation of this painting as a depiction of a nascent New Woman, see Holly Pyne Connor, "Not at Home: The Nineteenth-Century New Woman," in *Off the Pedestal: New Women in the Art of Homer, Chase, and Sargent,* ed. Holly Pyne Connor (Newark, NJ: Newark Museum, 2006), 20. Barbara Welter has described the mid-nineteenth-century ideal of "true womanhood" as pious, pure, and domestic. See Welter, "The Cult of True Womanhood: 1820–1860," *American Quarterly* 18, no. 1 (1966): 151–174.

Over the last thirty years, a number of scholars have questioned the degree to which women actually conformed to the ideal Welter described; however, it is precisely because there was no consensus about women's nature and proper role that the ideal of "true womanhood" was a powerful cultural tool—it presented the viewpoint of the white bourgeois elite as natural and universal.

25. Sarah Burns, "Winslow Homer and the Natural Woman," in *Victorian Americans and Virgin Nature,* ed. T. J. Jackson Lears (Boston: Isabella Stewart Gardner Museum, 2002), 18.

26. Jane H. Hunter, *How Young Ladies Became Girls: The Victorian Origins of American Girlhood* (New Haven, CT: Yale University Press, 2002). See also Sarah Burns, "Winslow Homer's Ambiguously New Women," in *Off the Pedestal: New Women in the Art of Homer, Chase, and Sargent,* ed. Holly Pyne Connor (Newark, NJ: Newark Museum, 2006), 53–90.

27. Elizabeth Johns, *American Genre Painting: The Politics of Everyday Life* (New Haven, CT: Yale University Press, 1991), 202.

28. As the symbolic anthropologist Mary Douglas has observed, cultures tend to associate social ills with bodily ailments. See Douglas, *Purity and Danger: An Analysis of Concepts of Pollution and Taboo* (New York: Praeger, 1966).

29. David M. Lubin, *Picturing a Nation: Art and Social Change in Nineteenth-Century America* (New Haven, CT: Yale University Press, 1994), 205–243; Lauren Lessing, "New Perspective: Rereading Seymour Joseph Guy's 'Making a Train,'" *American Art* 25, no. 1 (Spring 2011): 96–111.

30. Lucy Larcom, *A New England Girlhood* (Boston: Houghton, Mifflin, 1889), 166.

31. See Amy Ellis's catalogue entry on this painting in Elizabeth Mankin Kornhauser, *American Paintings Before 1945 in the Wadsworth Atheneum* (New Haven, CT.: Yale University Press, 1996), 2:515–516.

32. Richard Grant White, "The Unsociables of Society," *The Galaxy,* September 1869, 414.

33. Florence Hartley, *The Ladies' Book of Etiquette, and Manual of Politeness: A Complete Hand Book for the Use of the Lady in Polite Society* (Boston: Lee and Shepard, 1872), 151.

34. Joan Jacobs Brumberg, *The Body Project: An Intimate History of American Girls* (New York: Random House, 1997), 10, 23–24.

35. For the representation of melancholy in late nineteenth-century images of adolescents, see Gretchen R. Sinnett, "Envisioning Female Adolescence: Rites of Passage in Late Nineteenth- and Early Twentieth-Century American Painting" (Ph.D. dissertation, University of Pennsylvania, 2006), 60–67.

36. Thomas More Madden, "Puberty: Its Pathology and Hygiene," in John M. Keating, ed. *Cyclopaedia of the Diseases of Children, Medical and Surgical* (Philadelphia: Lippincott, 1889), 1:416.

37. "Legal Protection for Young Girls," *Philanthropist,* January 1886, 4. For a broader discussion of purity crusades and age of consent legislation in the United States, see Timothy J. Gilfoyle, *City of Eros: New York City, Prostitution, and the Commercialization of Sex, 1790–1920* (New York: Norton, 1992), 283–288; Mary E. Odem, *Delinquent Daughters: Protecting and Policing Adolescent Female Sexuality in the United States, 1885–1920* (Chapel Hill: University of North Carolina Press, 1995).

38. George Ellington, *The Women of New York; or, The Under-World of the Great City* (New York: New York Book Company, 1869), 109.

39. Sinnett, "Envisioning Female Adolescence," 41–51.

40. Alexis de Tocqueville, *Democracy in America,* trans. Henry Reeve (New York: Pratt, Woodford, 1848), 209. Both the original French edition and the English translation of *Democracy in America* were first published in two parts, the first in 1835 and the second in 1840. Tocqueville's observations about American girls appear in the second volume.

41. "The Spring Exhibition of the National Academy," *Appleton's Journal,* May 25, 1872: 579. See also Amy Ellis's catalogue entry on this painting in Kornhauser, *American Paintings Before 1945,* 2:427–428.

42. Louisa M. Alcott, *An Old-Fashioned Girl* (Boston: Roberts Brothers, 1870), 74–75.

43. John D. West, *Maidenhood and Motherhood; or, Ten Phases of Woman's Life* (Chicago: Law, King, and Law, 1887), 181.

44. Louisa M. Alcott, *Eight Cousins; or, The Aunt-Hill* (Boston: Sampson Low, Marston, Low, and Searle, 1875).

45. Idem, *Rose in Bloom: A Sequel to "Eight Cousins"* (Boston: Roberts Brothers, 1876).

46. Crista DeLuzio, *Female Adolescence in American Scientific Thought, 1830–1930* (Baltimore, MD: Johns Hopkins University Press, 2007), 71–72.

47. "Brush and Pencil," *New York Herald-Tribune,* January 26, 1880, 5; "Fine Arts," *New York Evening Post,* January 26, 1880, 2. Although Nicolai Cikovsky Jr., and Franklin Kelly have associated these reviews with the other version of *Peach Blossoms* formerly in the collection of Mr. R. Philip Hanes Jr., the girl in that painting wears a yellow dress and leans (rather than sits) on the wall. See Cikovsky and Kelly, *Winslow Homer,* exhibition catalogue (Washington, D.C.: National Gallery of Art, 1995), 168. See also Margaret C. Conrads, *Winslow Homer and the Critics: Forging a National Art in the 1870s,* exhibition catalogue (Princeton, NJ: Princeton University Press, 2001), 169–170.

48. Henry James, "On Some Pictures Lately Exhibited," *The Galaxy,* July 1875, 93.

49. Henry Adams, "The Identity of Winslow Homer's 'Mystery Woman,'" *Burlington Magazine* 132 (April 1990): 244–252.

50. See the letter from Hazel Lewis, William Macbeth Gallery, New York, to Clyde H. Burroughs, Detroit Institute of Arts, 2 August 1940, in which Lewis describes the sitter as a "local boy named Sanders." Lewis apparently gleaned

her information about the model for *Girl and Laurel* from Homer's family. See Patricia Hills's entry on the painting in *American Paintings in the Detroit Institute of Arts* (New York: Hudson Hills Press, 1997), 2:123–124.

51. Bailey Van Hook, *Angels of Art: Women and Art in American Society, 1876–1914* (University Park: Pennsylvania State University, 1996), 191–193; Constance A. Nathanson, *Dangerous Passage: The Social Control of Sexuality in Women's Adolescence* (Philadelphia: Temple University Press, 1991), 75.

52. Sinnett, "Envisioning Female Adolescence," 81–138. Elizabeth Lee has shown that Thayer's obsession with female purity also stemmed from widespread anxieties about immigration, urbanization, and disease. See Lee, "Therapeutic Beauty: Abbott Thayer, Antimodernism, and Fear of Disease," *American Art* 18 (Fall 2004): 32–51.

53. Thayer to Royal Cortissoz, undated, Thayer Papers, Archives of American Art, reel D200, cited in Ross Anderson, *Abbott Handerson Thayer,* exhibition catalogue (Syracuse, NY: Everson Museum, 1982), 64.

54. Thayer to Mrs. Henry Holt, April 13, 1919, Thayer Papers, Archives of American Art, reel D201, cited in Anderson, *Thayer,* 64.

55. Samuel Isham, *The History of American Painting* (New York: Macmillan, 1905), 472.

56. L. Mechlin, "American Figure Painters," *The International Studio,* January 1910, 187.

57. Elisabeth Luther Carey, "Four American Painters Represented in the Metropolitan Museum," *The International Studio* 35 September 1908: supp. xcii.

58. Roger Stein, "After the War: Constructing a Rural Past," in *Picturing Old New England: Image and Memory,* exhibition catalogue (Washington, D.C.: National Museum of American Art, Smithsonian Institution, 1999), 15–41.

59. George Fuller to Agnes Fuller, April 18 and 29, 1878, George Fuller Papers, Archives of American Art, reel 606.

60. John Greenleaf Whittier, "George Fuller," in *George Fuller: His Life and Works,* ed. Josiah B. Millet (Boston: Houghton, Mifflin, 1886), 71.

61. F. D. Millet, "George Fuller," *Harper's New Monthly Magazine,* September 1884, 520.

62. Martha Banta, *Imaging American Women: Idea and Ideals in Cultural History* (New York: Columbia University Press: 1987), 104–130; Van Hook, *Angels of Art,* 204–208; Sinnett, "Envisioning Female Adolescence," 31–34.

63. "The Education of Girls: Dr. Mary Putnam Jacobi Discusses Phases of It Before the Mothers' Congress," *New York Times,* November 21, 1897, 18.

64. Sylvia Yount, "Family Pictures," in *Cecilia Beaux: American Figure Painter,* exhibition catalogue (Atlanta, GA: High Museum of Art, 2007), 20, 26, 35.

65. "Paintings by Miss Cecilia Beaux," *The Critic,* December 25, 1897, 406.

66. Sinnett, "Envisioning Female Adolescence," 66; Barbara Dayer Gallati, *Children of the Gilded Age: Portraits by Sargent, Renoir, Cassatt and Their Contemporaries* (London: Merrell, 2004), 58.

67. William Walton, "Cecilia Beaux," *Scribner's,* October 1897, 481–482. The French writer who praised Beaux's portraits of American girls was the sculptor and art critic Paul Bion. See Bion to Augustus St. Gaudens, undated, in Cecilia Beaux, *Background with Figures* (New York: Houghton Mifflin, 1930), 347–349.

PLATES

Plate 1. Attributed to Ammi Phillips, *Mother and Child in Grey Dresses,* c. 1825. Oil on canvas, 33⅞ x 27⅞ in. Fenimore Art Museum, Cooperstown, NY N0267.1961. Photograph by Richard Walker

Plate 2. Ammi Phillips, *Portrait of Harriet Campbell,* c. 1815. Oil on canvas, 48½ x 25 in. Sterling and Francine Clark Art Institute, Williamstown, MA; Gift of Oliver Eldridge in memory of Sarah Fairchild Anderson, teacher of art, North Adams Public Schools, daughter of Harriet Campbell 1991.8. Image © Sterling and Francine Clark Art Institute, Williamstown, MA. Photograph by Michael Agee

Plate 3. Erastus Salisbury Field, *Mrs. Paul Smith Palmer and Her Twins,* 1835/1838. Oil on canvas, 38½ x 34 in. National Gallery of Art; Gift of Edgar William Garbisch and Bernice Chrysler Garbisch 1971.83.5

Plate 4. John Lewis Krimmel, *Quilting Frolic,* 1813. Oil on canvas, 16⅞ x 22⅜ in. Winterthur Museum; Museum purchase 1953.0178.002

Plate 5. Elizabeth Stone, *Sampler,* 1836. Wool, 17¼ x 17¼ in. Newark Museum; Gift of Mrs. Fred E. Sutton, 1922 22.219

Plate 6. Julia Ann Morris, *Sampler,* 1844. Wool, 18 x 17½ in. Newark Museum; Gift of Mrs. B. Altemus, 1956 56.9

Plate 7. Samuel S. Carr, *Every Little Bit Helps,* 1872. Oil on canvas, 14 x 11¹³⁄₁₆ in. Newark Museum; Purchase 1985, The Members' Fund 85.235

Plate 8. John George Brown, *Swinging on the Gate,* c. 1878–1879. Oil on canvas, 22½ x 14⅜ in. Taubman Museum of Art; Acquired with funds provided by the Horace G. Fralin Charitable Trust 2003.003

Plate 9. John George Brown, *Little Servant*, c. 1880. Oil on canvas, 30¼ x 25⅜ in. Private collection

Plate 10. Junius R. Sloan, *The Knitting Lesson,* 1866. Oil on canvas, 18⅝ x 15⅝ in. Brauer Museum of Art, Valparaiso University; Gift of Percy H. Sloan 53.01.126

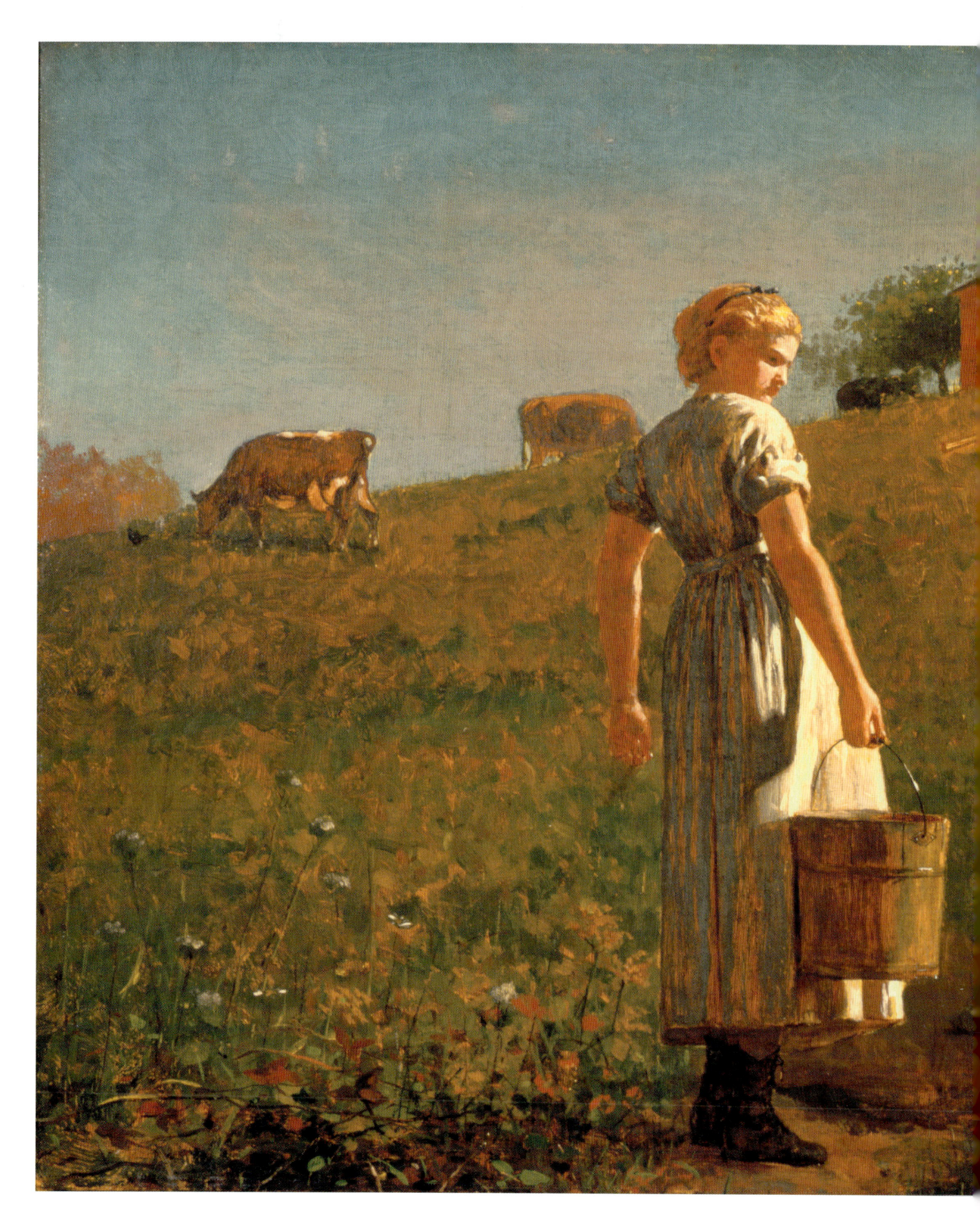

Plate 11. Winslow Homer, *A Temperance Meeting (Noon Time)*, 1874. Oil on canvas, 20⅜ x 30⅛ in. Philadelphia Museum of Art; Purchased with the John Howard McFadden Jr. Fund, 1956 1956.118.1

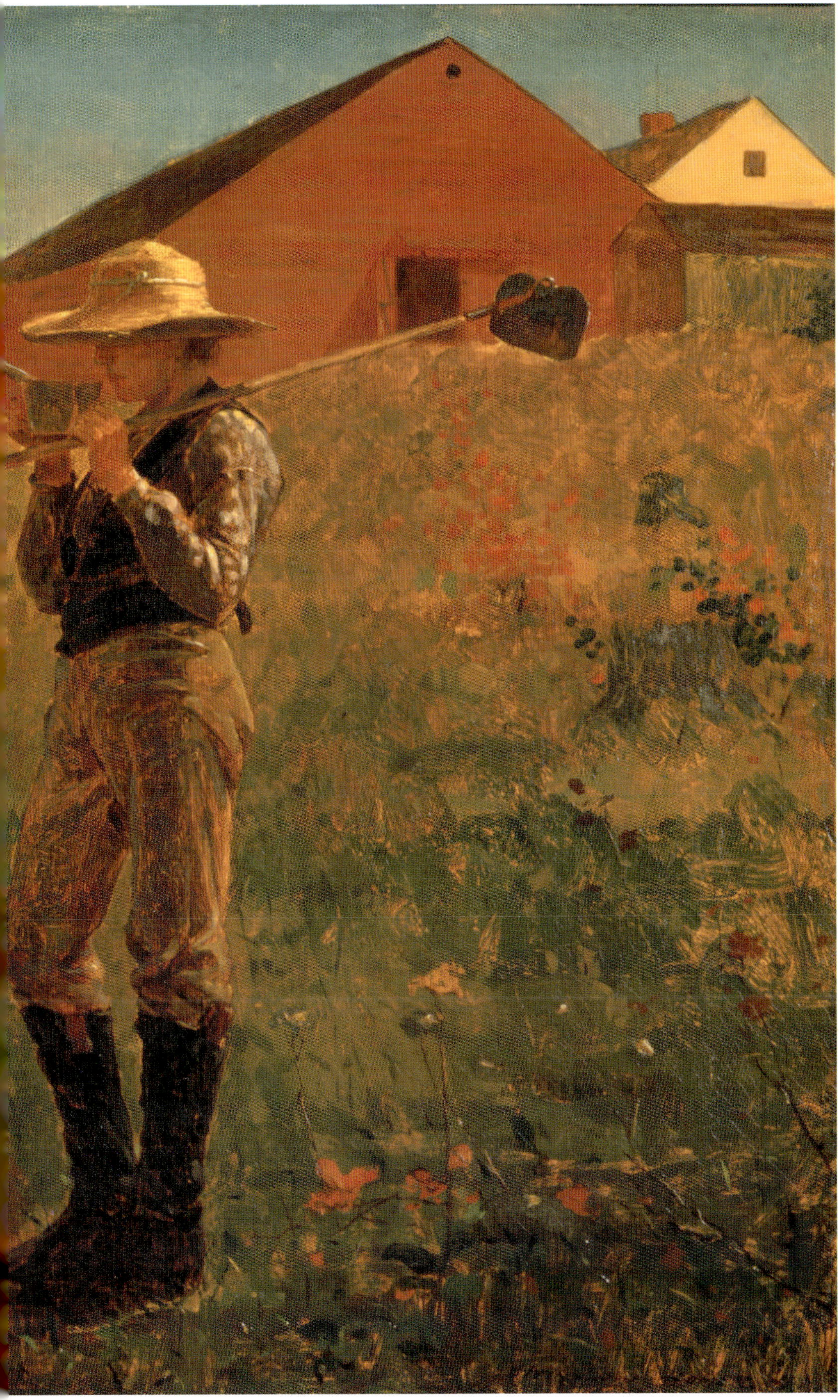

Plate 12. Winslow Homer, *Gathering Berries,* 1874, published in *Harper's Weekly,* July 11, 1874. Wood engraving, 9⅛ x 13½ in. The Old Print Shop

Plate 13. Eastman Johnson, *Kite Flying,* 1865. Oil on board, 21⅜ x 26 in. Colby College Museum of Art; The Lunder Collection

Plate 14. John Rogers, *The School Examination,* 1867. Plaster and paint, 20 x 13 x 8½ in. The Hyde Collection, Glens Falls, NY; Gift of Charles R. Wood 1992.4.61. Photograph by Jim McLaughlin

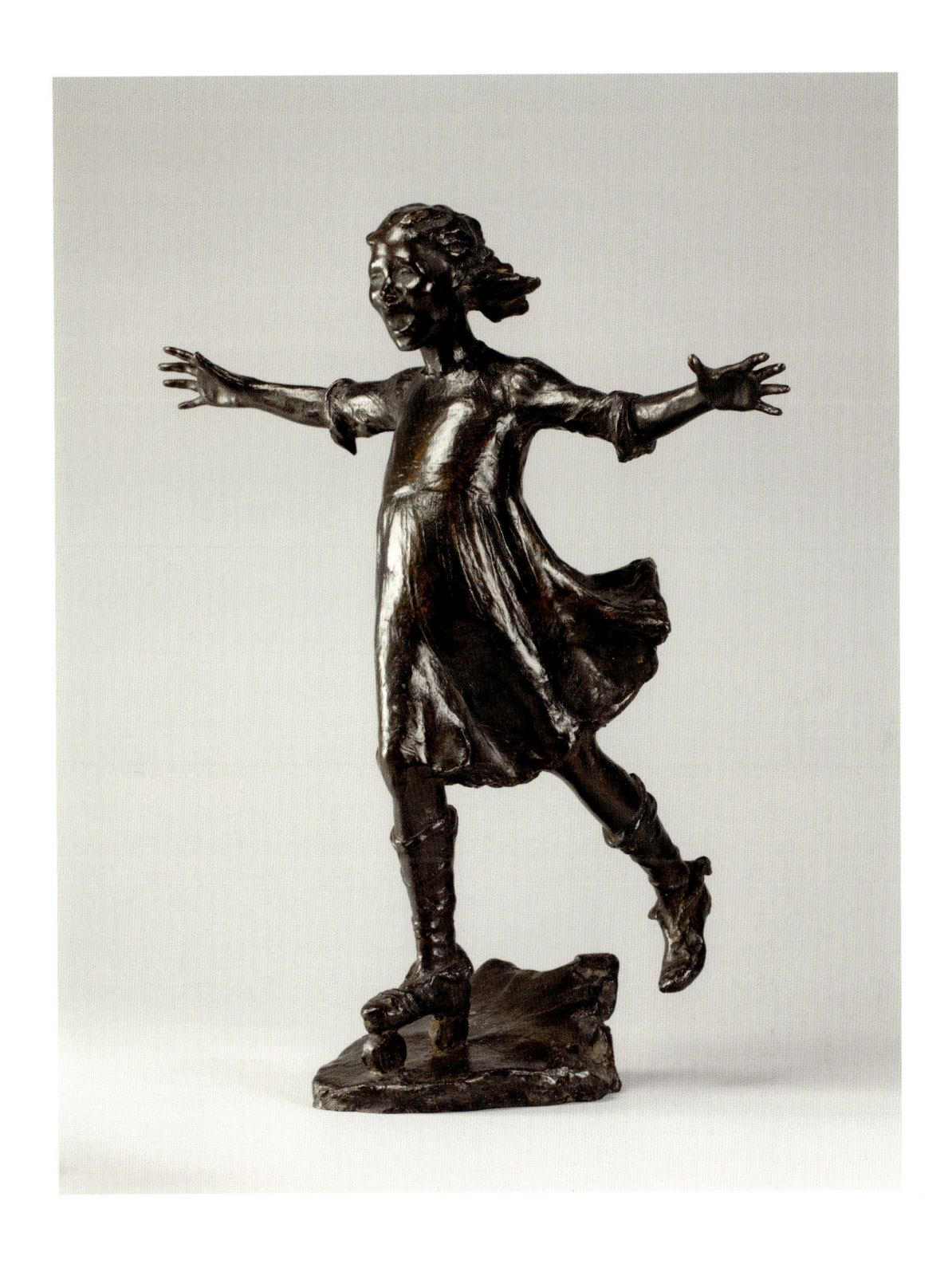

Plate 15. Mary Abastenia St. Leger Eberle, *Roller Skating*, 1906. Bronze, 13 x 11¾ x 6½ in. Whitney Museum of American Art

Plate 16. Edward Lamson Henry, *Kept In,* 1889. Oil on canvas, 13½ x 18 in. Fenimore Art Museum, Cooperstown, NY N0309.1961. Photograph by Richard Walker

Plate 17. Winslow Homer, *Reading by the Brook,* 1879. Oil on canvas, 15⅞ x 22¾ in. Memphis Brooks Museum of Art, Memphis, TN; Memphis Park Commission Purchase 43.22

Plate 18. William Hahn, *Learning the Lesson (Children Playing School)*, c. 1880. Oil on canvas, 34 x 27 in. The Oakland Museum of California; Kahn Collection

Plate 19. Ellen Kendall Baker, *The Young Artist,* 1885. Oil on canvas, 28 x 23 in. Detroit Institute of Arts; Gift of the Friends of the Museum. Image courtesy of The Bridgeman Art Library

Plate 20. Mary Cassatt, *The Reader*, 1877. Oil on canvas, 32 x 25½ in. Courtesy of Crystal Bridges Museum of American Art. Photograph by Robert LaPrelle

Plate 21. Edmund Charles Tarbell, *Josephine and Mercie,* 1908. Oil on canvas, 28⅛ x 32 1/16 in. Corcoran Gallery of Art, Washington, D.C.; Museum purchase, Gallery fund 09.2

Plate 22. Charles Courtney Curran, *Lotus Lilies,* 1888. Oil on canvas, 18 x 32 in. Terra Museum for American Art, Chicago; Daniel J. Terra Collection 1999.35. Photograph courtesy of Art Resource, NY

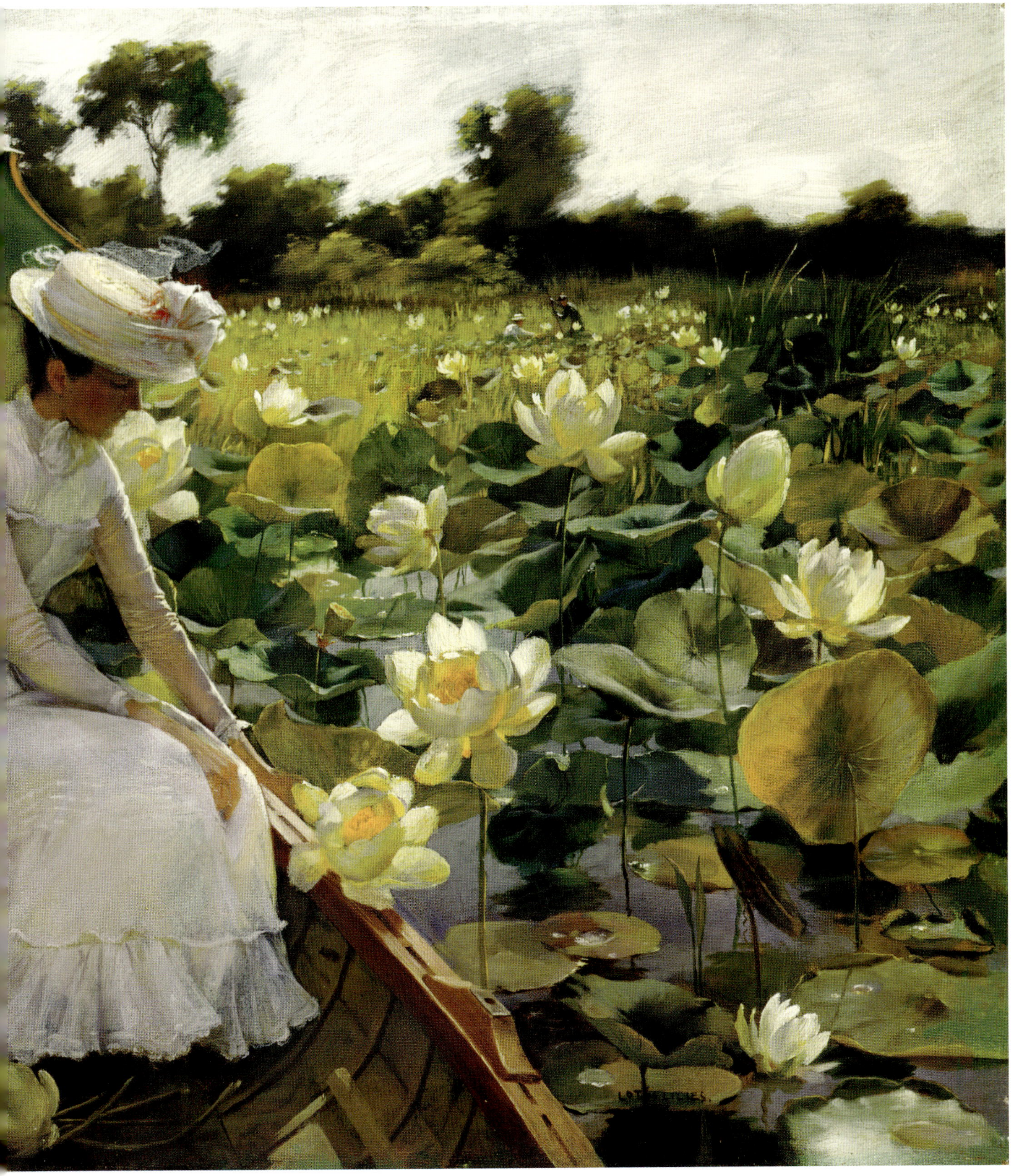

Plate 23. Ann Hall, *Louisa and Eliza Macardy,* c. 1845. Watercolor on ivory, 5½ x 4½ in. New-York Historical Society; Museum purchase, Louis Durr Fund 1946.297

Plate 24. Frank Weston Benson, *Gertrude,* 1899. Oil on canvas, 50⅛ x 40⅛ in. Museum of Fine Arts, Boston; Gift of Mrs. William Rodman Fay 54.596

Plate 25. Randolph Rogers, *Daughter Nora as the Infant Psyche,* c. 1871. Marble, 21½ x 14⅛ x 8⅜ in. The Chrysler Museum; Gift of James H. Ricau and Museum purchase 86.518

Plate 26. Chauncey Bradley Ives, *The Truant,* 1871. Marble, 36⅞ x 29 x 18 in. New-York Historical Society 1945.494

Plate 27. James Henry Cafferty, *The Encounter,* 1859. Oil on canvas, 20 x 16 in. New-York Historical Society 1983.39

Plate 28. (top) Jacob Riis, *I Scrubs,* c. 1890. Photograph printed from copy negative, 4 x 5 in. Museum of the City of New York; Jacob Riis Collection. **Plate 29.** (bottom) Jacob Riis, *Girl and Baby at Doorstep,* from *How the Other Half Lives,* c. 1890. Photograph printed from copy negative, 4 x 5 in. Museum of the City of New York; Jacob Riis Collection

Plate 30. Myron H. Kimball, *Emancipated Slaves Brought from Louisiana by Col. Geo. H. Hanks,* 1863. Photograph, 5¼ x 7⅜ in. New-York Historical Society, Negative no. 46085

Plate 31. (left) Holler (New Brunswick, NJ), *Portrait of a Baby,* c. 1890s. Photograph, 5 9/16 x 3 7/8 in. Collection of Tanya Sheehan, Providence, RI

Plate 32. (bottom left) Landy (Cincinnati, OH), *Portrait of a Young Boy,* c. 1870s. Photograph, 3 5/8 x 2 1/8 in. Collection of Tanya Sheehan, Providence, RI

Plate 33. (bottom right) Dunn (New Brunswick, NJ), *Portrait of a Young Child,* c. 1880s. Photograph, 5 1/2 x 4 in. Collection of Tanya Sheehan, Providence, RI

Plate 34. (left) Augustus Saint-Gaudens, *Sarah Redwood Lee,* 1881. Plaster, 26 x 11¼ x ⅞ in. Courtesy of Chesterwood, A National Trust Historic Site, Stockbridge, MA. Photograph by Paul Rocheleau.

Plate 35. (right) Gertrude Käsebier, *Blessed Art Thou Amongst Women,* 1899. Platinum print, 9½ x 5¹³⁄₁₆ in. Princeton University Art Museum; The Clarence H. White Collection, assembled and organized by Professor Clarence H. White Jr. and given in memory of Lewis F. White, Dr. Maynard P. White Sr., and Clarence H. White Jr., the sons of Clarence H. White Sr. and Jane Felix White CHWX 98

Plate 36. (above) Jean Baptiste Adolphe Lafosse, after Lilly Martin Spencer, *Height of Fashion,* 1854. Lithograph, 32⅜ x 24 in. Library of Congress, Prints and Photographs

Plate 37. (right) C. H. Gallup and Company (Poughkeepsie, NY), *Portrait of a Girl,* c. 1880s. Photograph, 5½ x 4 in. Collection of Tanya Sheehan, Providence, RI

EXHIBITION CHECKLIST

Ellen Kendall Baker (1839–1913)
The Young Artist, 1885
Oil on canvas, 28 x 23 in.
Detroit Institute of Arts
Gift of the Friends of the Museum
Image courtesy of The Bridgeman Art Library
(p. 153)

Cecilia Beaux (1863–1942)
Dorothea in the Woods, 1897
Oil on canvas, 53¼ x 40 in.
Whitney Museum of American Art
Gift of Mr. and Mrs. Raymond J. Horowitz 70.1587
(p. 128)

Cecilia Beaux (1863–1942)
Fanny Travis Cochran, 1887
Oil on canvas, 35½ x 28½ in.
Pennsylvania Academy of the Fine Arts
Gift of Fanny Travis Cochran 1955.12
(p. 40)

Cecilia Beaux (1863–1942)
Portrait of Harold and Mildred Colton, 1886–1887
Oil on canvas, 55⅞ x 42 in.
Pennsylvania Academy of the Fine Arts
Partial gift of Captain and Mrs. J. Ferrell Colton
Partial purchase, Academy Purchase Fund 1998.7
(p. 52)

Frank Weston Benson (1862–1951)
Gertrude, 1899
Oil on canvas, 50⅛ x 40⅛ in.
Museum of Fine Arts, Boston
Gift of Mrs. William Rodman Fay 54.596
(p. 159)

John George Brown (1831–1913)
The Cider Mill, 1880
Oil on canvas, 30 x 24 in.
Terra Foundation for American Art, Chicago
Daniel J. Terra Collection 1992.19
(p. 62)

John George Brown (1831–1913)
Crossing the Brook, 1874
Oil on canvas, 23 x 14½ in.
George Walter Vincent Smith Art Museum, Springfield, MA
George Walter Vincent Smith Collection
Photograph by David Stansbury
(p. 110)

John George Brown (1831–1913)
Little Servant, c. 1880
Oil on canvas, 30¼ x 25⅜ in.
Private collection
(p. 142)

John George Brown (1831–1913)
A Sure Shot, c. 1875
Oil on canvas, 20⅞ x 14¹³⁄₁₆ in.
Brooklyn Museum
Dick S. Ramsay Fund 48.139
(p. 85)

John George Brown (1831–1913)
Swinging on the Gate, c. 1878–1879
Oil on canvas, 22½ x 14⅜ in.
Taubman Museum of Art
Acquired with funds provided by the Horace G. Fralin Charitable Trust 2003.003
(p. 141)

John George Brown (1831–1913)
Vanity, 1899
Oil on canvas, 24 x 18 in.
Newark Museum
Gift of Dr. J. Ackerman Coles, 1920 20.1212
(p. 20)

James Henry Cafferty (1819–1869)
The Encounter, 1859
Oil on canvas, 20 x 16 in.
New-York Historical Society 1983.39
(p. 162)

Samuel S. Carr (1837–1908)
Every Little Bit Helps, 1872
Oil on canvas, 14 x 11¹³⁄₁₆ in.
Newark Museum
Purchase 1985, The Members' Fund 85.235
(p. 140)

Mary Cassatt (1844–1926)
The Reader, 1877
Oil on canvas, 32 x 25½
Courtesy of Crystal Bridges Museum of American Art
Photograph by Robert LaPrelle
(p. 154)

William Merritt Chase (1849–1916)
Idle Hours, c. 1894
Oil on canvas, 25½ x 35½ in.
Amon Carter Museum of American Art, Fort Worth, TX (p. 80)

William Merritt Chase (1849–1916)
Mrs. Chase and Cosy, c. 1895
Oil on canvas, 55¼ x 26¼ in.
Sheldon Memorial Art Gallery,
University of Nebraska–Lincoln
UNL–F. M. Hall Collection
Photograph © Sheldon Memorial Art Gallery
(p. 79)

William Merritt Chase (1849–1916)
Portrait of the Artist's Daughter, c. 1895
Oil on canvas, 32⅜ x 25⅝ in.
Hirshhorn Museum and Sculpture Garden,
Smithsonian Institution
Gift of Joseph H. Hirshhorn 1966.66.879
(p. 78)

William Merritt Chase (1849–1916)
Young Girl in Black: The Artist's Daughter in Mother's Dress, c. 1897–1898
Oil on canvas, 60⅛ x 36³⁄₁₆ in.
Hirshhorn Museum and Sculpture Garden,
Smithsonian Institution
Gift of Joseph H. Hirshhorn Foundation
1966.66.87
(p. 77)

C. H. Gallup and Company
(Active c. 1880s, Poughkeepsie, NY)
Portrait of a Girl, c. 1880s
Photograph, 5½ x 4 in.
Collection of Tanya Sheehan, Providence, RI
(p. 167)

Charles Courtney Curran (1861–1942)
Lotus Lilies, 1888
Oil on canvas, 18 x 32 in.
Terra Museum for American Art
Daniel J. Terra Collection 1999.35
(pp. 156–157)

Currier and Ives, publishers
After Louis Maurer
Into Mischief, c. 1857
Lithograph, 16½ x 12⅝ in.
The Old Print Shop
(p. 94)

Joseph Rodefer DeCamp (1858–1923)
Sally, c. 1907
Oil on canvas, 26 x 23 in.
Worcester Art Museum, Worcester, MA
Museum purchase
(p. 106)

Dunn (Active c. 1880s, New Brunswick, NJ)
Portrait of a Young Child, c. 1880s
Photograph, 5½ x 4 in.
Collection of Tanya Sheehan, Providence, RI
(p. 165)

Frank Duveneck (1848–1919)
Mary Cabot Wheelwright, 1882
Oil on linen, 50³⁄₁₆ x 33¹⁄₁₆ in.
Brooklyn Museum
Dick S. Ramsay Fund 40.87
(p. 48)

Thomas Eakins (1844–1916)
Home Scene, c. 1871
Oil on canvas, 21 7/16 x 18 in.
Brooklyn Museum
Gift of George A. Hearn and Charles A. Schieren, by exchange; Frederick Loeser Art Fund and Dick S. Ramsay Fund 50.115
(p. 72)

Mary Abastenia St. Leger Eberle (1878–1942)
Roller Skating, 1906
Bronze, 13 x 11 3/4 x 6 1/2 in.
Whitney Museum of American Art
(p. 149)

Erastus Salisbury Field (1805–1900)
Mrs. Paul Smith Palmer and Her Twins, 1835/1838
Oil on canvas, 38 1/2 x 34 in.
National Gallery of Art
Gift of Edgar William Garbisch and Bernice Chrysler Garbisch 1971.83.5
(p. 136)

Charles Dana Gibson (1867–1944)
The Nursery, 1906
From Charles Dana Gibson, *The Gibson Book,* Vol. 1 (New York: Charles Scribner's Sons, 1906)
Photomechanical print on paper, 9 1/2 x 6 1/2 in.
Newark Museum
Purchase 2005, Helen McMahon Brady Cutting Fund 2005.23.1 205 B
(p. 53)

Griffith and Griffith (Active c. 1900s, Philadelphia, PA)
"On Friday I play that they are taken ill," 1901
Photograph, 3 1/2 x 7 in.
Collection of Tanya Sheehan, Providence, RI
(p. 47)

Seymour Joseph Guy (1824–1910)
A Bedtime Story, 1878
Oil on canvas, 34 x 27 1/2 in.
Private collection
(p. 67)

Seymour Joseph Guy (1824–1910)
Children in Candlelight, 1869
Oil on canvas, 24 1/8 x 18 1/8 in.
Newark Museum
Purchase 1957
C. Suydam Cutting Special Gift Fund 57.74
(p. 66)

Seymour Joseph Guy (1824–1910)
The Crossing Sweeper, c. 1863
Oil on canvas, 12 1/8 x 8 1/2 in.
Metropolitan Museum of Art
Bequest of Collis P. Huntington, 1900 25.110.50
(p. 64)

Seymour Joseph Guy (1824–1910)
Dressing for the Rehearsal, c. 1890
Oil on canvas, 34 1/8 x 27 3/8 in.
Smithsonian American Art Museum, Washington, D.C.
Gift of Jennie Anita Guy 1936.12.5
(p. 68)

Seymour Joseph Guy (1824–1910)
Making a Train, 1867
Oil on canvas, 18 1/8 x 24 1/8 in.
Philadelphia Museum of Art
The George W. Elkins Collection, 1924 E1924.4.14
(p. 117)

William Hahn (1829–1887)
Learning the Lesson (Children Playing School),
c. 1880
Oil on canvas, 34 x 27 in.
The Oakland Museum of California
Kahn Collection
(p. 152)

Ann Hall (1792–1863)
Louisa and Eliza Macardy, c. 1845
Watercolor on ivory, 5 1/2 x 4 1/2 in.
New-York Historical Society
Museum purchase, Louis Durr Fund 1946.297
(p. 158)

EXHIBITION CHECKLIST

Edward Lamson Henry (1841–1919)
Kept In, 1889
Oil on canvas, 13½ x 18 in.
Fenimore Art Museum, Cooperstown, NY
N0309.1961
Photograph by Richard Walker
(p. 150)

Holler (Active c. 1890s, New Brunswick, NJ)
Portrait of a Baby, c. 1890s
Photograph, 5 9/16 x 3 7/8 in.
Collection of Tanya Sheehan, Providence, RI
(p. 165)

Winslow Homer (1836–1910)
Gathering Berries, 1874
Published in *Harper's Weekly,* July 11, 1874
Wood engraving, 9⅛ x 13½ in.
The Old Print Shop
(p. 146)

Winslow Homer (1836–1910)
Girl and Laurel, 1879
Oil on canvas, 22⅝ x 15¾ in.
Detroit Institute of Arts
Image courtesy of The Bridgeman Art Library
(p. 124)

Winslow Homer (1836–1910)
Reading by the Brook, 1879
Oil on canvas, 15⅞ x 22¾ in.
Memphis Brooks Museum of Art,
Memphis, TN
Memphis Park Commission Purchase 43.22
(p. 151)

Winslow Homer (1836–1910)
A Temperance Meeting (Noon Time), 1874
Oil on canvas, 20⅜ x 30⅛ in.
Philadelphia Museum of Art
Purchased with the John Howard McFadden Jr.
Fund, 1956 1956.118.1
(pp. 144–145)

Winslow Homer (1836–1910)
"Winter"—A Skating Scene, 1868
Published in *Harper's Weekly,* January 25, 1868
Woodcut, 9⅛ x 13½ in.
Private collection
(p. 89)

William Morris Hunt (1824–1879)
Girl with Cat, 1856
Oil on canvas, 42⅛ x 33⅜ in.
Museum of Fine Arts, Boston
Bequest of Edmund Dwight 00.504
(p. 45)

Henry Inman (1801–1846)
Children of Bishop George W. Doane, 1835
Oil on canvas, 25 x 31¼ in.
Newark Museum
Purchase 1959, Louis Bamberger Bequest
Fund 59.83
(p. 29)

Chauncey Bradley Ives (1810–1894)
The Truant, 1871
Marble, 36⅞ x 29 x 18 in.
New-York Historical Society 1945.494
(p. 161)

Eastman Johnson (1824–1906)
Kite Flying, 1865
Oil on board, 21⅜ x 26 in.
Colby College Museum of Art
The Lunder Collection
(p. 147)

Eastman Johnson (1824–1906)
The Party Dress (The Finishing Touch), 1872
Oil on composition board, 20⅝ x 16 11/16 in.
Wadsworth Atheneum Museum of Art
(p. 118)

Eastman Johnson (1824–1906)
Union Soldiers Accepting a Drink, c. 1865
Oil on canvas, 17½ x 21½ in.
Carnegie Museum of Art, Pittsburgh
Heinz Family Fund 1996.45
(p. 18)

Eastman Johnson (1824–1906)
Winter, Portrait of Child, 1879
Oil on canvas, 50¹⁵⁄₁₆ x 32 in.
Brooklyn Museum
Gift of the Charles M. Kurtz Trust 1992.108
(p. 70)

Gertrude Käsebier (1852–1934)
Blessed Art Thou Amongst Women, 1899
Platinum print, 9½ x 5¹³⁄₁₆ in.
Princeton University Art Museum
The Clarence H. White Collection, assembled and organized by Professor Clarence H. White Jr. and given in memory of Lewis F. White, Dr. Maynard P. White Sr., and Clarence H. White Jr., the sons of Clarence H. White Sr. and Jane Felix White
CHWX 98
(p. 166)

Myron H. Kimball (Active 1860s)
Emancipated Slaves Brought from Louisiana by Col. Geo. H. Hanks, 1863
Photograph, 5¼ x 7⅜ in.
New-York Historical Society
Negative no. 46085
(p. 164)

John Lewis Krimmel (1786–1821)
Quilting Frolic, 1813
Oil on canvas, 16⅞ x 22⅜ in.
Winterthur Museum
Museum purchase 1953.0178.002
(p. 137)

Landy (Active c. 1870s, Cincinnati, OH)
Portrait of a Young Boy, c. 1870s
Photograph, 3⅝ x 2⅛ in.
Collection of Tanya Sheehan, Providence, RI
(p. 165)

William Henry Lippincott (1849–1920)
Childish Thoughts, 1895
Oil on canvas, 32¼ x 45¹¹⁄₁₆ in.
Pennsylvania Academy of the Fine Arts
Gift of Mary H. Rice 1976.3
(p. 50)

William Henry Lippincott (1849–1920)
Infantry in Arms, 1887
Oil on canvas, 32 x 53¼ in.
Pennsylvania Academy of the Fine Arts
Gift of Homer F. Emens and Francis C. Jones
1922.10
(p. 51)

William J. McCloskey (1859–1941)
Feeding Dolly (If You Don't Eat It, I'll Give It to Doggie), 1890
Oil on canvas, 20 x 24 in.
Hudson River Museum
Gift of Mrs. Lillie H. Seaman 25.97
(p. 47)

Attributed to Samuel Miller (c. 1807–1853)
Picking Flowers, 1840–1850
Oil on canvas, 44½ x 27½ in.
Fenimore Art Museum, Cooperstown, NY
N0225.1961
(p. 39)

Julia Ann Morris (Active 1840s)
Sampler, 1844
Wool, 18 x 17½ in.
Newark Museum
Gift of Mrs. B. Altemus, 1956 56.9
(p. 139)

Ammi Phillips (1788–1865)
Boy in Red, c. 1832
Oil on canvas, 23½ x 20 in.
Princeton University Art Museum
Gift of Edward Duff Balken,
Class of 1897 Y1958-75
Photograph by Bruce M. White
(p. 34)

EXHIBITION CHECKLIST

Ammi Phillips (1788–1865)
Girl in a Red Dress, c. 1835
Oil on canvas, 32⅜ x 27⅜ in.
Terra Foundation for American Art, Chicago
Daniel J. Terra Collection 1992.57
(p. 33)

Ammi Phillips (1788–1865)
Girl in Pink, c. 1832
Oil on canvas, 23½ x 20 in.
Princeton University Art Museum
Gift of Edward Duff Balken,
Class of 1897 Y1958-74
Photograph by Bruce M. White
(p. 35)

Attributed to Ammi Phillips (1788–1865)
Mother and Child in Grey Dresses, c. 1825
Oil on canvas, 33⅞ x 27⅞ in.
Fenimore Art Museum, Cooperstown, NY
N0267.1961
Photograph by Richard Walker
(p. 134)

Ammi Phillips (1788–1865)
Portrait of Harriet Campbell, c. 1815
Oil on canvas, 48½ x 25 in.
Sterling and Francine Clark Art Institute,
Williamstown, MA
Gift of Oliver Eldridge in memory of Sarah
Fairchild Anderson, teacher of art,
North Adams Public Schools, daughter of
Harriet Campbell 1991.8
Image © Sterling and Francine Clark Art Institute,
Williamstown, MA
Photograph by Michael Agee
(p. 135)

Jacob Riis (1849–1914)
Girl and Baby at Doorstep, from *How the Other Half Lives,* c. 1890
Photograph printed from copy negative, 4 x 5 in.
Museum of the City of New York
Jacob Riis Collection
(p. 163)

Jacob Riis (1849–1914)
I Scrubs, c. 1890
Photograph printed from copy negative, 4 x 5 in.
Museum of the City of New York
Jacob Riis Collection
(p. 163)

John Rogers (1829–1904)
The School Examination, 1867
Plaster and paint, 20 x 13 x 8½ in.
The Hyde Collection, Glen Falls, NY
Gift of Charles R. Wood 1992.4.61
Photograph by Jim McLaughlin
(p. 148)

John Rogers (1829–1904)
Uncle Ned's School, 1866
Plaster, 19¾ x 14 x 9 in.
New-York Historical Society 1931.47
(p. 115)

Randolph Rogers (1825–1892)
Daughter Nora as the Infant Psyche, c. 1871
Marble, 21½ x 14⅛ x 8⅜ in.
The Chrysler Museum
Gift of James H. Ricau and
Museum purchase 86.518
(p. 160)

Augustus Saint-Gaudens (1848–1907)
Sarah Redwood Lee, 1881
Plaster, 26 x 11¼ x ⅞ in.
Courtesy of Chesterwood, A National Trust
Historic Site, Stockbridge, MA
Photograph by Paul Rocheleau
(p. 166)

John Singer Sargent (1856–1925)
Katherine Chase Pratt, 1890
Oil on canvas, 40 x 30⅛ in.
Worcester Art Museum, Worcester, MA
Gift of William I. Clark
(p. 42)

Junius R. Sloan (1827–1900)
The Knitting Lesson, 1866
Oil on canvas, 18⅝ x 15⅝ in.
Brauer Museum of Art, Valparaiso University
Gift of Percy H. Sloan 53.01.126
(p. 143)

Lilly Martin Spencer (1822–1902)
Engraving by Jean Baptiste Adolphe Lafosse
Height of Fashion, 1854
Lithograph, 32⅜ x 24 in.
Library of Congress, Prints and Photographs
(p. 167)

Lilly Martin Spencer (1822–1902)
The Home of the Red, White and Blue, c. 1867–1868
Oil on canvas, 24 x 30 in.
Terra Foundation for American Art, Chicago
Daniel J. Terra Art Acquisition Endowment Fund
2007.1 (p. 10)

Lilly Martin Spencer (1822–1902)
War Spirit at Home (Celebrating the Victory at Vicksburg), 1866
Oil on canvas, 30 x 32¾ in.
Newark Museum
Purchase 1944, Wallace M. Scudder Bequest Fund 44.177
(p. 96)

Alice Barber Stephens (1858–1932)
The Woman in Business, 1897
Cover for *Ladies' Home Journal,* September 1897
Oil on canvas, 25 x 18 in.
Brandywine River Museum
Museum purchase, 1982, made possible through Ray and Beverly Sacks
(p. 13)

Elizabeth Stone (Active 1830s)
Sampler, 1836
Wool, 17¼ x 17¼ in.
Newark Museum
Gift of Mrs. Fred E. Sutton, 1922 22.219
(p. 138)

Edmund Charles Tarbell (1863–1938)
Josephine and Mercie, 1908
Oil on canvas, 28⅛ x 32 1/16 in.
Corcoran Gallery of Art, Washington, D.C.
Museum purchase, Gallery fund 09.2
(p. 155)

Abbott Handerson Thayer (1849–1921)
Angel, 1887
Oil on canvas, 36¼ x 28⅛ in.
Smithsonian American Art Museum
Gift of John Gellatly 1929.6.112
(p. 74)

Unknown artist (Active 1840s)
Girl with Flowers, c. 1840
Oil on canvas, 36⅛ x 29 in.
Newark Museum
Purchase 1931, Felix Fuld Bequest Fund 31.145
(p. 37)

Unknown artist (Active 1830s)
The Goying Child, c. 1832–1835
Oil on wood, 42 x 25¼ in.
Newark Museum
Anonymous gift, 1938 38.213
(p. 36)

Bessie Potter Vonnoh (1872–1955)
Enthroned, 1902; cast 1906
Bronze, 12 x 8 x 10 in.
Colby College Museum of Art
The Lunder Collection
(p. 22)

CONTRIBUTORS

SARAH BURNS is Professor Emerita, School of Fine Arts, Indiana University. She is the author of *Pastoral Inventions: Rural Life in Nineteenth-Century American Art and Culture* (1989), *Inventing the Modern Artist: Art and Culture in Gilded Age America* (1996), and *Painting the Dark Side: Art and the Gothic Imagination in Nineteenth-Century America* (2004).

HOLLY PYNE CONNOR is the Curator of Nineteenth-Century American Art, the Newark Museum. She cocurated *Picturing America* (2001), the ground-breaking exhibition of the Newark Museum's permanent collection, and organized and coauthored *Off the Pedestal: New Women in the Art of Homer, Chase, and Sargent* (2006) and *Small but Sublime: Intimate Views by Durand, Bierstadt and Inness* (2006).

BARBARA DAYER GALLATI is Curator Emerita of American Art, Brooklyn Museum. She is the author of *William Merritt Chase* (1995), *Great Expectations: John Singer Sargent Painting Children* (2004), and *Making American Taste: Narrative Art for a New Democracy* (2011), and a coauthor of *Winslow Homer: Illustrating America* (2000) and *Kindred Spirits: Asher B. Durand and the American Landscape* (2007).

LAUREN LESSING is Mirken Curator of Education, Colby College Museum of Art. She is the author of "Ties that Bind: Hiram Powers' *Greek Slave* and Nineteenth-Century Marriage," *American Art* (Spring 2010), "New Perspective: Rereading Seymour Joseph Guy's *Making a Train*," *American Art* (Spring 2011), and "Angels in the Home: Adelicia Acklen's Sculpture Collection at Belmont Mansion," *Winterthur Portfolio* (Spring 2011).

INDEX

Page numbers in *italic* type refer to pages with illustrations. Page numbers within brackets indicate textual references to endnotes.

A

Abate, Michelle, 87, 104n10
Abell, Mrs. L. G., 87
Adams, Henry, 125
Advice to Young Ladies on Their Duties and Conduct in Life (Arthur), 23
Aestheticism, 125
African Americans, 17–19, 115–116. See also Civil War
Alcott, Louisa May, 38, 55n43, 90, 123
    Eight Cousins, 123
    Little Women, 15, 23, 24, 29, 35, 86–87, 90
    Moods, 24
    Old-Fashioned Girl, An, 41, 123
    Rose in Bloom, 123
Alexander, John White, 43
Allen, Bessie (fictional character). See "Little Mischief" story series
American Academy, 16
American Art Galleries, New York, 127
American Art-Union, 14, 16, 108, 130n3
American Society of Painters in Water Colors, 24
American Water Color Society, 25
Andrew Jackson Ten Broeck—Age One Year, Six Months (Phillips), *32,* 54n13
Angel (Thayer), *74,* 75, 125
Angels and Tomboys: Girlhood in Nineteenth-Century American Art exhibition, 6, 7–8, 168–174
Arthur, T. S., 23
    Advice to Young Ladies on Their Duties and Conduct in Life, 23
Arthur's Home Magazine, 100–101
Art Interchange, 14
At Her Ease (The Young Orphan, Study of a Young Girl) (Chase), *120,* 121
Atlantic Monthly, 23

B

Bacon, Ruth Sears, 49
Baker, Ellen Kendall, 153
    Young Artist, The, 153
Barbizon School painters, 19, 25
Barn Swallows (Johnson), 85, *86*
Baym, Nina, 16
Beauty and the Beer (Van Emery), *122*
Beaux, Cecilia, 41, 51–53, 127–129
    Dorothea in the Woods, 127–129, *128*
    Fanny Travis Cochran, 40, 41, 55n28, 55n29
    Portrait of Harold and Mildred Colton, 51–53, *52*
Bedtime Story, A (Guy), 65, *67*
Benson, Frank Weston, 41, 159
    Gertrude, 159
Bingham, George Caleb, 11

Bion, Paul, [129], 132n67
Blessed Art Thou Amongst Women (Käsebier), *166*
Blythe, David Gilmour, 11
Boose, Lynda, 69
Boy in Red (Phillips), *34*
Breton, Jules, 126
Brown, Charlotte (Lottie), 60, 61, 82n15, 82n16
Brown, Isabelle (Belle), 60, 61, 82n15, 82n16
Brown, John George, 11, 21, 24, 27n28, 60–61, 63, 90–91
    Cider Mill, The, 61, *62,* 63
    Crossing the Brook, 110, 111
    family, 27n31, 60, 61, 63, 69, 82n15, 82n16, 82n18
    Fishing—Fort Lee, New Jersey, 60
    Golden Locks, 63
    Little Servant, 142
    Peacemaker, The, 21
    Sure Shot, A, 84, 90–91
    Swinging on the Gate, 141
    Vanity, 20
    Watching the Woodpecker, 21, *60*
    We Can't Be Caught, 61
Brown, Mabel, 63
Brown, Mary Ann, 61
Burns, Sarah, 49, 84–105, 116, 175

C

Cafferty, James Henry, 162
    Encounter, The, 162
Calvin, John, 30
Campbell, Rose (fictional character). See Alcott, Louisa May: *Eight Cousins*
"Care of the Adolescent Girl, The" (Jacobi), 127
Carr, Katy (fictional character). See *What Katy Did* books
Carr, Samuel S., 140
    Every Little Bit Helps, 140
Cary, Elisabeth Luther, 125
Cassatt, Mary, 154
    Reader, The, 154
Century Association, 71
Chase, Alice Dieudonnée (Cosy), 25, 49, 56, 57, 77, 78, 79, 81, 83n47
Chase, Dorothy, 81
Chase, Hattie, 77
Chase, William Merritt, 24, 25, 41, 46, 49, 57, 77, 81, 121
    At Her Ease (The Young Orphan, Study of a Young Girl), 120, 121
    Did You Speak to Me?, 49, 56, *57,* 81
    family, 25, 49, 57, 77, 83n47
    Idle Hours, 80, 81
    Mrs. Chase and Cosy, 25, *79*
    My Little Daughter Dorothy, 81

176

Chase, William Merritt (*continued*)
   Portrait of the Artist's Daughter, 25, 77, *78*
   Young Girl in Black: The Artist's Daughter in Mother's Dress, 25, *77*
Cheney, John, and J. I. Pease, 107, 108
   "Maidenhood," *108*
C. H. Gallup and Company, 167
   Portrait of a Girl, 167
Child, Lydia Maria Francis, 38, 46, 54n17
Childish Thoughts (Lippincott), 49–51, *50*
Children in Candlelight (Guy), 65, *66*
Children of Bishop George W. Doane (Inman), 28, 31, 41, 54n10
Cider Mill, The (Brown), 61, *62*, 63
Civil War, 11, 17, 21, 23, 24, 58, 60, 85, 91, 97, 100–101
Clarke, Edward H., 121
Cochran, Fanny Travis, 40, 41, 55n28, 55n29
Cogan, Frances, 87
Cole, Thomas
   "Voyage of Life, The" series of paintings, 107–108
   Voyage of Life: Youth, 107
Colton, Harold, 51–53, 55n46
Colton, Mildred, 51–53, 55n46
Connor, Holly Pyne, 10–27, 28–55, 123, 175
Cook, Clarence, 17
Coolidge, Susan, 86, 88, 89, 102
Cooper, Helen, 25
Corcoran, William Wilson, 16
Corn Husking (Johnson), *19*, 27n26
Cosmopolitan Art Journal, 92–94
Cosy. *See* Chase, Alice Dieudonnée
Crayon, The (journal), 113
Crossing Sweeper, The (Guy), 12, 63, *64*
Crossing the Brook (Brown), *110*, 111
Crowell, Elizabeth, 24, 44, 71, 73, 119. *See also* Eakins, Thomas: family
Crowell, Frances, 71, 73, 119. *See also* Eakins, Thomas: family
Crowell, Kathrin, 55n35, 71. *See also* Eakins, Thomas: family
Crowell, William, 71. *See also* Eakins, Thomas: family
Cummins, Maria Susanna, 15–16, 38, 43
Curran, Charles Courtney, 156–157
   Lotus Lilies, 156–157
Currier and Ives, 15, 23, 94, 95, 97
   Training Day, 23, *97*

D
Daughter Nora as the Infant Psyche (Rogers), *160*
D'Avignon, Francis, 14
   Distribution of the American Art-Union Prizes at the Tabernacle, Broadway, New York, December 24, 1846, 14

Debby Ann (fictional character), 101
"Debby Ann" (Hallowell), 101
DeCamp, Joseph Rodefer, 107, 108
   Sally, 106
DeCamp, Sally, 106, 108
Detroit Institute of Arts, 125
Dewing, Thomas, 43
Dickens, Charles, 76, 112
   Dombey and Son, 76
   Little Dorrit, 76
Dickerman, Caleb, 115
Did You Speak to Me? (Chase), 49, *56*, 57, 81
Distribution of the American Art-Union Prizes at the Tabernacle, Broadway, New York, December 24, 1846 (D'Avignon; Matteson), 14
Doane, George Hobart, 31, 54n10
Doane, George W. *See* Inman, Henry: *Children of Bishop George W. Doane*
Doane, William Croswell, 31, 54n10
Dorothea in the Woods (Beaux), 127–129, *128*
Douglas, Ann, 21
Downes, William Howe, 75
"Dreadful Story of Pauline and the Matches, The." *See under* Hoffmann, Heinrich
Dressing for the Rehearsal (Guy), 44, 65, *68*, 69
Dunn (photographer), 165
   Portrait of a Young Child, 165
Durand, Asher Brown, 12
   Peddler, The, 12
Durand, John, 113
Duveneck, Frank, 48, 49
   Mary Cabot Wheelwright, 48, 49
Duverger, Théophile Emmanuel, 16

E
Eakins, Caroline (Caddie), 24, 44, 71, 72
Eakins, Frances, 71, 73
Eakins, Margaret, 24, 44, 71, 72, 73
Eakins, Thomas, 24, 25, 43, 44, 55n35, 71, 73, 75, 120
   Elizabeth Crowell with a Dog, 24, 44, *73,* 119, 120
   family, 24, 44, 71, 72, 73, 83n36, 119
   Home Scene, 24, 44, 71, *72,* 73
   Swimming Hole, The, 120
Eberle, Mary Abastenia St. Leger, 149
   Roller Skating, 149
Edmonds, Francis William, 12
   New Bonnet, The, 12, *13,* 26n7
Eleanora C. Ross (Stanley), *114,* 115, 130n21
Elizabeth Clarke Freake (Mrs. John Freake) and Baby Mary (unknown artist), *30*
Elizabeth Crowell with a Dog (Eakins), 24, 44, *73,* 119, 120
Ellington, George, 121

177

Emancipated Slaves Brought from Louisiana by Col. Geo. H. Hanks (Kimball), *164*
Encounter, The (Cafferty), *162*
Enthroned (Vonnoh), *22,* 23
Every Little Bit Helps (Carr), *140*

F
Fahs, Alice, 24
Fanny Travis Cochran (Beaux), *40,* 41, 55n28, 55n29
Feeding Dolly (If You Don't Eat It, I'll Give It to Doggie) (McCloskey), 46–47, *47*
Felter, John D., 114
    Olive Oatman with Tattoos on Chin, 114
    See also Oatman, Olive
Female Student; or, Lectures to Young Ladies on Female Education, The (Phelps), 38
Field, Erastus Salisbury, 136
    Mrs. Paul Smith Palmer and Her Twins, 136
Fi Fo Fum (Spencer), 59
First Polka, The (Lafosse; Spencer), *14,* 26n15
First Step, The: "Come to Mama" (Currier and Ives; Maurer), 95
Fishing—Fort Lee, New Jersey (Brown), *60*
Flagg, George Whiting, 11
Fourier, Charles, 59
Frère, Pierre Édouard, 16–17
    Supper with a Friend, 17
Fruit of Temptation (Lafosse; Spencer), *92,* 93, 94, 104n24
Fuller, George, 25, 125–126
    Hannah, 125–126, *126*

G
Gallati, Barbara Dayer, 56–83, 127, 129, 175
Gathering Berries (Homer), *146*
Gertrude (Benson), *159*
Gibson, Charles Dana, 53, 95
    Nursery, The, 53, 95
    "Seven Ages of Woman" series, 95
Gibson Girl, 53. See also New Woman
Gilder, Helena de Kay, 127
Gilder, Richard Watson, 127
Girl and Baby at Doorstep (Riis), *163*
Girl and Laurel (Homer), 41, *124,* 125, 131–132n50
Girl in a Red Dress (Phillips), 32, *33*
Girl in Pink (Phillips), *35*
Girl with Canary (The New Arrival) (Guy), 44, *46*
Girl with Cat (Hunt), 16, 44, *45*
Girl with Flowers (unknown artist), 34, *37*
Golden Locks (Brown), *63*
Goupil, Vibert, and Company, 16–17, 26n8
Goying Child, The (unknown artist), 34, *36*
Grandpa's Prodigies (Rogers; Spencer), *93,* 95
Greek Slave, The (Powers), 113

Griffith and Griffith (photographers), 47
    "On Friday I play that they are taken ill," 47
Guy, Anna, 65
Guy, Seymour Joseph, 15, 21, 24, 27n28, 43, 44, 55n36, 60, 63, 65, 69, 117, 119, 122
    Bedtime Story, A, 65, *67*
    Children in Candlelight, 65, *66*
    Crossing Sweeper, The, 12, 63, *64*
    Dressing for the Rehearsal, 44, 65, *68,* 69
    family, 63, 65, 69
    Girl with Canary (The New Arrival), 44, *46*
    Knot in the Skein, A, 122, 122–123
    Making a Train, 44, 65, *117,* 117–119
    Story of Golden Locks, 44
    Unconscious of Danger, 63, 65

H
Hahn, William, 152
    Learning the Lesson (Children Playing School), 152
Half-Orphan Asylum, Manhattan, 121
Hall, Ann, 158
    Louisa and Eliza Macardy, 158
Hallowell, Sarah C., 101
Hannah (Fuller), 125–126, *126*
Hanon, Jean Louis, 16
Harland, Marion, 29, 46
Harper's Bazaar, 119, 126, 127
Harper's Weekly, 88, 89, 146
Hartley, Florence, 119–120
Hatfield, Dot, 57
Hatfield, Joseph Henry, 57, 82n2
    Helping Papa, 57
H. C. White Co. (photographers), 102–103
    Private Investigations Lead to—, 102–103, *103*
Height of Fashion (Lafosse; Spencer), 26n9, 26n15, *167*
Helping Papa (Hatfield), *57*
Henry, Edward Lamson, 150
    Kept In, 150
Hidden Hand, The (Southworth), 87, 88, 104n10
Hoffmann, Heinrich
    "Dreadful Story of Pauline and the Matches, The," 98, 105n38
    Pauline and the Matches, 98
    Slovenly Peter, 97–98, 100, 102, 105n37, 105n38
Holler (photographer), 165
    Portrait of a Baby, 165
Holmes, Mary J., 86, 88, 89
Home of the Red, White and Blue, The (Spencer), *10,* 21, 23–24
Homer, Henrietta Benson, 24
Homer, Winslow, 17, 24–25, 41, 88, 89, 90, 91, 116, 123, 125, 131–132n50
    Gathering Berries, 146
    Girl and Laurel, 41, *124,* 125, 131–132n50

INDEX

Homer, Winslow (*continued*)
    Peach Blossoms, 123, 131n47
    Reading by the Brook, 151
    Sunday Morning in Virginia, 116
    Temperance Meeting (Noon Time), A, 144–145
    "Winter"—A Skating Scene, 88, *89*, 90, 116, 125
Home Scene (Eakins), 24, 44, 71, *72*, 73
Hoppin, Martha, 21, 82n16
Houghton Farm, 25
Hunt, William Morris, 16, 24, 43, 44
    Girl with Cat, 16, 44, *45*
    Violet Girl, The, 16
Hunter, Jane H., 87, 105n46, 116
Huntington, Daniel, 108

I
Ice Skater (Johnson), 17, *88*, 89
Idle Hours (Chase), *80*, 81
Illick, Joseph E., 30
Infantry in Arms (Lippincott), *51*
Infant Samuel, The (Reynolds), 119
Inman, Henry, 28, 31, 41, 54n10
    Children of Bishop George W. Doane, 28, 31, 41, 54n10
In the Hayloft (Johnson), *85*, 86, 88
Into Mischief (Currier and Ives; Maurer), *94*, 95, 102
I Scrubs (Riis), *163*
Isham, Samuel, 125
Ives, Chauncey Bradley, 161
    Truant, The, *161*

J
Jacobi, Mary Putnam, 127
James, Henry, 24, 27n37, 27n39, 38, 125
    Daisy Miller, 27n37, 27n39, 38
    Portrait of a Lady, The, 27n39, 38
    "Turn of the Screw, The," 27n39, 38, 55n46
    Watch and Ward, 24, 27n39, 54n20
Johns, Elizabeth, 11, 13, 15, 26n12, 71, 104n23, 117
Johnson, Eastman, 11, 12, 16, 17, 19, 21, 24, 27n27, 43,
    69, 71, 85, 86, 88, 89–90, 119
    Barn Swallows, 85, *86*
    Child with a Rabbit, 69
    Corn Husking, 19, 27n26
    family, 27n27, 69, 71, 88, 89–90
    Freedom Ring, The, 17, 26n20
    Hannah amidst the Vines, 17
    Ice Skater, 17, *88*, 89
    In the Hayloft, *85*, 86, 88
    Kite Flying, *147*
    Party Dress (The Finishing Touch), The, *118*, 119
    Pets, The, 16, 26n20, 43, *44*
    Union Soldiers Accepting a Drink, 17–19, *18*
    Winter, Portrait of Child, 69–71, *70*, 88, 89–90

Johnson, Ethel, 27n27, 69, 71, 88, 89–90
Josephine and Mercie (Tarbell), *155*

K
Käsebier, Gertrude, 166
    Blessed Art Thou Amongst Women, *166*
Kasson, Joy, 113–114
Katherine Chase Pratt (Sargent), *42*, 43, 55n30
Katz, Wendy J., 15, 26n12
Kendall, William Sergeant, 69
    Statuette, A, *69*
Kept In (Henry), *150*
Kimball, Myron H., 164
    Emancipated Slaves Brought from Louisiana by Col. Geo. H. Hanks, *164*
Kite Flying (Johnson), *147*
Knight, Margaret, 101, 105n44
Knitting Lesson, The (Sloan), *143*
Knot in the Skein, A (Guy), *122*, 122–123
Krimmel, John Lewis, 12, 26n7, 46, 55n37, 137
    Quilting Frolic, 55n37, *137*

L
Ladies' Book of Etiquette, and Manual of Politeness
    (Hartley), 119–120
Lafosse, Jean Baptiste Adolphe
    First Polka, The, *14*, 26n15
    Fruit of Temptation, *92*, 93, 94, 104n24
    Height of Fashion, 26n9, 26n15, *167*
    Oh!, *15*, 26n15
    Young Teacher, The, *14*, 26n15, 58
    See also Spencer, Lilly Martin
Lamplighter, The (Cummins), 15–16, 43
Landy (photographer), 165
    Portrait of a Young Boy, *165*
Larcom, Lucy, 35, 63, 119
Learning the Lesson (Children Playing School)
    (Hahn), *152*
Lee, Elizabeth, 75, 132n52
Lee, Rosa (fictional character). See *Meadow Brook*
Lessing, Lauren, 35, 106–132, 175
Lewis, Dio, 89, 104n13
Lippincott, William Henry, 49, 51
    Childish Thoughts, 49–51, *50*
    Infantry in Arms, *51*
Little Mischief (unknown artist), *100*
Little Mischief-Maker, and Other Stories, The
    (Woodworth), 92–93, 98
"Little Mischief" story series, 100, 105n41
Little Servant (Brown), *142*
Little Women. See under Alcott, Louisa May
Locke, John, 31
Longfellow, Henry Wadsworth, 107–108

Lotus Lilies (Curran), 156–157
Louisa and Eliza Macardy (Hall), *158*
Lowell High School Girls' Basketball Team, The—New England Champions, 108, *109*
Lowell Offering: A Repository of Original Articles, Written by "Factory Girls," 112
Lubin, David, 15, 104n23, 105n29

M
Madden, Thomas More, 121
"Maidenhood" (Cheney and Pease), 107, *108*
Making a Train (Guy), 44, 65, *117,* 117, 119
March, Jo (fictional character). *See* Alcott, Louisa May: *Little Women*
Marling, Jacob, 111
  May Queen, The, 111
Martin, Angélique, 82n9. *See also* Spencer, Lilly Martin: family
Martin, Angélique Marie. *See* Spencer, Lilly Martin
Mary Cabot Wheelwright (Duveneck), *48,* 49
Match Girl, The (Flagg), 11
Mathews Gallery, 123
Matteson, T. H., 14
  Distribution of the American Art-Union Prizes at the Tabernacle, Broadway, New York, December 24, 1846, 14
Maurer, Louis, 94, 102
  First Step, The: "Come to Mama," lithograph by Currier and Ives, *95*
  Into Mischief, lithograph by Currier and Ives, *94,* 95, 102
May Queen, The (Marling), *111*
McCloskey, Eleanor, 46, 55n42
McCloskey, William J., 46–47, 55n42
  Feeding Dolly (If You Don't Eat It, I'll Give It to Doggie), 46–47, *47*
Meadow Brook (Holmes), 86, 88, 89
Mechlin, Leila, 125
Mignon. See Thayer, Abbot Handerson: *Angel*
Miller, Samuel, 38, 41
  Picking Flowers, 38, *39,* 41
Millet, Jean-François, 16, 25, 44, 126
Mischief-Maker Discovered, The (unknown artist), *92*
Morris, Julia Ann, 139
  Sampler, 139
Mother and Child in Grey Dresses (Phillips), *134*
Mothers' Congress of the City of New York, 127
Mount, William Sidney, 11–12, 13, 26n5, 26n9
Mrs. Chase and Cosy (Chase), 25, *79*
Mrs. Paul Smith Palmer and Her Twins (Field), *136*
Mulready, William, 60
Murray, Freeman Henry Morris, 115–116
My Children (Mary, Gerald, Gladys Thayer) (Thayer), *76*

N
Napolitano, Laura, 94–95
Nast, Thomas, 126, 127
  Wife of the Period, The, 126, *127*
National Academy of Design, 16, 26n3, 26n5, 26n20, 82n10
National Police Gazette, The, 121–122
Native Americans, 113–115, 130n20, 130n21
New Bonnet, The (Edmonds), 12, *13,* 26n7
New England Girlhood, A (Larcom), 35, 63, [119]
New Woman, 24, 27n37, 53, 95, 102, 127, 130n24
New York Evening Post, 123–124, 131n47
New York Times, 16–17, 58, 97, 114
New York Tribune, 123
North American Review, 24
Northwestern Female College (Northwestern University), 90
Nursery: A Monthly Magazine for Youngest Readers, The, 100
Nursery, The (Gibson), *53,* 95

O
Oatman, Olive, 114, 130n18
Oh! (Lafosse; Spencer), 15, 26n15
Olive Oatman with Tattoos on Chin (Felter), *114*
"On Friday I play that they are taken ill" (Griffith and Griffith), *47*
Optic, Oliver (William Taylor Adams)
  Dolly and I, 102
  What Katy Did, 102

P
Palmer, Erastus Dow, 113–114
  Indian Girl, 113, *115*
  White Captive, The, 113–114, *113*
Paris Salon of 1891, 57
Party Dress (The Finishing Touch), The (Johnson), *118,* 119
Pauline and the Matches (Hoffmann), 98
Peach Blossoms (Homer), *123,* 131n47
Pease, J. I. *See* Cheney, John, and J. I. Pease
Peddler, The (Durand), *12*
Pets, The (Johnson), 16, 26n20, 43, *44*
Phelps, Mrs., 38
Philanthropist, The, 121
Phillips, Ammi, 32, 34, 38, 54n12, 54n13
  Andrew Jackson Ten Broeck—Age One Year, Six Months, 32, 54n13
  Boy in Red, 34
  Girl in a Red Dress, 32, *33*
  Girl in Pink, 35
  Girl in Red Dress with Cat and Dog, 32
  Girl in Red Dress with Dog, 32
  Mother and Child in Grey Dresses, 134
  Portrait of Harriet Campbell, 135

INDEX

Picking Flowers (Miller), 38, *39*, 41
Pollard, Josephine, 98–100
    Tomboy Kate, 98–100, *99*
Portrait of a Baby (Holler), *165*
Portrait of a Girl (C. H. Gallup and Company), *167*
Portrait of a Young Boy (Landy), *165*
Portrait of a Young Child (Dunn), *165*
Portrait of Harold and Mildred Colton (Beaux), 51–53, *52*
Portrait of Harriet Campbell (Phillips), *135*
Portrait of the Artist's Daughter (Chase), 25, 77, *78*
Powers, Hiram, 113
Pratt, Katherine Chase, 42, *43*, 55n30
Private Investigations Lead to— (H. C. White Co.), 102–103, *103*
Pumpelly, Elise, 125
Puritans, 30

Q
Quilting Frolic (Krimmel), 55n37, *137*

R
Raleigh Academy, 111–112
Reader, The (Cassatt), *154*
Reading by the Brook (Homer), *151*
Redwood, Clara (fictional character). See *Little Mischief-Maker, and Other Stories, The*
Reed, Luman, 11
Reynolds, Sir Joshua, 119
Riis, Jacob
    Girl and Baby at Doorstep, *163*
    I Scrubs, *163*
Rogers, John, 115, 116
    School Examination, The, *148*
    Uncle Ned's School, 115–116, *115*
Rogers, Randolph, 160
    Daughter Nora as the Infant Psyche, *160*
Rogers, T., 93, 95
    Grandpa's Prodigies, *93*, 95
    See also Spencer, Lilly Martin
Roller Skating (Eberle), *149*
Roof, Katherine Metcalf, 57
Ross, Eleanora, 114, 115
Ross, John, 115
Rousseau, Jean-Jacques, 31, 59
Ruth Sears Bacon (Sargent), *49*

S
Saint-Gaudens, Augustus, 166
    Sarah Redwood Lee, *166*
Sally (DeCamp), *106*
Sampler (Morris), *139*
Sampler (Stone), *138*
Sarah Redwood Lee (Saint-Gaudens), *166*

Sargent, John Singer, 25, 41–43, 46, 49, 55n30
    Carnation, Lily, Lily, Rose, 25, 41
    Daughters of Edward Darley Boit, The, 25
    Katherine Chase Pratt, 42, *43*, 55n30
    Ruth Sears Bacon, *49*
Saturday Evening Post, 114
Schaus, William, 13, 14, 15, 26n8, 26n9, 95, 130n19
Schaus's Art Gallery, 113
School Examination, The (Rogers), *148*
Second Great Awakening, 109
Sex in Education (Clarke), 121
Shaw, Fanny (fictional character). See Alcott, Louisa May: *Old-Fashioned Girl, An*
Sheldon, George, 25
Shinnecock Summer School of Art for Men and Women, 81
Simpson, Marc, 71
Sinnett, Gretchen, 121–122, 125, 127, 129
Sloan, Junius R., 143
    Knitting Lesson, The, *143*
Slovenly Kate (unknown author), 98
Society of American Artists, 71
Southworth, E. D. E. N., 87, 88, 104n10
Spencer, Angélique Caroline, 58
Spencer, Benjamin, 91
Spencer, Lilly Martin (born Angélique Marie Martin), 11, 13, 14–15, 16, 21, 23, 24, 26n2, 26n9, 26n12, 26n15, 57–59, 69, 82n6, 82n10, 82n11, 91–94, 95, 97, 101, 103, 104n23, 105n29, 105n32
    Don't Touch, 92–93
    family, 57–59, 82n6, 82n9, 91–94, 105n32
    Fi Fo Fum, 59
    First Polka, The, 14, 26n15
    Fruit of Temptation, *92*, 93, 94, 104n24
    Grandpa's Prodigies, 93–95, *93*
    Height of Fashion, 26n9, 26n15, *167*
    Home of the Red, White and Blue, The, *10*, 21, 23–24
    Oh!, 15, 26n15
    War Spirit at Home (Celebrating the Victory at Vicksburg), 21, 23, 57, 58, 59, *96*, 97
    Young Teacher, The, 14, 26n15, 58
Stanley, John Mix, 114, 115, 130n21
    Eleanora C. Ross, 114, *115*, 130n21
Statuette, A (Kendall), *69*
Stein, Roger, 126
Stephens, Alice Barber, 12, 13
    Woman in Business, The, *13*
Stone, Elizabeth, 138
    Sampler, *138*
Stowe, Harriet Beecher, 23
Sunday Morning in Virginia (Homer), *116*
Supper with a Friend (Frère), *17*
Sure Shot, A (Brown), *84*, 90–91
Swinging on the Gate (Brown), *141*

181

T

Tait, Arthur Fitzwilliam, 11
Tarbell, Edmund Charles, 155
    Josephine and Mercie, 155
Temperance Meeting (Noon Time), A (Homer), 144–145
Thayer, Abbott Handerson, 41, 75–76, 83n44, 125, 132n52
    Angel, 74, 75, 125
    family, 75–76, 125
    My Children (Mary, Gerald, Gladys Thayer), 76
    Virgin Enthroned, 75, *76*
Thayer, Gerald, 75, 76
Thayer, Gladys, 75, 76, 125
Thayer, Kate, 75
Thayer, Mary, 75–76, 125
Thompson, Jerome, 21, 27n28
Tocqueville, Alexis de, 122
Tomboy Kate (fictional character), 98–100
Tomboy Kate (Pollard), 98–100, *99*
Too Many Presents (unknown artist), 100, *101*
Training Day (Currier and Ives), 23, *97*
Truant, The (Ives), 161

U

Uncle Alec (fictional character). *See* Alcott, Louisa May: *Eight Cousins*
Uncle Frank. *See* Woodworth, Francis Channing
Uncle Ned's School (Rogers), 115–116, *115*
Unconscious of Danger (Guy), 63, *65*
Union Soldiers Accepting a Drink (Johnson), 17–19, *18*
unknown artists
    Elizabeth Clarke Freake (Mrs. John Freake) and Baby Mary, 30
    Girl with Flowers, 34, *37*
    Goying Child, The, 34, *36*
    Little Mischief, 100
    Mischief-Maker Discovered, The, 92
    Too Many Presents, 100, *101*

V

Van Emery, Edward, 122
    Beauty and the Beer, 122
Vanity (Brown), *20*
Virgin Enthroned (Thayer), 75, *76*
Vonnoh, Bessie Potter, 22, 23
    Enthroned, 22, 23
Voyage of Life: Youth (Cole), *107*

W

Walsh, Judith, 41
Walton, William, 129, 132n67
Wanamaker, John, 12
Ward, Samuel, Jr., 107
Warner, Susan, 15–16, 38, 54n20
War Spirit at Home (Celebrating the Victory at Vicksburg) (Spencer), 21, 23, 57, 58, 59, *96,* 97
Watching the Woodpecker (Brown), 21, *60*
Webster, Thomas, 60
We Can't Be Caught (Brown), *61*
Weisberg, Gabriel P., 17
West, John D., 123
Westbrook, Raymond, 85–86
What Katy Did (Optic), *102*
What Katy Did books (Coolidge), 86, 88, 89, *102*
Wheelwright, Mary Cabot, 48, 49
White Captive, The (Palmer), 113–114, *113*
Whittier, John Greenleaf, 126
Wide, Wide World, The (Warner), 15–16
Wife of the Period, The (Nast), 126, *127*
Willard, Frances E., 90, 91, 101
Willard, Mary, 90
Willard, Oliver, 90
"Winter"—A Skating Scene (Homer), 88, *89,* 90, 116, 125
Winter, Portrait of Child (Johnson), 69–71, *70,* 88, 89–90
Woman in Business, The (Stephens), 13
Women of New York, The (Ellington), 121
Women's Christian Temperance Union, 90
Woodville, Richard Caton, 11
Woodworth, Francis Channing (Uncle Frank), 92–93, 98, 105n28
World's Columbian Exposition of 1893, 57

Y

Young Artist, The (Baker), *153*
Young Girl in Black: The Artist's Daughter in Mother's Dress (Chase), 25, *77*
Young Teacher, The (Lafosse; Spencer), *14,* 26n15, 58
Yunginger, Jennifer, 31, 54n11

Z

Zwinger, Lynda, 76–77

TRUSTEES OF THE NEWARK MUSEUM ASSOCIATION

EX OFFICIO
The Honorable Chris Christie
Governor of New Jersey

The Honorable Cory A. Booker
Mayor of Newark

The Honorable Joseph N. DiVincenzo Jr.
Essex County Executive

The Honorable Donald M. Payne Jr.
President, Newark Municipal Council

Ms. Cami Anderson
Superintendent, Newark Public Schools

OFFICERS
Mrs. Arlene Lieberman
Chair

Mr. Andrew H. Richards
President

Mrs. Gloria Hopkins Buck
Vice President

Mr. Peter B. Sayre
Treasurer

Mrs. Mary Sue Sweeney Price
Secretary, Director, and Chief Executive Officer

Mrs. Meme Omogbai
Assistant Treasurer and Chief Operating Officer

Ms. Susan M. Baer
Mr. Dave Barger
Mr. Clifford Blanchard
Mrs. Gloria Hopkins Buck
Mr. Joseph L. Buckley
Mr. Jacob S. Buurma
Mrs. Sheila Nugent Carter
Mrs. Eleonore K. Cohen
Mrs. Patricia Hall Curvin
Mr. Samuel A. Delgado
Ms. Ann B. Dickinson
Mr. Robert H. Doherty
Mr. Keith Dolin
Ms. Caroline Dorsa
Mr. Stephen R. Ehrlich
Mrs. Wilma Gelfand
Mr. Angelo J. Genova
Mrs. Mona Gibson
Mrs. Christine C. Gilfillan
Mrs. Stephanie Glickman
Mr. Jerome W. Gottesman
Mr. Paul M. Graves
Mrs. Kathy Grier
Mrs. Joan Kalkin
Mr. Donald M. Karp
Hon. Thomas H. Kean Jr.
Ms. Poonam Khubani
Mr. Theodore G. Koven
Mrs. Dorothy D. Lewis
Mrs. Arlene Lieberman
Mrs. Judith Lieberman
Mrs. Ruth C. Lipper
Ms. Patricia P. Lunka
Mr. Joseph J. Melone
Mrs. Jazz J. Merton
Mr. D. Nicholas Miceli
Mr. Ronald M. Ollie
Mrs. Meme Omogbai
Mrs. Ashley M. Pertsemlidis
Mrs. Mary Sue Sweeney Price
Mr. Andrew H. Richards
Dr. Linda M. A. Rodrigues
Mr. Seth L. Rosen
Mr. Peter B. Sayre
Mr. Gary Shaw
Mrs. Sophia Sheng
Mr. William F. Taggart
Ms. Grizel Ubarry
Mr. Gurdon B. Wattles
Mr. Richard K. Weinroth
Dr. Francis A. Wood

NEWARK MUSEUM COUNCIL

OFFICERS
Mr. Kevin Shanley
Chair

Mrs. Dana Dowd Williams
Vice Chair

MEMBERS
Mrs. Carole Angel
Mr. Jake Angell
Mr. Andrew Ballantine
Rt. Rev. Mark M. Beckwith
Ms. Patricia A. Bell
Miss Sally G. Carroll
Mr. Raymond G. Chambers
Mrs. Barbara Bell Coleman
Mr. Christopher Forbes
Rabbi Matthew D. Gewirtz
Hon. Joseph A. Greenaway Jr.
Mr. John Jacoby
Mr. James L. Johnson
Mr. Daniel Karslake
Mr. Gregory Matthews
Ms. Catherine M. McFarland
Mr. Samuel C. Miller
Director Emeritus
Mrs. Beverly K. Nadler
Dr. Winsome J. Parchment
Mr. B. Waring Partridge
Rabbi Emeritus Norman R. Patz
Ms. Christine Pearson
Ms. Lisa Richards
Mr. William C. Robinson
Ms. Jacqueline R. Rocci
Mrs. Patricia E. Ryan
Ms. Susan Satz
Mrs. Joyce M. Sharkey
Ms. Linda Singletary
Mr. Paul St. Onge
Hon. Daniel P. Sullivan
Mr. Quincy Troupe Jr.
Mrs. Christabel Vartanian
Hon. Alvin Weiss
Mr. Christopher M. Wiedenmayer
Ms. Junea Williams-Edmund